Bottom-Line Call Center Management

Creating a Culture of Accountability and Excellent Customer Service

**IMPROVING
HUMAN
PERFORMANCE
SERIES**

Series Editor: Jack J. Phillips, Ph.D.

Accountability in Human Resource Management
Jack J. Phillips
Achieving the Perfect Fit
Nick Boulter, Murray Dalziel, Ph. D., and Jackie Hill, Editors
Bottom-Line Call Center Management
David L. Butler
Bottom-Line Training
Donald J. Ford
Corporate Performance Management
David Wade and Ronald Recardo
Developing Supervisors and Team Leaders
Donald L. Kirkpatrick
The Global Advantage
Michael J. Marquardt
Handbook of Training Evaluation and Measurement Methods, 3rd Edition
Jack J. Phillips
Human Performance Consulting
James S. Pepitone
Human Performance Improvement
William J. Rothwell, Carolyn K. Hohne, and Stephen B. King
The Human Resources Scorecard
Jack J. Phillips, Patricia Pulliam Phillips, and Ron D. Stone
HR to the Rescue
Edward M. Mone and Manuel London
HRD Survival Skills
Jessica Levant
HRD Trends Worldwide
Jack J. Phillips
Learning in Chaos
James Hite, Jr.
Linking Learning and Performance
Toni Krucky Hodges
Managing Change Effectively
Donald L. Kirkpatrick
The Power of 360° Feedback
David A. Waldman and Leanne E. Atwater
The Project Management Scorecard
Jack J. Phillips, G. Lynne Snead, and Timothy W. Bothell
Return on Investment in Training and Performance Improvement Programs, Second Edition
Jack J. Phillips
Bottom-Line Organization Development
Merrill Anderson
Managing Employee Retention
Jack J. Phillips and Adele O. Connell
The Diversity Scorecard
Edward E. Hubbard

FORTHCOMING TITLES
Building a World-Class First-Level Management Team
Jack J. Phillips and Ron D. Stone

Bottom-Line Call Center Management

Creating a Culture of Accountability and Excellent Customer Service

David L. Butler

ELSEVIER
BUTTERWORTH
HEINEMANN

Amsterdam   Boston   Heidelberg   London   New York   Oxford   Paris
San Diego   San Francisco   Singapore   Sydney   Tokyo

Elsevier Butterworth-Heinemann
200 Wheeler Road, Burlington, MA 01803, USA
Linacre House, Jordan Hill, Oxford OX2 8DP, UK

∞ Recognizing the importance of preserving what has been written, Elsevier prints its books on
acid-free paper whenever possible.

Library of Congress Cataloging-in-Publication Data
Application submitted.

British Library Cataloguing-in-Publication Data
A catalogue record for this book is available from the British Library.

ISBN: 0-7506-7684-1

For information on all Butterworth-Heinemann publications
visit our Web site at www.bh.com

04 05 06 07 08 09 10 9 8 7 6 5 4 3 2 1

Printed in the United States of America

Dedication

A toast to all people who have earned success and choose to risk that success in order to create something new, unique, and even more successful. Cheers to us entrepreneurs!

Contents

Foreword, xi

Preface, xiii

Acknowledgments, xxi

C H A P T E R   1

Culture 1
From Boot Camp to Teamwork, 1. Human Capital, 4. From the Mountain
to the Trenches, 5. Positive Culture Companies, 7. Earning Their
Respect, 8. Humans and Human Nature, 8. Are You the Boss?, 9. Respect
and Distance, 9. The Names, 13. The Open Door, 14. Incentives, 15.
Final Thoughts, 15. References, 16. Further Reading, 16.

C H A P T E R   2

Accountability 17
Accountability, 17. Goals, 17. Assets to Achieve Goals, 24.
Current Status, 25. SWOT Analysis, 25. Scenarios of Success, 29.
Final Thoughts, 31. References, 32.

C H A P T E R   3

Location, Location, Location 33
Where to Locate a Call Center, 33. Site Selection, 33. Commuting, 35.
Labor Shed, 35. Buildings, 40. Clusters, 42. Incentives, 43.
Technologies, 44. Community Colleges, 44. Labor—The Recurring
Cost, 47. How to Find a Labor Shed, 49. Labor Sheds and

Geographical Information Systems, 51. Final Thoughts, 55. References, 56. Further Reading, 56.

CHAPTER 4

Hiring 57
Hiring, 57. Skills, 61. Competency Model, 62. Attitude, 62. Recommendations for Filtering, 66. Employees Come First, 68. Final Thoughts, 69. References, 69. Further Reading, 70.

CHAPTER 5

Your Reps 71
Why Do Your Reps Work at Your Center?, 71. Choosing a Call Center Manager, 75. Empowering Employees, 80. The Whole Person, 82. Financial Transparency, 83. Employee Satisfaction, 83. Measuring Job Satisfaction, 84. How to Hire a Consultant, 87. Performance Measures, 87. Final Thoughts, 89. References, 90.

CHAPTER 6

Pay, Benefits, and the Dreaded Labor Unions 91
What Do You Pay?, 93. What Does Your Competition Pay?, 96. What Is Culture Worth?, 96. Spatial Fix, 97. Unions Yikes!, 98. By the Numbers, 99. Union Avoidance, 99. Unionization! Now What?, 102. Final Thoughts, 109. References, 109.

CHAPTER 7

The People and the Technology 111
Technology as a Panacea, 112. Adopting New Technologies, 113. Technological Change and Resistance, 117. Measuring Technology Change Success, 120. An ROI of Technological Change, 120. Who Controls the Technology?, 123. Technology as an Enabler or a Wall?, 124. Final Thoughts, 126. References, 126. Further Reading, 126.

CHAPTER 8

Return on Investment (ROI) 128
By the Numbers Accountability, 128. Return on Investment, 129. Why ROI?, 129. The Approach, 131. The ROI Model, 133. Barriers to Implementation, 138. Benefits to Implementation, 139. ROI Candidate?, 141. Final Thoughts, 144. References, 145. Further Reading, 145.

CHAPTER 9

ROI Case Study at Happy Airways 146
Culture Matters! Retaining Employees and Showing a Strong ROI, 146.
Are Your CSRs There for the Money?, 155. What Do You Produce?, 156.
Positive Culture and ROI, 158. Final Thoughts, 165.

CHAPTER 10

From the Present to the Future 166
State of the Industry, 166. Call Center Life Cycle, 168. Positioning the
Center, 169. Final Thoughts, 173. References, 174.

Index, 175

About the Author, 179

Foreword

Imagine this…you walk into a huge room, that looks like a gutted retail store—no merchandise, no personality. The lighting is overly bright. At the front of this enormous room stands a big, burly man holding a vertical drum. You can tell he is anxious to get on with the drumming. There are hundreds of people sitting at desks and then you hear it…he begins to beat the drum; it is reminiscent of those Tyrone Power and Erroll Flynn swashbucklers. Only these people are not rowing in time with the drum beat, they are picking up their headsets, attaching them to their ears, and in sync with the drum saying "Good Morning. How may I help you?" The only thing missing is the familiar "Oh wee Ohhhh…" chanting.

When asked what a call center is like, the aforementioned may be the response from the uninitiated. Those of us who have spent a couple of decades working, learning, and growing in "the business" have different perceptions of a call center. We understand, or should understand, that a call center is a community. Many of these centers contain a population akin to a small town and as such represent all the issues and concerns that can occur in that small town. There are births, deaths, baby showers, birthday parties, disastrous failures, and incredible success stories. There are politics, popularity polls, and photo opportunities as well. It is, after all, a community.

Great managers understand this well, and know how to work within the boundaries of their corporate confines while still maintaining and creating a local flavor for their operation. Great managers also know that the industry has changed dramatically over the past 10 years and is continuing to change. The reality is that while we are still trying to find time for that concept of "balance," we also need to stay on top of our game, continue our education about the industry, and proffer care to our associates.

While running large inbound and outbound shops at several outstanding Fortune 500 companies such as Citicorp, American Express, and Bank of America I scanned through industry publications, met with call center alliance members, and called and worked hard to locate great information to do my job more effectively. David Butler's book *Bottom-Line Call Center Management* can assist anyone working in the environment much more expeditiously because he has completed the research for us.

The requirement to stay up-to-date and share best practices quickly is tantamount to our success, and one read through Dr. Butler's book will open your eyes to opportunities you can implement to increase productivity, reduce turnover, and increase your "fun" factor at the place we have come to know as our home away from home. It covers everything from how to identify a location for a new call center, to running a profitable center, to keeping your employees happy. Please, save yourself 20 years…read this book!

Ann John
Leading Edge Consults, LLC
annjohnlec@aol.com

Preface

Forget everything you learned in school about management – we are starting fresh!

REALITY

Businesses exist to make money. If they didn't, they'd go bankrupt. Therefore, this book focuses on both tactics and strategies for improving the bottom-line performance of call centers directly, and parent corporations' bottom line indirectly, while simultaneously improving the quality of service offered to clients/customers. A manager of a center within the United States and Britain would be wise to read this book thoroughly and then implement a strategy to improve the quality of customer service offered in his or her center while simultaneously decreasing the expensive high turnover rate that plagues the industry at present. The double punch of high labor costs and high turnover is a major push factor of outsourcing call centers to developing nations around the world. Which center is next?

Managers of call centers outside the United States and Britain, but serving these two large markets, would also be wise to read this book thoroughly to understand the American and British customer service marketplaces and corporate logic. Many companies have outsourced just a few of their total centers to developing markets, but not all of them. This means that outsourcing is still in its infancy and thus is still being tested. To be considered a success, these centers must deliver the service levels expected by customers and keep labor costs and turnover rates low as required by corporations. Recent reports suggest that India is beginning to have similar problems of turnover rates and cannibalization of labor between centers that drive up labor costs. Though preliminary, reports such as these begin to question the future success of this experiment. If these outsourced centers fail to provide the expected benefits to both the customers and organizations, the companies will relocate the center to another region with a track record of excellence in customer service and lower labor costs or back to the United States or Britain to ensure oversight and management of the customer service function by headquarters staff. The next five years will determine whether the experiment is successful or not. This book crosses many national, cultural, and linguistic boundaries by mapping out success for all call center managers, no matter if the center is in Baltimore, Birmingham, or Bangalore.

RESEARCH

Since 1991, the author has extensively researched the relationship between information technology and organizations. Since 1996, the research narrowed to focus specifically on the international call center industry. This book is a manifestation of specific research on this unique industry, but in no way is this book intended to be exhaustive or the definitive text. The research and insights are ongoing and thus dynamic. The purpose of this book is to inform the reader of actions that can be taken to improve overall call center performance and thus increase the bottom line of the center based on solid research data and years of experience. Few, if any, books on the subject of call center management can make this claim. The intended structure of this book is to balance both the rigor of academic research, which underpins the information contained with these pages, with practical advice and examples, while making the book readable without lengthy endnotes, footnotes, and citations commonly found in academic publications.

AUDIENCE

There are multiple audiences for this book worldwide. The call center industry is not just based in the United States or Europe. The industry, like the information flow it supports, is global. The largest and most articulated audience for this book is the hundreds of thousands of call center managers in the United States, England, Wales, Scotland, Ireland, South Africa, Panama, India, China, the Philippines, Australia, Malaysia,

Canada, New Zealand, and countless other locations throughout the world where call centers are evolving. Many of the successful strategies and techniques outlined in this book will be most effective for call center managers if they receive "buy in" by executives in their organization. Therefore, executives in organizations with call centers are the second major audience for this book. In fact, ideally, this book should be read by both the upper management of a company and all their call center manager(s) simultaneously to ensure that the total organization fully understands how effective call center management directly impacts the whole organization's bottom line. Executives would be wise not only to read this book, but to buy a copy for each manager and supervisor in each of their centers to ensure that these managers understand that their actions and decisions directly affect the company's bottom line and that the level of performance and accountability are high.

Other audiences for this book include instructors and students in institutions of learning throughout the world, economic and community developers who wish to recruit a call center(s), or communities currently with call centers who desire to retain or expand their center over time. Furthermore, many of the thoroughly researched techniques outlined in this book are equally applicable to both back office industries and industries with a high labor cost structure and high turnover such as the food and beverage and entertainment industries. Managers in thee industries can easily replicate the programs outlined in this text to enable success. Finally, I would be remiss if I failed to mention that strongly motivated call center supervisors, who wish to be promoted to run their own call center, would be wise to read this book thoroughly and to map out a strategy of effective management techniques to use when they are given the green light to sit in the manager's seat at a center.

STATE OF THE INDUSTRY

The call center industry is a little over 40 years old, and its history parallels the development and implementation of advanced information technologies. At present there are approximately 4,500 call centers in Britain and between 90,000–140,000 (uncountable to date) call centers within the United States – the largest market for call centers in the world. However, Canada, Ireland, and other European, African, Asian, and American nations have established call centers serving both the large US and UK markets as well as their smaller but growing domestic markets.

CALL CENTER HISTORY

The author has created an overlapping multi-phase history of the call center industry from research.

Phase I: **Local phase 1960s–Mid 1980s**
             Early call centers 1960s to 1984
             Airlines reservation systems
             Banking systems
             Centralized computing and concentrated labor at point of computer processing and storage
             Emerging new technologies

Phase II: **Regional phase Mid 1980s to early 1990s**
             US Long-distance deregulation 1984–1990
             New switching and routing technologies available
             Increase use of call centers due to lower costs of long distance
             Expansion of existing call centers
             Growth of new call centers in information dependent industries

Phase III: **International Expansion Phase Early 1990s- to late 1990s**
             Growth of IT in developed nations
             Call center growth in developed nations
             Higher levels of mobility for call centers within countries
             Call centers as development policy
             New industries using call centers

Phase IV: **Globalization Phase Late 1990s–present**
             Outsourcing of call centers to developing nations
             Expansion of call centers worldwide
             Highly flexible location criteria for call centers
             New industries developing call centers including professional services

Each of these phases is separated according to substantial changes, growth, and new developments of the call center industry. Phase I includes the birth of the call center where a handful of workers in these centers collected and disseminated information from fixed locations near a base of operations or in a corporate headquarters. These centers were found mostly in information dependent industries such as airlines and banking. As computers began to be used by corporations, these organizations were the first to purchase large main frames to handle the increasing volume of data collected, organized, and disseminated.

Phase II was ushered in by the deregulation of the United States long distance phone service and emerging technologies in switching and routing. With competition, cost to consumers and businesses for long distance dropped significantly, allowing for the first time a level of flexibility in the location of evolving call centers. Industries such as catalog sales, telemarketing, etc., could produce a business model that would earn a profit given the lowered costs of long distance. Therefore, during Phase II the call center industry matured and grew substantially.

Phase III of the call center industry indicates the rapid improvements of both computers and communication systems commonly known as information technology (IT) today. As IT advanced, more powerful and less expensive technology could be brought to bear on the large volume of information needed to be processed and evaluated within call centers. In Phase III call center growth continued in traditional industries, new industries began to open call centers or outsource them to third party companies, and the emergence of the overseas call center to serve the "English-speaking" world was just beginning.

In Phase IV, the call center industry still continued to expand. New businesses including professional services (doctors, lawyers, accountants, engineers, etc.) can now be reached nationally and internationally through call centers. A growing number of call centers have either been relocated from the United States and the UK to English-speaking India, the Philippines, Panama, and other locations, or new center growth has emerged in these countries. The end of Phase IV or the beginning of Phase V will be determined by the long-term success or failure of the overseas call centers, emerging inexpensive and flexible digital information technologies, and the desires of consumers in the developed world with ample disposable income and expected levels of service.

TODAY

There are two major trends in the global call center industry. The first trend is the movement of select call centers from more mature labor markets, such as the United States and Britain, to less mature and lower cost labor regions of the world to service the developed nation's markets. For example, many national or international companies will have multiple sites worldwide. They may have five in the states and two overseas. Such is the case for America Online and other similar companies. The trend of US and British-based call centers relocating or growing overseas centers is not without critics. Reports indicating that up to 97,000 jobs will be lost in the UK call center industry to India, increasing the level of tension around this issue. Outsourcing of call centers overseas can be accomplished reliably and affordably through real-time global telecommunication infrastructure. The largest market growth is in regions that have a relatively high level of education, strong English-language skills, and those which have the necessary infrastructure and support networks to ensure consistent level of reliable service.

The second trend is the emerging new markets for call centers in professional services such as doctors, lawyers, pharmacist, accountants, and many more areas. As companies seek more efficiency, many find the ability of call centers to easily interact directly with the customer intriguing. This trend is expected to continue, and both new and old industries are expected to see opportunities for both revenue growth and cost saving with call centers in the near future.

DEFINITIONS

Words have meaning, and the same words mean different things to different people. Given this reality, this section will briefly review some key words that recur often in this book to ensure that both the author and the reader are working from the same definition.

Representative. A person in a call center who works the phones as his or her primary job responsibility. Other interchangeable words in this book include **employee, customer service representative, CSR,** and **rep.**

Call Center. This word is used generically throughout the book. This book does not specifically distinguish between inbound and outbound centers. Call centers are also referred to as **customer contact centers, customer support centers, helpdesks,** and derogatorily, as **cost centers.** The word "**center**" is used throughout this book as a shortened version of call center.

Organization. A group of people working toward a similar purpose or goal in an organization. Sometimes an organization is a call center itself, possibly groups of call centers, or maybe a large **company** with call centers as only a subset of one division. The organization can be government, public, private, for-profit, and non-profit. However, the word organization and **business** are frequently used interchangeably in the text because no matter the status of a center, for profit or non-profit, or government, the goal is to reduce costs and generate the highest return on investment possible.

Manager. This is the head person in a call center. Depending upon the call center size, function, and the type of organization it is embedded in, the head of the call center may be called a **director,** manager, or some other title. Either way, the word manager in this book refers to the highest level of authority in a single center.

OUTLINE OF THE BOOK

This book is divided into ten chapters, each with its own unique focus. This text intends to fill the large gap in the literature by providing a solid authoritative research base for call center managers that allows them to make incremental steps to improve the environment and culture of their center while lowering overall center costs.

Chapter 1 examines the role of culture within a call center, specifically suggesting that creating a positive work environment in a call center can lead to a decrease in turnover and a simultaneous increase in the return on investment.

Chapter 2 articulates that a call center manager must be accountable to both his or her upper management as well as to the reps in the center. With this burden of accountability comes the requirement to produce results and align goals to ensure success at all levels.

Chapter 3 examines the relationship between the location of a specific call center and the capacity to hire and retain employees in a center. This is a key relationship that all managers should be aware of because if a center is poorly located, it can have a difficult time attracting and retaining employees. However, there are specific tools and techniques a manager can use to determine the effective recruiting labor shed of their center, improving the performance of recruiting employees, and retaining them for a longer period of time.

Chapter 4 examines the specific hiring, skills, and training of employees. This chapter does not outline a training module, but instead suggest ways in which a manager should examine the skill sets, hiring parameters, and training regime of the employees to ensure both the most knowledgeable and productive workforce possible.

Who are all of these people who work for you? Do you actually know much about your representatives? **Chapter 5** examines this question in detail suggesting that many employees may have excellent talents that have so far gone unused by the center. The chapter suggests ways to utilize the full range of your representative's talents while simultaneously building a positive and productive work atmosphere. The chapter also examines the motivation of employees to work in a call center.

Is pay the problem or the solution? **Chapter 6** examines the pay structure and benefits of the call center industry and suggests that while pay is important, it is only one measure of employee satisfaction. In fact, cases will be cited where people have opted for lower paying jobs just to work in a more positive and productive environment. Labor Unions. The name alone sends shivers down many managers' backs. **Chapter 6** continues by examining labor unions in call centers. It discusses when it is most advantageous for centers to avoid unions and also discusses how a manager faced with unionizing can enable the best return on investment possible.

Do you need to purchase that new technology system? Will new system really improve performance? **Chapter 7** examine the relationship between technology and your employees. The chapter suggests that instead of imposing new technologies on your representatives in the hopes that they will perform at a higher rate, managers should ask employees what they would like in a new technology to improve their own performance.

Chapter 8 takes a common return on investment model used by a successful consulting team and outlines the strategies on why ROI is important and gives examples of how ROI works within a call center.

Chapter 9 begins where Chapter 8 left off and applies the ROI model theorized in chapter 8 and applies it to a call center case study to demonstrate that even if a center does not generate revenue directly for an organization, it can show a strong (or weak) ROI in is programs. This ROI report is invaluable to a call center manager articulating the importance of the center to the full organization.

Chapter 10 concludes the book by examining recent trends in the global call center industry specifically examining the movement of call centers from the US and UK to various other countries and what this trend means and does not mean. Furthermore, the chapter examines the Call Center Life Cycle Model and suggests that managers need to keep their position in the model in mind when developing the best strategy for their center within their industry.

David Butler can be reached at Butler and Associates, Inc., 100 South 22nd Avenue, Hattiesburg, Mississippi 39401, 601-310-9372 (phone), ButlerandAssociates@yahoo.com.

Acknowledgments

Though this book has a single author listed on the cover, in reality there is a team of people who helped this book come to fruition. The driving philosophy behind this book and head cheerleaders are Drs. Patricia and Jack Phillips. If it were not for many engaging dinner conversations, this book would not be a concept nor a product in print.

I am forever indebted to Joyce Alff who edited the original manuscript. It would take a full chapter to explain how important the support Joyce provided was, and then that chapter would have to be marked-up with editing corrections to be ready for submission.

Karen Maloney at Butterworth Heinemann was instrumental in working with me for the original contract for this book. Her patience with me and my endless questions went beyond the call of duty. Others at Butterworth Heinemann/Elsevier who were instrumental in making this book a reality include Dennis McGonagle, Paul Gottehrer, Ailsa Marks, and countless others who I never worked with directly but whose efforts substantially improved the quality of the work submitted for publication.

I cannot forget to thank my wife Leslie and my daughters Elizabeth and Alyssa for their support. Many nights were spent with a computer in my lap at home asking to be left alone to meet manuscript deadlines. Without my family's patience, this project would never have been completed.

CHAPTER 1

Culture

Culture, or more precisely business culture, is the environment in which the practice of business takes place. This environment includes both physical and psychological spaces. The culture of these spaces is initially set by a leader of an organization and is then reformed and replicated in daily work activities by people within the organization. The goal of any business should be to create the best and most productive culture possible to enable the highest possible bottom-line return on investment (profitability). How this culture is created and what it entails differs greatly from company to company, manager to manager, and organization to organization. This chapter examines specific approaches to creating a positive and profitable culture within a call center.

A positive business culture is not easy to create and, once created, can be undermined quickly in the early development stages of a business. With a concerted effort, however, a strong and positive work environment can be created for call center employees. Though building a positive work culture takes a large initial input of effort, time, and energy, especially from leaders of an organization, if initiated correctly, success will pay ample dividends in employee retention and recruitment, accountability, and, of course, productivity.

FROM BOOT CAMP TO TEAMWORK

Managers do not have to run their organizations like military drill sergeants to achieve employee loyalty and dedication to the company and product(s). Because the goal of business should be to have self-motivated and engaged employees with a dedication to the products and services produced by the company, managers need to move beyond the boot camp model of barking commands and move rapidly toward a culture of teamwork.

Unfortunately, much of what is practiced and called "management" has more in common with a 15th- and 16th-century overseer model of agricultural production than a modern understanding of human interaction within an information- and technology-dependent industry. Archaic management models still in place assume that employees, given the opportunity, will exploit the company they work for at every opportunity. This model takes as truth that to "keep an employee in line" requires the use of a heavy hand and someone looking over the employee's shoulders at all times (an overseer). Whether managers consciously choose to use the overseer model, replicate what they have witnessed/experienced in the past, or actually believe that the overseer model is effective, the reality is that managers who use such models commonly make statements such as:

"If I don't watch them, then they will. . . ."
"If I don't show up for work, nothing will get done."
"I have to watch over them constantly, if not, nothing will get done."
"You have to keep an eye on them or they will rob you blind."
"If I am not in the office today, I know they will take a long lunch and sneak out early."

Each of these statements, and countless others, all presume the employee to be lazy, shiftless, thieving, lacking intelligence, and without individual initiative—cornerstones of the overseer model. These phrases also suggest that one must be tough on employees or else they will act in their own interest, diametrically opposed to the interests of the company. This type of management sets up the employee and manager in an adversarial relationship. Managers who choose to develop and reinforce an adversarial model when relating to employees should ask themselves the following questions:

1. Why did I hire these employees if I think so little of them?
2. What is it about my management practices that makes my employees want to escape the confines of my establishment given the slightest opportunity?
3. If I am a hardworking and loyal employee, why do I think that my employees are so different from me?
4. Is my management model the most effective for the bottom line of the call center?

Too often, managers believe that through intimidation and pressure employees will perform at high levels, thus producing the desired results of increased productivity. This is not the 15th century, and this is not the most effective model to use for profitability within an organization.

The globalizing economy is reinventing itself constantly as it continues to evolve. Creative destruction is common and requires companies to adapt or die. Companies who succeed in this dynamic environment are those that have the best capacity to identify and then to adapt to the changes as they occur. Ideally, if a company is well positioned within the market, it will be the initiator of change in its industry instead of responding to other companies' market movements.

Two necessary ingredients for a business to respond and adapt to rapidly changing market conditions are flexibility and the ability to think creatively (outside the box). The method to achieve this level of flexibility and creativity is the creation of a business culture (place and people) that not only allows, but actively encourages and fosters, employee development at all levels of business—from the janitorial broom closet to the boardroom. This means that old models of management, especially those related to the overseer type of model, must be discarded and new models that embrace a team approach must be adopted and used if an organization is to compete effectively in a dynamic market.

Research indicates that most employees, given a reasonable level of responsibility, rise to the occasion and bring their varied talents to bear on the tasks at hand if the necessary business culture is set up to help enable success. Therefore, for an organization to prosper, managers must trust their employees with the success of their business. Conversely, to become an effective team with a set of clear objectives and goals, employees must trust their managers to lead them with experience through daily difficulties in achieving the team's goals. If this balance between management and employees is not achieved, the full relationship cannot be developed, and thus, the company will not be in a position to rapidly and effectively respond to market changes (i.e., it will lose market share and be supplanted by another business). If employees trust their managers, but managers do not trust the employees, the business model will break down. If managers trust their employees blindly, but do not give them a reason to trust the management, then employees collectively will walk all over management by exerting their own idea of an employee–management plan, which is also a recipe for disaster. The trust between management and the employees must be reciprocal for effective business operations to occur.

The goal of a manager is to have a team of employees that can produce successes with or without management's direct and daily presence. However, creating this type of teamwork, as well as individual and collective responsibility, takes practice, patience, and time. When effective, the old math of productivity no longer works: $1 + 1$ does not $=$ 2. Instead, with an effective team of employees using their collective talents focused on a task, $1 + 1 = 2.5$ or even 3, since each person can build from the strengths of team members and increase his or her own abilities (a positive multiplier). If the unique skills of employees are not effectively utilized and poor management reigns, then the potential exists to have a high level of inefficiency in the system, making $1 + 1$ not even equal 2, since inefficiencies and conflicts within the system can reduce both individual and group performance.

HUMAN CAPITAL

Human capital is the total set of human assets that any business has at its command. In a small firm this may be 10–15 total employees; in a large corporation it may be 20,000 employees. Human capital, like physical capital, is an investment that should produce a return on investment for a business. This means that if an organization pays an employee $12 an hour, that employee should produce at least $12.01 per hour in tangible and intangibles for the company directly or indirectly. Like physical assets, the right human capital should be used for the particular need in the most efficient and effective means possible. Historically, businesses have thought of ways to use physical objects (usually identified as technologies) in a new mode, method, or manner to produce an efficiency yielding increased revenue generation. However, too often employers forget that they should use similar knowledge/technology when examining human capital. In fact, increasing the efficient use of both human and physical capital should be viewed as seamless, since human capital should not be examined without examining the necessary physical capital and vice versa. When employees are hired, no matter the level, they bring in certain sets of skills, abilities, and disabilities with them. The goal of the manager, in concert with other employees, is to maximize the use of every employee in the most effective, efficient, and flexible means possible.

In short, human capital, like physical capital, must be understood in all of its manifestations to fully utilize its potential for an organization's bottom line. Unlike most physical capital that depreciates in value over time and thus decreases in value as it is used, human capital should be developed to increase in value (through learned experiences and skills),

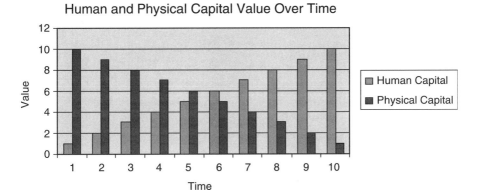

Figure 1-1. Human and physical capital value over time. (Source: David L. Butler.)

thus causing the employee to appreciate in value over time to the organization. Therefore, it is to a business's advantage to develop its human capital as early as possible to ensure that the business obtains the maximum value of its employees during their tenure with the company (see Figure 1-1).

FROM THE MOUNTAIN TO THE TRENCHES

There are many ways to earn an employee's respect and trust. However, one sure way to earn it and to have the respect spread like a wildfire to all employees is to ensure that every employee knows that a manager is willing to get his or her hands "dirty." It is critically necessary to come down off the management mountain periodically and into the trenches with the rest of the employees. Usually, when peak call load occurs at a center, managers spend their time "managing" employees. This usually entails watching the performance screen to see the average time spent per call and the number of calls in queue or possibly passing out popsicles to the reps to keep them cool. Each one of these responses to peak call demand is understandable; however, managers should ask what type of dividend does each response pay. Sure, managers can spend time viewing the metrics on the screen; however, the chances of modifications to the numbers during this window of opportunity are minimal. In reality, the metrics will be reviewed and evaluated, and new procedures will be created only after the fact. What type of dividends would it pay if once a week or maybe just once a month, during a peak call time, the manager sat down in a cubicle next to his/her employees and began answering calls or making calls for an outbound center (of course, utilizing the best skills and techniques taught in training classes)? If the employees have enough training, experience, and knowledge, as well as flexibility and trust from management, the need to oversee each employee during this period will be substantially minimized. Supervisors can handle all routed problem calls. This allows the manager time to sit down with employees, at their level, and to do the job of the center, that is, to communicate with customers one-on-one. Imagine the talk in the break room the day after employees saw their manager answering calls. Getting down in the trenches is especially important for managers who may be new to call centers. No amount of reading and training will substitute for sitting in a cubicle, putting on the head phones, and answering (dialing) call after call after call with the highest level of customer service possible for several hours. Not only will the manager gain invaluable experience about how the center works (in reality, not in abstract terms), but he or she will also build an invaluable bridge between management and the call reps that will be hard to destroy.

Quite often, executives and managers object to the suggestions of "going down into the trenches" with their employees because they fear that their employees would lose respect for them. Others suggest that working one-on-one with the employees will appear to the employees as an attempt to curry favor and will damage the appropriate distance managers should keep. Both of these reactions are unfounded. Any employee who has been hired by a company knows the boss is the person who hires and fires. No matter the distance between the boss and the employee, the manager is in charge by definition and action. The willingness of the manager to take on the role of an employee during a peak time shows the manager's ability to do the tasks effectively and efficiently and also gives the manager more credibility from employees. The manager also increases his/her level of information and knowledge of daily activities in the center, which, in turn, strengthens the manager's statements about performance and productivity numbers for the center.

If a manager chooses to "get dirty" with the employees, the manager is not expected to "beat" the other employees in production numbers. Most managers are selected based on their potential to effectively manage people, not because they produced the best metrics as a rep. The goodwill earned by showing a willingness to do the tasks of employees will pay substantial dividends later. This task will show the team that the supervisor is not only a leader, but a good leader and is empathetic to their needs and problems.

POSITIVE CULTURE COMPANIES

At leading cultural-friendly businesses, it is customary for almost all employees to work in various parts of the company and at all levels for a specific period of time. The purpose of this activity is not only an empathy-building exercise, but also a way to get everyone in the company acting in concert as a team. What better way to have a group of people come together to work toward the same larger goals than to literally "walk in each others' shoes" for miles and miles? This type of exercise ensures all employees that people from the top to the bottom know their job and know what they are doing for the company. Similarly, this allows people at the bottom of the pay ladder to see that management does work and works hard, quite often to the tune of 60–80 hours a week in most good companies. This type of interaction ensures that everyone is clear on what the others are doing and that everyone collectively is doing their best to pull their own weight and possibly a little more.

JetBlue is a relatively new airline within the United States led by its CEO David Neeleman. On his website, Neeleman states, "One of the most enjoyable parts of my job is meeting customers onboard when I fly JetBlue each week" (www.jetblue.com). Outside of Southwest Airlines, JetBlue is one of the most profitable airlines and is known to have a great business culture. As Neeleman said, he actively flies on his planes, meets and greets his customers, serves drinks and food, and listens. Imagine if you were a flight attendant for an airline and the CEO of the company decided to join you on your flight and acted in the capacity as a co-worker with you to serve the customers on the plane. What type of loyalty would this instill in you? Would the CEO seem aloof and not in touch with the average worker? How much extra effort would you put into your job knowing that the CEO of the company was willing to work with you at your level, doing your job? The situation is the same at a call center. Willingness to sit and work the phones at peak times will help instill employee loyalty to both the management team and the corporate organization.

Earning Their Respect

How do managers know their employees respect them? Should they ask? Does the employee's behavior exhibit respect for management? If managers do not know if their employees respect them, there is a good chance that the employees do not. The only way to be sure that employees respect their managers is to witness it through the actions of the employees and managers, that is, their collective behavior and performance, especially during busy times with increased performance stress. Proof is in the actions, not just the statements.

The goal of good managers is to be respected by their employees, whether or not the employees like them on a personal level. Respect is earned through actions over time. This respect can be transformed into higher levels of focused productivity. Therefore, earning the respect of the reps can bring a manager dividends which can positively influence the bottom line.

Humans and Human Nature

Human beings need specific substances to physically survive. Food, water, and shelter are cited most often as the three basic requirements of human survival. However, beyond these basic physical needs there are also psychological and social factors that humans desire and seek out as part of their nature. Humans are inherently social beings. We tend to live in families or groupings and seldom do we crave a full solitary existence. Clearly, some of us are more social than others, but we all seek some level of communication, companionship, and interaction with other humans to fulfill a basic human instinct. If it were not for this natural desire for closeness and proximity, none of us would be here right now. Managers need to fully understand this necessary social contact and the desire to communicate with and be positively reinforced in this social environment before they can fully understand how to create an ideal positive environment for their call centers. In call centers, more so than in most industries, people can be in very close proximity, but working thousands of miles away from each other. To help smooth this possible disconnect, employees should be allowed and encouraged to work in groups, some large, some small, and to work collaboratively. This usually results in some interesting and unique successes that would otherwise not be achieved if every person was working as a single and separate unit.

Are You the Boss?

Managers usually answer "Yes" to this question, but how do they know that they are the boss? Is it because the sign on their doors says "manager?" Or is it because they are understood to be the respected leader of the call center? Where does a manager's power and influence within the center come from? Is the power granted only from the top, or is it supported by the reps from the bottom? Manager is not only a title, it is a state of being.

Respect and Distance

Too often, managers believe that an effective method of showing management skills is to distance themselves from their employees. In a call center, this could manifest itself in a separate and large office, in the form of a high-back leather chair, in a phone with too many buttons, and in other similar trappings. However, these are only symbols, and symbols often mean more to the person who has them than to the people who view them. This is not to say that having nice manager comforts makes someone a poor leader. What is does say is that these symbols do not make a person a good manager. It is not the objects; it is the employees, their performance on the job, and their respect for the manager that matters most and has the largest influence on profits.

To be effective as a manager, and for a company to be effective as an organization, a policy of equal respect for all employees must be in place and practiced. For example, the manager at one call center was speaking to a researcher in the employee break room during a shift change. In the middle of a sentence, the manager walked away from the researcher without saying a word and made a beeline to an employee coming through the door about to start a shift. He walked straight up to her, asked her a question, and then proceeded to give her a big hug. The researcher was shocked. His initial thought was "this manager is going to get sued." When the manager of the center came back to the researcher several minutes later, he apologized for leaving so abruptly and explained that this worker's mother was terminally ill in the hospital and he was checking up on her and her mother in her time of emotional turmoil.

There are several important management lessons in this one simple scenario. First, the manager of this center not only knew this employee by name and sight, but also knew that she had a seriously ill mother. This means that two important events occurred. One, the employee had enough confidence in her manager to disclose something so personal, thus making herself vulnerable. Two, the manager listened to the employee, understood the needs of the employee, and actively sought the employee out—above a researcher to his facility—to ensure that the employee was okay that day. This indicates that this center had a culture where communication and respect flow freely throughout and that the employees come first in the eyes of the management.

The second lesson from this scenario is that when the manager hugged the employee, he indicated sympathy—a rational action given the circumstances. If the manager chose not to hug the employee, but indicated sympathy, that would have been fine as well. However, if the manager instinctively was about to hug the employee, then at last moment due to fear, perception, or litigious reasons backed away from the employee, he would have made the situation worse, not better. A negative signal would have been sent, indicating an element of distrust or fear of action between the manager and the employee. Instead, given the events and the circumstances, everyone in this call center understood the manager's reaction, which was correct for the occasion and fully within the character of the manager and the center, giving solitude and support to employees in need.

The manager in this example was genuine in his concern for his employees. However, this genuineness also benefits the center and will pay dividends. The employee with the ill family member knows she works in an environment where she did not have to appear at work with a false face hiding a painful event. She did not check her life at the door. If the work culture were not as positive, there would be a good chance that she would not have come to work or she possibly might have quit. If this happened, the center would be short a rep and thus performance would slow. However, knowing the manager knew of her grief and knowing that she could trust management enough to share her grief with them, she was able to come to work and perform the best that she could with the realization that any poor performance would not be held against her. Having the employee at work, doing the best job possible, with a sympathetic management team is the most efficient and productive scenario for the center in this situation. A distracted employee with a sympathetic management team is more effective than an unsympathetic management team that would cause an employee not to show up or possibly quit her job. Furthermore, the goodwill generated by the policy of mutual respect for every employee will pay dividends in the future when this employee promotes the great work environment and the support she received to potential hires.

Not all management decisions are as extreme as the one outlined above. A simple communication skill of walking around the center saying "hi" to reps, patting them on the back, telling them to keep up the good work, and verbally encouraging them to go for a record day goes a long way. Communicating to employees in this manner conveys that managers are human and not some distant people outside of their reach. E-mails are nice, especially when they are personalized, but nothing goes as far as someone taking the time to look at an employee, shake her hand, and tell her that she is doing a great job and it is good to have her as a member of the team. This type of positive feedback will actually increase productivity because the employees will know that the manager knows them and knows what they are capable of, and out of respect for the manager, they will want to perform well so that they can earn even more positive visits from that manager and satify their desire for success at the same time. It is human nature to desire positive reinforcement.

Dan Coen, in his book *Building Call Center Culture* (2001), outlines five approaches managers should use when agents enter the call center. These approaches include:

1. Condition your agents to expect something when they walk through the door.
2. Train agents to accept your objectives.
3. Consistently penalize agents who fail to meet initial company objectives.
4. Make it a point of communicating with each agent in the same way each time.
5. Be prepared to motivate early—it pays dividends.

In number 1, Coen is talking about communicating every day to agents. As they walk through the door and enter the center to begin their shift, new information from yesterday's production numbers to today's goals will be listed. If there is a training session occurring, the reps will report to their respective supervisors for their time, etc. By posting important information for the employees daily, they will begin to expect objectives to be set by the managers on a daily basis, which is the basis for approach number 2. Consistency for all employees is at the core of approach number 3. If one agent fails to show up for work on time or fails to meet performance measures everyone is expected to meet, then this agent needs to be penalized in such a way that all employees know that there is a punishment for not meeting the objectives. If the behavior is not modified through disciplinary action, then the employee needs to be fired. Knowing that an agent can directly communicate with the manager often gives comfort to employees, thus Coen suggests in approach number 4 that the manager seek an opportunity each day to communicate with each employee through a variety of mediums. The final approach, number 5, outlined by Coen is employee motivation. Every employee from the highest performer to the lowest, needs to be motivated. Each needs reinforcement to improve their abilities and for the successful work done to date.

Interestingly, Coen's number one approach is reflected in the example of the call center with the grieving employee. The manager was at the door to greet all the reps as they walked through the door for their shift when he saw the employee with the ill mother. The other approach that requires expansion is number four.

Coen states that managers of call centers should realize that "agents desire to have an opportunity to communicate with management in non-telephone communication" (Coen, 2001, p. 17). To this Coen adds five specific ways to communicate to agents.

1. Go to an agent, say "hello," and ask them how they are doing.
2. Send a voice mail to each agent.
3. Send an e-mail to each agent.
4. Leave a message on the chair of each employee.
5. Leave a personalized note on the desk of each employee.

Coen continues, "[a] little communication when it is not required is always welcome. What you go out of your way to do in three to thirty minutes' time pays dividends in every way imaginable" (Coen, 2001, p. 17). Research for this book confirms Coen's idea that constant and effective communication from the call center manager to employees is an absolute necessity to build and sustain a positive culture. There is one caution, however, in Coen's five daily communication channels—keep it genuine. Agents in a call center, like all employees in an organization, talk, chat, and gossip. If a manager sets out to leave a voice mail, an e-mail, and a note on each agent's desk every day, it becomes routine, predictable, and trite. Agents will begin to expect the communication as a matter of course, not as something special or unique, and thus it will lose its positive effect. Therefore, a manager should communicate in person to select agents each week, giving each agent his/her time when appropriate. This way the attention will be neither rare nor continuous and thus trivial.

THE NAMES

Whether a manager employs a center of 10, 200, or 3000 representatives, he or she should know the first names of all of the employees from day one. Yes, day one! This is best done by taking a photo of new employees (either an immediate picture such as a Polaroid or a digital image). This picture becomes a flash card for the manager to memorize all employees' names. A manager should also know whether the employee goes by a nickname or shortened name to ensure that Jonathan is not called Jon or Elizabeth is not called Lizzy. Why is it so important to know the employees name so soon? Imagine the following two scenarios:

1. A new employee comes in the door for his shift. The manager walks up to the employee and welcomes him to work. He says, "Welcome…. what was your name again, Steve was it?" The employee retorts, "No, my name is Carlos, Mr. Van Horn."
2. A new employee comes in the door for her shift. The manager walks up to her and welcomes her to work. She states, "Welcome Sharon. I sure hope your first day is a rewarding challenge." Sharon replies, "Thank you Ms. Delillo. I am looking forward to working here."

In Scenario 1, the employee is nervous because it is his first day. He is afraid he will mess up and will not be able to make friends, and he is a bundle of nerves. In fact, the manager who just signed his papers to hire him could not even remember his name. Carlos thinks that maybe he was not as impressive in the interview as he thought and thus will be worried and less productive due to this worry all day.

In Scenario 2, the nervous new employee is greeted by name by the manager when she walks in the door. This tells Sharon that she is known and the expectations are high. Though the employee may be nervous, she will rise to the challenge put forth to her by the manager. Sharon realizes that the manager knows who she is and will be watching her progress. This gives her a reason to work hard because it is clear that the manager is fully in tune with the workings of the center since she knows every employee by name, even the brand new ones.

The sooner the names are remembered, the sooner the positive results will emerge from knowing the people who work to help make the center more productive. Simply stated, "attention is a strong aphrodesiac that makes people want to do for other people" (Coen, 2001, p. 83).

THE OPEN DOOR

One of the most effective means of communicating a positive business culture is to have a stated, and literally, open door policy. Most open door policies indicate that any employee at any level has the right to come into the manager's office and talk confidentially about any issue without fear of punishment or disclosure. This is not to say that employees should not use the existing chain of command; however, having an open door policy allows the employees access to the top quickly when necessary, when going through the chain of command would be too burdensome and time consuming, or when the issue is so personal that they do not want it shared with every supervisor and assistant manager. It is best for the manager with an open door policy to have an office close enough for all employees in the center to see the open door and know that at any time when that door is open, they are free to access the manager without question. Interestingly, even if there is an open door policy, few people will take advantage of it, except when it is a real necessity. Most employees will not abuse the system, but the knowledge that they can have this access is often enough to ensure a level of confidence in the management and to invite a positive culture throughout the organization. Furthermore, a call center manager should encourage assistant managers and supervisors to adopt the same open door policy. This will achieve two specific goals. (1) Every employee will know that the full management team has an open door and thus respects them enough to give them free and full access all the way to the top in the center. (2) If a manager has an open door policy, but the assistants and supervisors do not, then the only place an employee will feel comfortable taking a special issue will be straight to the top, discounting the rest of the management team. This could lead to an inefficient use of the management team and a dual level of trust in the management. All employees should know that any and every manager and supervisor can be approached and talked to confidentially.

A follow-up issue to the open door policy is respect for privacy. This means that if an employee comes to a management team member with a specific issue, that employee should have the confidence that this information will remain with that person unless stated otherwise. All it takes is one success, and that employee will become a positive and productive employee as well as a great recruiting tool for the call center. Likewise, if only one employee confides something to a manager and the information is leaked to other employees in the center, then that employee will never trust the management again, will never be fully productive, and will probably leave the call center, eventually becoming an anti-recruiting tool for the center. Therefore, a manager must absolutely ensure that all of the management team knows the policy of confidentiality and strictly abides by it, promoting a strong and productive work environment.

INCENTIVES

Many authors suggest that offering incentives is the ONLY way to get maximum performance from call center reps. However, experience shows that although there may be a rise in performance when the incentive is first offered, once the incentive is gone, so goes the performance. To sustain this level of performance, the manager would need to consistently offer not just incentives, but ever-increasing and more expensive incentives just to maintain the performance level. As Table 1-1 shows, the best approach for maximum performance is to ensure the right culture in the center where everyone is working their best to benefit both themselves and their center, simultaneously creating a win–win proposition.

Another problem with incentives is that they are temporally limited, meaning that employees work hard for a specific amount of time during the program, but not before or after. The effort is put forth, if at all, for the prize, not for improving individual or collective performance in the center. Changing the culture where each employee mutually reinforces each other in a positive manner to perform at their maximum does not have a limited shelf life as do incentive programs.

FINAL THOUGHTS

This chapter suggests that a key to an economically successful call center is to create a positive culture within an organization. Once created, this

Table 1-1. Effect on Performance of Incentive Program vs. Cultural Change

Single Incentives			
Old production	Incentive production	Post-incentive production	Total
8	10	7	25

Overall Cultural Change			
Overall production	Overall production	Overall production	Total
9	9	9	27

positive culture can begin to replicate itself through the employee's day-to-day experiences. The goal of each call center manager should be to have the most successful center possible. To accomplish this goal, this chapter outlines some key concepts a manager can implement within his/her center, such as knowing all reps by name, having an open door policy, working side-by-side with the reps on the phones each month, and more. These positive culture-building activities set the environment for success. Once a manager has enabled the creation of a positive and sustainable culture, both reps and customers will know its success.

REFERENCES

Coen, D. *Building Call Center Culture*. Tarzana, CA: DCD Publishing, 2001.

FURTHER READING

Bave-Kerwin, J. "The Role of Corporate Culture in Agent Commitment." *Call Center Agent Turnover and Retention*. Annapolis, MD: Call Center Press, 2002.

Freiberg, K., and J. Freiberg. *Nuts: Southwest Airlines' Crazy Recipe for Business and Personal Success*. New York, NY: Bard Press, 1996.

Phillips, J. J. *The Consultant's Scorecard*. New York, NY: McGraw-Hill, 2000.

CHAPTER 2

Accountability

ACCOUNTABILITY

The manager of a call center is accountable to two groups of people. First, the manager is accountable to the executives in the company or organization to meet goals, deadlines, and requirements set forth by the company. Second, the manager is accountable to his/her employees and staff. To be successful, a manager must ensure both groups' needs are accounted for to create a positive culture in the call center and ideally throughout the whole organization (a major theme of this book).

The *Oxford English Dictionary* (2003) defines the word accountable as the "quality of being accountable; liability to give account of, and answer for, discharge of duties or conduct; responsibility, amenableness" (www.OED.com). The key words a manager should pay attention to in the above definition are to give an account of, answer for, and responsibility. Many call centers are islands of power for a manager, away from a centralized headquarters location. Therefore, the manager must be accountable for all activities that occur within his or her center. This includes having the necessary information and data to account for his/her actions and the actions of the full call center vis-à-vis the goals, deadlines, and requirements set forth.

GOALS

If a manager is accountable for specific achievements in his/her center, the manager must set goals to ensure that accountability is ensured. Goals are an extremely critical tool for any manager, both for the center's performance standards and for the manager's personal achievement.

Setting goals accomplishes two things:

☐ Goals force people to identify what is important. If something is unimportant, then it should not be associated with a goal and possibly not be part of the mission of the center.
☐ Goals give people a mark to strive toward, to accomplish, and to measure success.

What do most employees in a company strive for or toward? If a goal is in place, then it will be clear when a person or people within an organization reach that goal. Similarly, if the goal is not reached within a particular time frame, it is fully necessary to ask "why was the goal not reached?" By fully examining this question (and answering it), new insights into an organization's efficiencies and inefficiencies will be illuminated, thus giving the manager the opportunity to turn a potential negative into a positive through necessary changes. The problems that may stop a manager from reaching a goal are possibly the same problems that have prevented the call center from being the top center in the organization to date.

The *Oxford English Dictionary* (2003) defines a "goal" as the "object to which effort or ambition is directed; the destination of a (more or less laborious) journey." This means that there is an endpoint somewhere in the future when a person perceives completion of a particular task—a goal (Figure 2-1). Without a clearly defined endpoint, goals will never be fully realized.

Another part of goal setting is laying out the strategy, the pathway, which will be traversed en route to the endpoint goal. What decisions have to be made? What people have to be in place? What events must transpire to continue movement toward the goal? All of these questions must be thoroughly explored and understood before a goal can be successfully achieved. While each of these questions are answered, the pathway to the goal is being set, and a type of road map is being created (Figure 2-2).

Figure 2-1. Goals must have an endpoint. (Source: David L. Butler.)

Figure 2-2. The pathway to a goal must be set. (Source: David L. Butler.)

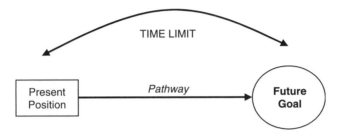

Figure 2-3. A time limit must be set to reach a goal. (Source: David L. Butler.)

The final piece of a goal is to set a temporal limit on when the goal should be achieved. Once a goal is defined and/or described and a map has been constructed to reach the goal, then a set time limit must be imposed to achieve this goal. Time frames can be as short as within the next hour or as long as within the next five years (Figure 2-3). No matter the duration, time must be a critical piece of the equation. If not, a goal may never be reached because there is no sense of urgency to accomplish the goal. Success for most people and organizations is measured by achievements. Without set goals, pathways to reach the goals, and a time frame to accomplish the tasks, success will be fleeting and the manager will have little or no level of accountability.

Levels

Goals are set at various levels for a multitude of reasons. A person may have personal goals for her/himself, for a relationship, for children, for a career, and for life. Likewise, a company can have a set of stated or unstated goals. These may include being the most successful company in a given market; increases in sales volume; increases in revenue; the ability to stay out of bankruptcy for another quarter, to hire more people, and to lower recurring costs; and many more. Similarly, a call center manager may set goals for a center. These may be to handle more calls faster with a higher level of customer service, to retain more employees, to convince an executive that a new piece of equipment is needed, and many others. Within a call center, each rep will have a set of personal goals not directly related to the center and a set of goals related to work within the center. This means in any given call center there will be scores of goals at various levels sometimes overlapping in the same space and time. The critical management piece is to harness the potential of all of these goals at one time through the call center.

Alignment

What are the chances of success in a call center if the many and varied goals are neither spoken, written, nor aligned all at levels (Figure 2-4)? This would mean that each person could have goals that have no commonality in terms of success, pathway, or completion time. Imagine the force that could be brought to bear if the various levels of goals from the corporate to the rep's personal goals were all in alignment seeking to achieve the same goal with the same road map within the same time frame? If success for your call center is what you seek to achieve, then this type of goal alignment in your call center is absolutely necessary, as Figures 2-4 and 2-5 demonstrate.

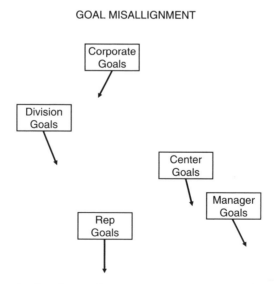

Figure 2-4. Goal misalignment. (Source: David L. Butler.)

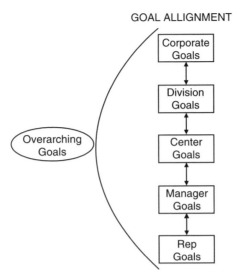

Figure 2-5. Goal alignment. (Source: David L. Butler.)

It is not enough just to have goals at various levels in an organization, these goals need to be aligned and parallel to ensure maximum chances of success in achieving the goals. For example, if a corporate goal is a 10% increase in revenue, a call center manager's goal is recruitment, and a rep's goal is a pay raise. Each of these disparate goals could pull the total expended labor effort in different, and sometimes opposing, directions. Imagine how disheartening it could be for a rep who has set a personal work goal for achieving success only to find out that another rep's goals runs counter to theirs, thus eliminating any potential gains the one person was hoping to achieve for the center. Instead of the potential for no goals or scattered goals, a manager needs to be fully cognizant of a corporation's or organization's stated and implied goals and to ensure alignment throughout. This requires the manager to be savvy enough to fully understand his or her total organization, the *motus operendi*, and their center's unique position within the total structure.

A call center manager should have a set of 3–5 clearly defined and articulated goals for his/her center. Most of these goals should parallel (be in alignment with) the goals of the parent company. For example, if a clearly defined goal of the parent company is a 10% growth rate in the next 2 years, the call center should have as its goal to bring to bear its ability to help in the 10% growth. Depending upon the type and focus of the center, this could be accomplished in a number of ways, including:

1. Revenue growth.
2. Decreases in spending.
3. Increases in productivity per unit input of labor.
4. Some mix of the three above.

Moreover, the manager may choose to increase the level of customer service by at least 10% in the same period, demonstrating that increasing customer service to this level directly adds to the growth rate of the company through customer loyalty to the company and/or products.

However, as Bruton notes, "business goals are a stumbling block; it is here that so many support departments come unstuck, and not necessarily by their own fault. Too often, the problem starts higher up the chain, where the business goals should be defined. Business goals are often unclear; either the company, its businesses, or in these acquisitive days its management is changing too quickly, so the goals move too fast. Another reason might be poor communication channels, rendered that way by accident or deliberately in some misguided attempt to control the workforce as opposed to involving them" (Bruton, 2002, p. 7). If a manager of a call center has some of the problems described by Bruton, then it is even more critical that the manager penetrate the veil of the upper management to discern what the actual goals of the business are so that he or she can strategically place the center on the path for success within the organization.

An effective manager should operate with a written set of solid, well thought out, and clearly articulated goals that specify what must be achieved in the next month, the next year, and the next 5 years. Operating without goals will leave the center without direction and thus at the mercy of others' agendas.

Ellis and Hawk (2002, p. 11) suggest that it is critical for the manager to effectively communicate to all employees the purpose and role the specific call center plays. The authors argue that "if you want your call center to be competitive, your agents need to fully understand the mission they're being asked to undertake. For call center leadership, this means clearly stating why their unit exists, what it contributes to the larger business and what appropriate measures will be used to assess its success."

A possible goal for the parent company may be to acquire similar companies over the next 5 years (mergers and acquisitions). This means that one goal for a call center manager should be to create an environment of flexibility that allows potential absorption of other call centers or similar divisions into the organization as new acquisitions occur, or, through acquisitions, as the parent company takes on new products and services. The manager should ensure that the environment in place allows his or her center to rapidly and successfully take on new functions of customer service to ensure a quick road to profitability for the parent company, reducing the transition time associated with mergers and acquisitions.

If the parent company has as a short-term goal to reduce operational costs, then the manager must do his or her utmost to increase the return on investment (see Chapter 8 on ROI) for the center and, if possible, to demonstrate that the center can be linked to the profitability of the parent company either directly or indirectly.

Employees at all levels should be encouraged to set personal performance goals that align directly with those of the center, the headquarters, and the center manager. Other goals can also be set for the rep, but it must be understood and communicated to the reps that these goals are secondary to the main alignment goals. Coaching, training, and mentoring on goal setting, mapping, and achievement may be necessary for any reps who are unfamiliar with goal setting and accomplishment.

In his chapter entitled "Tips to Make Agents Successful," Dan Coen (2001) summarized the full concept of goal setting from both the manager and the employee's perspective. One of the seven tips is "Make Goals Simple." Specifically, Coen states, "Agents can meet and exceed simple goals. They can't meet or exceed goals they cannot understand. In the telesales and customer service environments, management must simplify exactly what they want from their agents. Then, they must communicate those goals to their agents, and support those goals by managing around them" (Coen, 2001, p. 84). Building upon Coen's statements, not only should the goals of the organization, center, and manager be communicated to the reps, but the rep's point of view on their own goals and center goals should be taken into consideration. A self-set goal is more appealing and motivating than a goal set by someone else. Therefore, ensure that the reps are fully engaged in the goal setting process for themselves and the center.

Achievement

If a manager has walked through the goal setting for accountability standards logically, the goals of the company, the center, the manager, and the reps will be put in place. Likewise, a map of how to get to the goal has been delimited, as has the required time frame to meet the goals.

The critical question then becomes how does a manager or a rep know when the goal is achieved? If the date set for meeting the goal comes, how can a group of people know immediately whether or not the goal was reached or missed and by how much? The answer to the question is measurement. A goal, and mile markers along the path to the goal, must be set in a way that is measurable. Both quantitative and qualitative data/information can be turned into numerical measurements. For example, if a goal for the center, manager, and reps is to decrease the time callers are in queue, then this is easily measured with existing technology. If, at present, the average is 5 minutes, then the goal may be to reduce it to 2 minutes. Each day, week, and month the data will exist and can be seen by all. However, if a more qualitative goal is set, such as improved customer service, a different measure must be created. The manager must ask how customer service is measured? Is it through call backs? Satisfaction surveys? Time in queue? Repeat customers? Whatever is chosen as the surrogate measure, data must be collected to represent the improvement or non-improvement of customer service.

Not only do goals need to be measurable, they also need to be fully transparent to all. This means that if a goal is to increase the number of calls per minute for each rep, then a scoreboard must be set up in a location in the center that allows the reps to view the measurable improvements of their efforts on a daily basis. This means that pieces of reports will need to be displayed, and possibly explained, to the reps. Daily, weekly, and monthly data can be shown as well as trend lines, indicating potential success or non-success on the pathway to the goal. This way when a goal is achieved, it is a success for everyone collectively and individually.

ASSETS TO ACHIEVE GOALS

Whether a manager is new to a call center or has been there for years, he or she should immediately take an accounting of the assets of the center and compare those against the short- and long-term goals for the center. To make an assessment, first the manager should write down all of the capital at his or her disposal, making a list of the physical capital including building size, number of stations, software, routers and switches, furniture, etc. He or she should also make a reckoning of human capital at his or her disposal. How many people work at the center? Who comprises the management team, and what are their strongest skills and abilities? This will determine what is in the center's arsenal and aid in making the center the best call center in the region and within the organization.

Once a manager has established that the goals of the center are linked with the goals of the parent company, the manager needs the human capital necessary to achieve these goals. If the goals are articulated clearly, with specific numerical benchmarks to be met within a specific time frame, the human capital needed will be hired to meet and hopefully exceed these goals. In this manner, the goals become the defining factor for hiring the right people. For example, if the goal is to expand service on a particular product by 35%, then a manager must hire aggressive reps who can understand the goal and reach it within the time allotted. If the goal is to reestablish relationships with 10,000 customers who left or who may leave the organization, then it is necessary to hire people with skills who can articulate the "feelings" that the company would like to see customers come back. So instead of hiring just "any representative," now human resources can be tapped to hire specific people for the specific tasks that need to be achieved, reaffirming alignment within the full center.

CURRENT STATUS

Besides taking an account of the physical and human assets, an effective manager must know the center's current status. What is happening in the center at present, what occurred yesterday, and what is on the schedule for tomorrow? As important as "what" is occurring is knowing "why" it is occurring. Why are the events from yesterday, today, and tomorrow going on? Who set them in motion? Do they fit into the goal of being the best center in the region and within the organization? If a manager cannot answer these questions, then it is necessary for him or her to take some specified amount of time to fully understand the workings of the center from the bottom up and the top down. Only then can a manager fully maximize the performance of the center and create the highest return on investment for the company.

SWOT ANALYSIS

A SWOT analysis is an effective means to make a quick assessment of a person or organization's current position and avenues of potential strategic action. SWOT is an acronym for Strengths, Weaknesses, Opportunities and Threats. A SWOT analysis, like goals, can be completed and examined at many scales from the individual to the group

AN ORGANIZATION'S STRENGTHS

dedicated workforce

excellent management

location of facilities

Figure 2-6. A sample SWOT analysis. (Source: David L. Butler.)

or organizational level. Often, groups hire a neutral person to facilitate SWOT analyses to ensure maximum participation by all members of the organization. Within a center, this means that they would either need to bring in a neutral party (consultant) or, if the manager feels confident, he/she can lead the session. The key to most SWOTs is to allow all the brainstorming up front and to enable all voices to be heard.

During a SWOT analysis, most facilitators write down group decisions in each category: "What is the organization's strengths?" "What is the organization's weaknesses?" etc. (see Figure 2-6 as an example). Strengths and weaknesses are listed as internal factors, and threats and opportunities are considered external factors. With these concepts written down, a person or organization can then list action steps to enable forward movement and eventual success. After completing a traditional SWOT analysis, a slight addition to the existing analysis can bring a more complete picture of an organization's current position and can help determine its position and strategy for action (Lassen, 2003).

To create this added piece of a SWOT analysis, a 3×3 matrix needs to be created (see Figure 2-7).

After the matrix is created, the words "strengths" and "weaknesses" need to be printed across the top middle and right boxes. Next, the words "opportunities" and "threats" need to be placed on the left middle and bottom boxes with the summary list of items from the traditional SWOT analysis (Figure 2-7).

Once this table template is created, each of the four internal boxes need to be labeled 1 through 4. Each of these boxes will represent the intersection of the box directly above and to the far left. For example, box 1 will represent the summary list of strengths and opportunities, box two will represent the summary list of weaknesses and opportunities, and so on (see Figure 2-8).

Answers to boxes 1–4 need to be completed. Each box will more than likely include at least one item, and several boxes will be filled with many items, potentially overflowing the available space of the box.

SWOT MATRIX

	STRENGTHS 1. _____ 2. _____ 3. _____	WEAKNESSES 1. _____ 2. _____ 3. _____
OPPORTUNITIES 1. _____ 2. _____ 3. _____		
THREATS 1. _____ 2. _____ 3. _____		

Figure 2-7. A SWOT matrix. (Source: David L. Butler.)

Once complete, take a break, come back, and examine the full box. Does your organization have a dominant box? Does your organization have a box with little or no writing? Each box and the information contained within is a message about your organization, its current position, and the abilities or disabilities it has in a manager's road to success.

Box 1 represents an aggressive posture with many opportunities and strengths, and thus, you are in a position to move your center forward rapidly. This is the ideal position for most businesses. Box 4, weaknesses and threats, is a defensive posture. External threats are high, and your organization is riddled with weaknesses. Quite often, the best strategy for a business in this category for an extended period is to sell the business and start anew. If your organization fits into either box 1 or 4, the options are clear: keep an aggressive stance and reform or close, respectively. However, if a call center is dominant in box 2 or 3, options are less clear. In box 2, weaknesses exist, but so do opportunities. The ideal

SWOT MATRIX

	STRENGTHS 1. _____ 2. _____ 3. _____	WEAKNESSES 1. _____ 2. _____ 3. _____
OPPORTUNITIES 1. _____ 2. _____ 3. _____	1 strengths-opportunities 1. _____ 2. _____ 3. _____	2 weaknesses-opportunities 1. _____ 2. _____ 3. _____
THREATS 1. _____ 2. _____ 3. _____	3 strengths-threats 1. _____ 2. _____ 3. _____	4 weaknesses-threats 1. _____ 2. _____ 3. _____

Figure 2-8. A SWOT matrix with strengths and weaknesses. (Source: David L. Butler.)

goal here is to determine how to overcome the weaknesses that allow the organization to take advantage of the opportunities at hand. On the flip side, a dominant box 3 suggests that the external threats are high, but so are the internal strengths. The goal for a manager in this box would be to use the internal strengths to mitigate the threats as much as possible. Often, the external threats are high levels of competition, thus creating a niche market would be one of the action steps to move from box 3 to box 1. Sometimes an organization in box 2 or 3, when examining the assets required to move into box 1, realizes that the costs associated with this transformation are prohibitively high. Given this situation, and the expected slide into box 4 status, a organization will choose to sell while the negatives are not too strong to allow a decent return on the investment (Lassen, 2003).

A manager must remember that the SWOT analysis accomplishes two items. One, it helps to clarify the position of the center in the mind of the manager and gives the manager some information to communicate up the chain of command. Two, by allowing employees to engage in the processes, the employees can see the position of the center and what needs to be accentuated and strengthened to place the center in the best business position possible. Allowing the employees to participate will increase the likelihood that they will actively help to initiate the changes necessary for success and accountability in the center.

SCENARIOS OF SUCCESS

Every company has the same *motis opperendi*: to make a profit, and ideally, the highest profit possible. Though qualitative measures are good and legitimate, in the end the quantitative measures are what count, literally, as the return on investment for the company. Therefore, it is absolutely imperative that a manager measure as much as possible within the organization, including how goals will be achieved. Ellis and Hawk (2002) suggest that if goals are set and clearly articulated to all workers, then success from these goals should be measured. "Developing a wider range of success measures allows call centers to reap dual benefits: 1) top management views them as a more critical part of the business; and 2) they are able to motivate their staff with much more engaging missions and goals" (Ellis and Hawk, 2002, p. 11).

Quite often, managers put in place numeric goals, for example, 100 calls per employee per shift. Numeric goals are good, but they need a philosophical underpinning that illuminates the purpose. For example, if a manager said the call center was doing well, that manager should be able to explain why the center is doing so well, how he knows it is doing well, and what he is comparing the center's performance to. The manager should have some form of metric to measure the center's success. To fully make an argument, to achieve a goal, or to fully perform at the maximum ability and achieve the largest return on investment (ROI) for an organization, it is necessary for a manager to have numerous measures throughout the organization. Many managers have at their disposal some form of evaluation and scheduling software for their center. This is a start, but there is much more data that can be collected that will positively influence the decision-making process within the center. A manager should fully measure the cost of training, the return on investment (ROI) per employee, the turnover rate, the cost of turnover, and employee satisfaction. It is imperative to accurately and regularly track specific data in the center that are related to specific goals. If this data is not collected and goals are not tracked, there will be no mechanism in place to determine when goals are achieved and success is established or, if the goal is not reached, what variable(s) hampered the successful completion of the goal.

Imagine the following scenarios in which an executive from the company headquarters arrives to asses the status of the call center.

Scenario 1

The executive asks the center manager, "How are things?" The manager says they are fine for the most part. He shows energy and enthusiasm, but gives no specifics. Following up, the manager suggests that there are some problems to overcome, but once again gives no specifics. A portrait of a center manager emerges that shows he is enthusiastic, but without vision.

The outcome of the visit is that the manager will never be promoted beyond his current position in the center.

Scenario 2

The executive asks the center manager, "How are things?" The manager says that she set three goals for the center to achieve by midyear, with each of them paralleling the larger goals of the organization. These goals were set two months ago and the center has accomplished goal 1 during the first month, is striving to achieve goal 2 this month, but goal 3 does not seem to be achievable by midyear because of four major obstacles that she is attempting to overcome. She (the manager) asks the executive if he has any suggestions or can offer any help in removing some of the obstacles to achieve goal 3. The manager shares with the executive that as soon as goal 3 is achieved, her plan is to initiate a new set of goals with a particular focus to achieve an even more customer-friendly call center, a high level of accountability, and, of course, the largest ROI possible for the center. As a result of this conversation, the executive places her on his "person to watch" list and will monitor the center's success more closely and potentially target the manager for future promotions within the company.

The outcome of the visit is that the manager has just distanced herself from the competition and is on the fast track for promotion.

Clearly, articulated goals and objectives are important not only for the executives in the organization, but also for the rank-and-file employees in a call center. Imagine the following two scenarios as they relate to call center goals.

SCENARIO 1

The goal set by the manager for the employees in the center is an average number of calls completed per employee and achieved with a specific level of customer service. Each employee individually works toward his/her goal. Once achieved, the employee can then rest comfortably on his/her laurels for a while before a new goal is set next month. Those that have not reached their goal must work more diligently near the end of the month to ensure they meet the goal by the deadline. As long as they meet their goal, their job is secure.

SCENARIO 2

The manager sets three goals for the center. This has been communicated to everyone in the center in four mediums: memo, e-mail, posted displays, and announcements during an employee meeting. The goals are clear, reasonable, and achievable. It will take the concerted effort of everyone individually and collectively to reach the goals. Posters in prominent locations throughout the building have the goals listed for all to view daily. There is a thermometer next to each goal on the posters that is filled in as the center nears its goal. Similarly, there is a sheet next to the thermometer to insert a date when each goal is met. Each representative is assigned a responsibility to achieve his/her respective portion of the goal. This means that the center's success rests on everyone's shoulders collectively and that every person needs to fulfill his/her duties to achieve both personal and center goals. Instead of reaching a goal and stopping, the reps will over-achieve to ensure that the center meets its goals.

In Scenario 1, there is no collective vision or goal. Each person is looking out for themselves, but not the total center. This can be productive, but only in a limited scope and limited time, just like the incentive program. In Scenario 2, the goals are achieved as a team. Though the team is composed of individuals, it is the collective team effort that enables the success to occur. As the team continues to meet its goals, higher goals and standards are set.

FINAL THOUGHTS

This chapter has articulated that a call center manager has two groups he/she is accountable to and for: executives in the headquarters and reps in the center. To be accountable, a manager must have a clearly defined set of goals that are achievable, a road map to get to the goals, benchmarks along the way, a set time to reach the goals, and the ability to measure when the goals have been achieved. The goals being achieved should be in full alignment throughout the organization from the CEO all the way down. If not, then maximum efficiency cannot be found. Understanding what assets are available and how to bring them to work on a problem is needed in each center. However, before taking action, a manager should spend the necessary time and money to bring in an outside expert to run a SWOT analysis for the center with full employee participation. Once the manager is clear on the current status of the center, then he/she can use the available assets to set the goals and move forward to success.

REFERENCES

Bruton, N. *How to Manage the IT Helpdesk: A Guide for User Support and Call Centre Managers*, 2nd ed. Woburn, MA: Butterworth-Heinmann, 2002.

Coen, D. *Building Call Center Culture*. Tarzana, CA: DCD Publishing, 2001.

Ellis, C. M., and E. J. Hawk. "Improving Call Center Performance." *Call Center Agent Motivation and Compensation*. Annapolis, MD: Call Center Press, 2002.

Lassen, G. E. Author interview with Gregg Lassen, August 19th, 2003.

Oxford English Dictionary. London: Oxford University Press, 2003.

CHAPTER 3

Location, Location, Location

This chapter examines a common issue faced in business: What is the best location for a particular facility that will help maximize profitability? Since call centers require a large input of labor, critical factors in site location are the size and type of labor available. The right mix of labor helps managers hire successfully, thus meeting the objectives of the center. The location of a call center will by default determine the number and type of employees it can hire and retain. Conversely, the number and type of employees sought to fill the center should strongly influence the location of the call center.

WHERE TO LOCATE A CALL CENTER

There is an art and science to locating business activities. Site selection is a major industry because where a business is placed can help influence its success or failure, no matter how well the business is managed (see the Site Selection box).

SITE SELECTION

According to author Brendan Read (2000, p. 203) and site selection consultants, there are many factors to consider when locating a call center. These factors fall into three major categories: labor, legislation, and community.

LABOR

Availability
Wage structures

Local fringe benefits
Education
Language skills
Labor force participation

LEGISLATION

Telemarketing laws
Taxation policies and rates
Unemployment insurance and workers' compensation rates and
  rules
Right-to-work laws
Incentives, such as training grants and tax credits

COMMUNITY

Time zones
Climate
Telecom and electrical infrastructure
Transportation (roads, mass transit, and inter-city air and rail
  access)
Cost of living, including housing
Public safety
Property and site availability
Local business attitudes (e.g., whether the community is pro-
  business)

Though Read is correct that these factors, and many others, help one
location to succeed over another in site selection of call centers, what
is not clear is how to weigh each of these factors against one another.
In other words, is the climate of a community as important as the educational level of the labor pool? Clearly, legislation and community
are important elements in call center site selection. However, are they
the most important? This researcher's interviews with executives in
companies with multiple call centers as well as interviews with call center directors have delineated a top three list of variables that strongly
influence call center location decisions. These include:

1. Labor costs/labor pool
2. Tax incentives
3. Labor skills

Without an available and affordable labor pool that has the necessary skills, the call center will not be able to function, no matter the community or legislative environment. Therefore, Read suggests that many factors help influence call center site selection decisions, and each center has unique requirements; however, three major site selection factors consistently rise to the top, suggesting that not all site selection variables are weighted equally.

Call center managers do not have to worry about a storefront to attract walk-in customers to sell a service or product. Thus, there is a fundamentally different set of location requirements for a Wal-Mart than for a call center. Most call centers are back offices, and thus, the products/services are sold/acquired over the phone or by e-mail. The only reason to have a large and highly visible class-A office building would be for public relations, advertising, and/or company policy. However, even though call centers will not attract walk-in customers, the location of a call center is still extremely important and will help determine the success or failure of the center.

COMMUTING

Most people dislike a long commute to work; some actually despise it. Even if a commuter leaves his/her car at home because access to an effective and efficient public transit system exists, there are still crowds, delays, and time spent in commuting to contend with. Despite the pain associated with commuting, people traverse long distances all the time in all of the large- and medium-sized cities over the world. Even though people do commute and realize this is just a cost associated with "doing business," there is a threshold distance where they will choose not to commute—an invisible line where a location is too far to commute to given the particular job and pay. It is this threshold that determines the labor shed of each call center. The labor shed for each center is unique (see the Labor Shed box).

LABOR SHED

What is a labor shed? A labor shed is usually represented in the form of a map that delimits a given distance or time from a point that people are willing to commute to and from. For example, imagine a red dot on a map representing a call center. Now imagine driving 5 minutes in one direction from the call center. Stop. Mark a white dot on the map. Go back to the red centroid call center dot. Drive 5 minutes in the opposite direction. Stop. Mark a white dot on the map. Repeat this exercise along major and minor roads leading from the center. Now connect the white dots together in a circle-like figure. This is a crude labor shed map representing a 5-minute commute to/from the call center. This process can be repeated for 10, 20, or 30 minutes, and so on. Eventually, the labor shed will become elongated along interstates and major thoroughfares and less elongated on small roads in neighborhoods. This labor shed, if used correctly, can help a manager effectively recruit and retain employees and market his/her center toward a specific demographic profile as well.

Commuting, especially non-productive commuting, makes people feel that they are wasting time, money, energy, and patience. Likewise, most employees in a call centers are paid when they clock in and cease being paid when they clock out. Thus, reps are not paid to commute to and from work, and so the time and money spent on the commute is lost. Furthermore, commuting costs money. There are real costs, such as fuel, oil, parking permits, tires, and bus and metro passes, and opportunity costs, such as time spent on other activities. Therefore, each person has a maximum distance and/or time they are willing to commute for a particular job before they believe they are losing more from the commute than they are gaining from the job. It is at this threshold when many employees choose either not to take a job or soon find themselves seeking other job opportunities in locations nearer their homes. The long and difficult commute will lead to an unwanted turnover rate in the call center, especially if there is a negative business culture or a manager who is not respected by the employees.

The maximum commuting distance someone is willing to travel differs from person to person. Some people choose to use a formula to make their decisions. For example, a person can calculate the price of fuel, wear and tear on the vehicle, parking, etc. per day, per week, and per month to determine the commuting cost as a percentage of his/her total take-home pay. If the ratio of commuting cost to take-home pay grows, then the likelihood of attracting this type of employee to a center that is far away decreases (see Table 3-1).

The best opportunity for the employee in Table 3-1 would be to take the job closer to home which pays less because the cost of commuting would eat into any potential gains from an additional 50¢ an hour.

Table 3-1. Ratio of Commuting Cost to Take-Home Pay

Job 1—$8 Per Hour Pay and 30-Mile Commute

Cost of travel per week:
    Travel costs = 30 cents per mile
    30 miles each way, 60 miles roundtrip per day
    6 days per week × 30 cents per mile = $108 per week
Weekly pay:
    40 hours per week × $8 an hour = $320 per week
Take-home pay:
    $320 per week − commute cost ($108) = $212 per week

Job 2—$7.50 Per Hour Pay and 20-Mile Commute

Cost of travel per week:
    Travel costs = 30 cents per mile
    20 miles each way, 40 miles roundtrip per day
    6 days per week × 30 cents per mile = $72 per week
Weekly pay:
    40 hours per week × $7.50 an hour = $300 per week
Take-home pay:
    $300 per week − commute cost ($72) = $228 per week

Source: David L. Butler.

In fact, the employee would earn an extra $16 a week, plus the benefit of a shorter commute, taking the closer job.

Other people evaluate commuting in terms of lost opportunities. For example, some people want to work very close to home so they can be home as much as possible with children, be near a daycare, or be able to reach someone at home quickly if there is an emergency. As Table 3-2 shows, once again the best opportunity for a potential rep is to take the position at the location only 10 miles from home, even though it pays $2 less per hour. The reason is that by commuting 25 miles to work, there is a high likelihood that traffic will cause this person to be late picking up his/her child(ren) from daycare. The costs associated with those delays are not worth the increased costs of the more distant job. In fact, what should become clear is that, traditionally, to attract people from farther away, a business must pay more, making the commute and costs associated with the commute negligible. However, there are exceptions to this rule, such as a great work environment, that can influence people to commute very long distances.

Other employees like a short commute distance because they want to be able to get home to attend various functions or activities. The activity

Table 3-2. Ratio of Commuting Time to Lost Opportunities

Job 1—$9 Per Hour and 25-Mile Commute

Cost of travel per week:
  Travel costs = 30 cents per mile
  30 miles each way, 60 miles roundtrip per day
  5 days per week × 30 cents per mile = $90 per week
Weekly pay:
  40 hour per week × $9 per hour = $360 per week
Other costs:
  Daycare late fee = $35 per hour
Take-home pay:
  $360 per week − commute cost ($90) − daycare late fee ($35) = $235
  per week
  Chances of being late increases with distance

Job 2—$7 Per Hour Pay and 10-Mile Commute

Cost of travel per week:
  Travel costs = 30 cents a mile
  10 miles each way, 20 miles roundtrip per day
  5 days per week × 30 cents a mile = $30 per week
Weekly pay:
  40 hour per week × $7 per hour = $280 per week
Other costs:
  No daycare late fee due to proximity
Take-home pay:
  $280 per week − commute cost ($30) = $250 per week
  Chances of being late decreases with proximity.

Source: David L. Butler.

may be a soccer game, a church or reading group, or to just sit down, rest, and watch their favorite television show. People who dislike being in a car for an extended period of time usually hate sitting in traffic. Many of these people will take a route to or from work that may take 10–15% more time, just to keep the vehicle moving forward. This type of person would likely not seek a job too far from work along a congested thoroughfare. Others, however, are not bothered by a long commute. As long as the commute is not eating into a large percentage of their income, some employees do not mind traveling to earn an advanced income. These people usually consider commuting as a productive activity.

Table 3-3 shows the ratio between distance and costs of commuting. In Scenario 1, the commuter takes roads and pathways that are less

Table 3-3. Ratio of Distance to Costs of Commuting

	Travel Time	Travel Distance	Cost per mile	Total Costs
Scenario 1—Longer distance, less time (roundtrip)	1.5 hours	70 miles	$0.30	$21
Scenario 2—Shorter distance, more time (roundtrip)	2 hours	50 miles	$0.30	$15

Source: David L. Butler.

direct, but likewise not as filled with traffic. This commuter hates to sit in stop-and-go traffic and would rather trade off time over distance just to ensure that he/she is in continual motion and seems to be making progress. Though a bit farther, this commuter can usually shave off time from the more direct route, but at a cost of more money to travel the longer distance.

In Scenario 2, the commuter takes the most traditional and direct route to work. This also happens to be the same route that most other commuters take. Therefore, traffic is heavy and quite often he/she hits bottlenecks on the road that lead to stop-and-go traffic. The distance is shorter, though, and thus he/she burns less fuel, even including idling, and spends less direct money on commuting costs, an average of $15 per day.

Though these scenarios are hypothetical in nature, they do illuminate differences in commuter patterns. An effective call center manager should know not only the commuter distance of his/her employees, but also which type of commuter scenario each fits into. The reason this knowledge is important is that if some employees travel at the farthest extent of the center's labor shed and the manager assumes they do not mind the commute, when in reality they do, the chances of retaining those employee decreases significantly. Why? There are three main reasons. One, these employees hate to sit in traffic and therefore will go out of their way to avoid traffic, suggesting they will become tired of the commute quickly. Two, this avoidance increases the cost of their commute to the center. Since a center's labor shed is based partially on the economics of travel to and from the center, these employees' circuitous routes increase their costs of traveling, disabling the labor shed model. Thus, if these representatives live at the edge of the center's established labor shed, there is a high likelihood that the costs associated with taking the longer route will cut into their earnings, pushing them to find employment closer to home.

Three, if these employees notice that they are paying too high a percentage of their wages for commuting, they are left with two options: they can either take the more direct route, which will decrease their commute costs, increase their commute time, and put them in the traffic situation they wished to avoid or they can seek employment closer to home or move closer to the employment.

Buildings

Call centers are found almost everywhere and in every type of building imaginable, from downtown skyscrapers to strip shopping centers to malls, to old Wal-Marts. Call centers can even be found in homes and in aircraft hangers above maintenance bays. Call center buildings come in all sorts of sizes, shapes, and locations. Whether a center is above an airline hanger in Chicago or in an old abandoned church, the important consideration is whether a center's size, layout, and location help in effectively managing the center.

Read (2000) presents a list of items to examine when looking at a particular property. These items include:

1. Access
2. Competition
3. Security
4. A healthy building
5. The shape of the building
6. Voice/data/power reliability
7. Expansion and contraction rights

By access, Read means the ability for workers to find the center within a reasonable commute time. Too much competition in a market will naturally lead to cannibalization of centers and will drive up labor costs. To avoid this problem, the center should not be too close to other centers and overlap multiple labor sheds, but at the same time, it should not lose the vital access variable. Security, especially after 9–11, is a necessary requirement of doing business. It is important to find a building that is healthy and in good shape. The appropriate building should allow for effective management with its current layout/configuration. If the building's design inhibits an open and communicative atmosphere that would leave reps feeling isolated, then it is not a good choice. Voice/data/power reliability, or to state it another way, redundancy, is critical to operations of a call center. Most organizations with more than one center will have built into their call centers' architecture the concept of redundancy, allowing one center to go offline with an automatic switching of calls to another center without losing a call. If there is only one center in an organization, the idea of redundancy takes on more important challenges.

EXAMPLE 1

A hotel reservation center in the South was receiving the standard allocation of calls during a normal mid-week day. Suddenly an alarm sounded from the manager's computer. The manager went to the computer and saw the problem. The Midwestern sister call center of their organization was now under a tornado warning. A tornado had been spotted near their center, a tornado warning had sounded, and all employees of the Midwestern center were heading for the basement for protection. Before the Midwestern manager left for the basement, all operations were suspended in the center and calls were routed to the nearest center, the one the South. Call volume peaked at the Southern center. Within 30 minutes, the threat of the tornado passed, the Midwestern center was back online, and calls were declining at the Southern center as the network was routing calls back to Midwestern center. Tornadoes are not predictable, and therefore, redundancy is necessary, ideally through multiple centers in multiple locations.

EXAMPLE 2

A call center in the West was experiencing unusual weather, a lightening storm. This was the only center open for this organization since it was late in the day. As the electrical storm strengthened, lightening began striking nearby, testified by the increased volume and frequency of thunder. A few minutes later, a loud boom was heard and the lights of the center dimmed, but operations continued. One glance outside indicated that the nearby blocks had gone black; the lightning strike hit a nearby transformer. Having foreseen this type of emergency, this center was equipped with two backup diesel generators, which could be heard humming through the back walls outside the center. These generators enabled the center to remain online through the power outage, saving all calls in queue and all data in the system. After approximately 40 minutes, the power company had the power back on and the sound of the generators faded as the lights came back up to full illumination. Though the center staff was a bit shaken, customer service continued uninterrupted.

The final item on Read's list of finding property for a call center is expansion contraction rights. Remember, any number of opportunities and challenges face call center managers on a daily basis.

Organizations are always in a state of flux, which includes mergers, divestments, acquisitions, restructuring, consolidation, expansion, and more. This means that each call center should be in a position to maximize on the opportunities presented. Ideally, this should enable the expansion of an already successful center. Thus, it is vital to fully understand the full constraints, both physical and contractual, to expansion.

An additional item to add to Read's list would be parking. Many managers forget that if they have a 250-seat center, at any given time they would need a parking lot that accommodates at least 250 spaces. This is a lot of concrete and asphalt. Consider the following equation:

$$250 \text{ employees} = 250 \text{ parking spaces}$$

Each parking space is 10 feet wide and 22 feet long (to accommodate backing out of the parking spot)

$$10 \text{ feet} \times 22 \text{ feet} = 220 \text{ square feet per parking space}$$

$$220 \text{ square feet} \times 250 \text{ needed space} = 55,000 \text{ square feet of space at}$$
$$\text{minimum for parking}$$

$$55,000 \text{ square feet} = 1.26 \text{ acres}$$

It becomes obvious then that proposed location for a center should ensure ample parking nearby and in a safe location. If not, the center might end up like a cell phone call center in a city on the Gulf Coast. This center chose a scenic location due the availability of labor (and a little politics). Once the center was opened and then quickly expanded, it became apparent that there were not enough parking spaces to accommodate the employees' vehicles. Because of this bottleneck, the call center had to lease land for parking. The local economic developer was finally brought in and an agreement was worked out between the cellular service call center and nearby establishments with parking. Unless a call center is located in a major metropolitan area with an advanced, reliable, and safe public transportation system with a stop nearby, expect at least 95% of employees to drive to work with one person per vehicle. Research on call center reps indicates that the majority drive themselves to work, as Table 3-4 indicates.

CLUSTERS

When locating a call center, it is important to determine what types of services are available and where these services are located. For example, will the center need copying services? Will it need regular maintenance of

Table 3-4. Survey of Employee Transportation to Work

How do you get to work?	Percent
Drive	95
Dropped off	1.95
Public transport	1.10
Carpool	1.95
Total	*100*
n = 359	

Source: David L. Butler

equipment? What would happen if some of the computer systems went down or the backup generators did not function? Is a list of the service providers available? Are they on the same side of town as the center or in another town? The good news is that the services that a center needs are probably in most medium-sized metropolitan areas. The bad news is that that these service companies like to locate near a large cluster of call centers since they are major clients. Therefore, to get close to the service providers a center has to get closer to other centers, potentially encroaching into their labor sheds. This means that a manager will have to balance the proximity to service providers for fast and easy access if a problem occurs with being too close and possibly overlapping several other centers' labor shed. "Many locations are already saturated with too many positions for the available labor supply, both in total and in different fields, such as call center work" (Read, 2001, p. 170). Balance wisely.

INCENTIVES

Almost any new call center can take advantage of incentives from the local community and/or the state. Common incentives include free land, low-interest loans, tax breaks on large equipment purchases, free training for reps, and more. The question is not whether to take advantage of the incentives, but what mix of incentives a manager should choose to take advantage of? Instead of having the incentives drive the center, the wisest course of action is to have the center's strategy outlined first and then chose the specific incentives from the buffet of options offered by the state or local municipality. It is not wise to have the incentives drive the center, since the goals of the center may not be parallel to those of the state or community. A manager should keep the center's priorities front and center. Most local economic developers/chambers of commerce can help a new center take advantage of these opportunities.

TECHNOLOGIES

What technological infrastructure is necessary for a call center? What type of bandwidth does it need? Depending upon the location, the options may be many or few. For example, in large- and medium-sized cities within the United States, a center should have multiple options of long distance, data, and voice carriers. Furthermore, there is a good chance that there are multiple redundancies within each system, so if one fiber line is cut, the other part of the loop continues transmitting without a loss of contact or bandwidth. In more rural states, the options and choices may be few. In developed nations, the level of technology will be similar to that of the United States; however, you may have only one provider—the national carrier. Developing nations provide some challenges. Locations such as India, the Philippines, China, South Africa, Panama, and others have fewer data and voice lines and even fewer redundancies. However, specific locations within these nations have been targeted as "technology centers," such as Bangalore in India, where the necessary information technology infrastructure has been placed to ensure connectivity. However, as more centers locate in these lower labor cost areas, more pressures will be placed on the existing infrastructure and bandwidth, necessitating the need for continued investment by both private and public entities if this growth trend is to continue. There are a number of books that address call center technology in superb detail, including Bocklund and Bengston's *Call Center Technology Demystified* (2002) and Waites' *A Practical Guide to Call Center Technology* (2001). The purpose of this section is to inform managers that there are multiple trade-offs in call center location, including the availability, accessibility, and redundancy in the information technology infrastructure. It is wiser to choose the conservative side of too much bandwidth and voice capacity because chances are in the near future the center will need to draw on these reserves.

COMMUNITY COLLEGES

Community colleges can be one of the greatest assets to a call center. Community colleges, as their name implies, were created for and focused upon the development of a local community. This includes the economic development of the community and the personal development of people within the community. These two foci of community colleges can be used in a positive and productive manner to develop a call center. First, the community college brings expertise to the particular problems centers may be having. Just one look at the roster of faculty and administrators at the local community college should indicate the wealth of information and expertise that is usually available to the center with just a phone call to the community college. Most of this expertise can be accessed very inexpensively (if not for free) and can offer solutions or troubleshooting for any of the myriad of problems a center might be experiencing.

Many community colleges also have centers for workforce development. This may be in the form of job placement, retraining, research, and/or ongoing classes. Often, call centers can outsource their training, or at least the initial stages of training, to the local community college. "Placing a center in an area that has one or more colleges or even a single large university can give you ongoing flow of admittedly transient workers. They won't stay around long, but they are often available on short notice, and they can work odd shifts" (Dawson, 2001, p. 19). These colleges offer at least one filtering layer for potential employees to work in the call center, saving the center both time and money in recruitment and training.

Besides the workforce component and expertise, community colleges are also a reserve of labor in the form of students. Students often make excellent call center employees for the following reasons:

1. They are intelligent.
2. They come with skills.
3. They have flexible schedules.
4. They are not seeking full-time employment.
5. They usually have insurance with their parents.
6. They are trainable.
7. They are motivated with excitement and energy.
8. They are not likely to unionize.

Most call centers managers seek trained (or trainable) and motivated people who can learn, show up to work, and are not likely to cause serious concerns with performance or union activity. Because students are transient and often have very flexible schedules and extra time on their hands, they are often sought after by many call centers. Furthermore, since most students have some level of skills and training already, Levin (2001, p. 48) suggests that this can lead to substantial savings for call centers in reduced training.

The same reasons that make students attractive to call centers as a source of labor makes them eventually leave the center. Because students are transient, they work at the center because it is near the college. Thus, when they leave the college or university, they leave employment at the center. Levin (2001) and others have articulated that call centers should be viewed not as "just a job," but as a career. If this philosophy was implemented, it would cause a disruption of the flow of students into the centers. For example, imagine that a call center recruits from a local college or university for part of its labor force. These students show up to work, do their job well, earn their paycheck, and enjoy their classes at the college and time spent with their peers. Now interject the idea of the call center as a career. If the manager told one of these students working at the center that this is not just a job, it is a career, the manager would get two possible responses. Response one would be, "If this is a career, why am I going to college if I am performing these functions as required very well with my current level of education? I am wasting time and money on college." Response two is, "I am going to school to be able to avoid just this type of job. I can do this job now; there is little possibility of promotion that I can see. I would rather be a manager of a company, not make a career as a customer service representative."

Herein lies the problem. The skills required and pay level offered at call centers are ideal for someone beyond high school with some college. However, with a full college degree, too often the employee becomes bored with little chance for challenge or promotion (i.e., pay raise and responsibility) and thus seeks employment more in line with their degree. Therefore, if call centers truly want to make call center employment a career path for educated and degreed people, they will by necessity have to raise wages, entrance requirements, and transparency of promotion throughout the full corporate organization. If customer service rep positions were viewed as entry-level management, sales, or marketing tracks within an organization, then the possibility of making a call center rep position a career would begin to take on new light. However, this would entail recreating the job description of most call center reps to include a higher level of autonomy for employees to utilize their skills. Considering the level of automation in the industry, it appears that, in fact, the industry is going in just the opposite direction, where the technology takes on the major skills so that reps can come in with fewer skills and less training time.

LABOR—THE RECURRING COST

The single most important variable for most call centers is labor. Labor costs, over a short period of time, easily eclipse costs associated with new equipment, a new building, and land. Controlling labor costs means controlling the success of a center and, by association, the success of the manager of the center. Table 3-5 demonstrates the awesome power of labor costs.

Using the scenario in Table 3-5, recurring labor costs per month are more than the full cost of equipment and the recurring cost of the long distance contract per month combined. If you compare only recurring costs such as labor and services, labor then becomes an even greater percentage of total call center costs.

Alternatively, imagine if the cost of labor per quarter in the previous example exceeded $1.3 million and the cost of the land and facility was $1.5 million. This would mean that the amount spent on labor cost in one year could allow the building of approximately four new call centers, of course with no employees. Therefore, managers with the focus on the highest ROI possible for their call centers must be able to control and manage labor costs, at all costs. If a manager cannot effectively control labor costs, the call center will not have an effective ROI for the parent organization. In fact, given the limited time available to managers, most of their time should be spent managing their labor, not on the other service costs,

Table 3-5. Call Center Labor Costs

300-Seat Center	
Infrastructure	
Cost of land and building (one time cost)	$1,500,000
Equipment and services	
Cost of long distance per month	$135,000
Cost of equipment (one time cost)	$250,000
Labor[a]	
Cost of labor per hour per rep	$9
Cost of labor per day per rep (8-hour day)	$72
Cost of labor for all reps per day	$21,600
Cost of labor for all reps per week (40-hour week)	$108,000
Cost of labor for all reps per month	$432,000
Cost of labor for all reps per quarter	$1,296,000

[a] Excludes taxes and benefits which often contribute an additional 25% to labor costs.

because in the end the stability or instability of the labor force, and thus labor prices, will either make the center a success or failure.

Because labor is the driving force of investment in call centers, employee recruitment and retention should be at the very top of the list of concerns for a call center manager. To illustrate this point, consider the following example. A particular call center had a manager who was both bright and experienced in the call center industry; however, his relationship with his employees was one of distance. The major project this manager was working on was a concept for reducing long distance calls for his center. Though the approach this manager created was interesting and innovative, the chances of success were slim due to the changing nature of long distance and key information technologies. However, this manager, who clearly put time and effort into this project, was not aware of the severity of his labor problems. This particular call center was unionized. Management was about to initiate longer hours (at night) in the center, unbeknown to the employees and labor reps at the time. The mixture of the manager's dislike of the union (and unionized employees), plotting for increased shift hours, and the union's problems with management all pointed to one distinct conclusion: the manager should have been spending more time communicating with his employees directly instead of working on a plan to possibly save a percentage of their long distance cost. The potential costs savings of his project were minute compared to the costs associated with the labor union demanding an increase in pay and benefits if the company was going to require the employees to work longer shifts. Table 3-6 demonstrates the projected costs of overtime labor in this situation.

Table 3-6. Comparison of Current Labor Costs with Projected Costs for Overtime Labor

100-Seat Center
Current labor costs at $10 per hour for 30 hours per rep
$10 \times 100 \times 30 = \$30,000$ per week for labor
If employees worked 39 hours per week per rep
$10 \times 100 \times 39 = \$39,000$ or an increase of $9,000 or almost 30% per week
If the union demanded high wages to accommodate this need for extended hours at $11.50 an hour the total cost would be
$11.50 \times 100 \times 39 = \$44,850$ or an increase of $14,850 per week.

The difference in labor costs per week between the manager's ideal and the union's demands are $14,850 - $9,000 = $5,850$ per week or $23,400 per month. The manager's plan for long distance savings would have to save the center at least $23,400 per month just to break even and to justify his attention on issues other than his employees. Furthermore, factor in the likelihood of success of his project, which was small, and it is possible to state that the cost of this inattentive manager could cost his center $23,400 per month, since this was what he was not saving through effective communication as a manager.

How to Find a Labor Shed

The beginning of this chapter defined a labor shed and offered some basic descriptions on how a labor shed is constructed. This part of the chapter examines how a labor shed is created for a center and examines what benefits a manager can glean from knowing the labor shed for his/her organization.

Location = Employees, Employees = Location

The bottom line is that no matter the call center's location, the size of the building, or the marketing used to recruit employees to the center, a manager will be limited by both time and space (labor shed) to a finite number of people they can potentially employ in their center. To maximize resources, recruitment, and retention, all focused on the bottom line, the manager needs to be aware of the labor shed in all of its nuances and should know how to maximize labor participation in the center within this area.

First, the manager must have quality data to work with. This is best accessed through a research consulting firm that will offer the best value for money spent on obtaining quality data. Once the data is acquired, tables and graphs such as those in Tables 3-7 and 3-8 and Figure 3-1 can be constructed.

Tables 3-7 and 3-8 and Figure 3-1 indicate the existing labor shed of multiple call centers in a Southwestern city. It is very clear from both tables and the figure that the majority of the employees of these centers drive under 40 minutes and 25 miles to work. Beyond these limits, the number drops off dramatically. This means that the chance of recruiting and retaining an employee from 50 miles and/or 50 minutes from the center is slim.

Table 3-7. Distance Traveled to Call Center in Miles

Distance	Number of Commuters
0–5	85
6–10	110
11–15	71
16–20	32
21–25	25
26–30	14
31–35	4
36–40	8
41–45	4
46–50	3

$$n = 356$$
Average miles traveled 12.86

Source: David L. Butler

Table 3-8. Commute Time to Call Center in Minutes

Time	Number of Commuters
0–5	16
6–10	52
11–15	81
16–20	88
21–25	51
26–30	26
31–35	15
36–40	15
41–45	13
46–50	1
51–55	0
56–60	2
61–65	1

$$n = 361$$
Average commute time 20.41

Source: David L. Butler

Just as the location of the center helps define the employee base of a call center, where potential employees live helps to define the call center as well. For example, imagine that each person at home held up a powerful flashlight pointing directly up into the night sky. The manager then gets into an airplane and flies over the area with a camera and takes

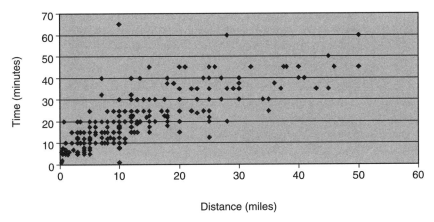

Figure 3-1. Commute time and distance to call center. (Source: David L. Butler.)

a picture. When the picture is developed, thousands of little dots of light will appear representing potential employees at their homes. Some areas of the town or city would have many people closely clustered together if they lived in apartments, condos, dormitories, or similar areas of high-density residencies. Other parts of the map would represent more exclusive neighborhoods with fewer dots in an area, representing larger houses and associated acreage. Farther out of the city, into more rural areas, the map would indicate areas with no dots, just complete blackness.

Using this map with the points of light, it becomes easier to narrow potential locations for call centers based on labor availability. Even though the most inexpensive land would probably be found in the black area where there was no light, of what use is a call center on inexpensive land if there are no people nearby to work in it? A light map showing a highly concentrated urban area like New York City would indicate that that city would be an ideal location for labor. However, prices for building space and business operations can be prohibitively expensive, even if millions of people live within a close distance to the center. This is the balance that is negotiated, with each call center trying to determine an optimal location based on labor availability.

LABOR SHEDS AND GEOGRAPHICAL INFORMATION SYSTEMS

Since the mapping project outlined above is a fantasy, how can managers find their labor shed and make the best use of this knowledge?

First, managers must create a realistic labor shed for their centers. This can be done any number of ways; however, the most efficient way to provide the best information and graphic interface is to use a Geographical Information System (GIS).

Geographical Information Systems, commonly referred to GIS, are tools that allow data and data analysis to be used in a powerful spatial medium, usually through overlaying multiple maps with different sets of data and analysis. These tools can be invaluable to a call center manager when utilized correctly with good data.

EXAMPLE

To create the labor shed, good data must be collected first. Though many local development agencies may have data and charts on labor patterns available, for purposes of accuracy and unbiased results, it is suggested that the data either be collected anew or be the current U.S. census data. These data come in different spatial areas including census tracks and zip codes. Since most people know their zip code, quite often this is the easiest unit to collect data from. The next step is to determine concentric zones of time/distance from the call center. This can be accomplished easily by traveling along major and minor roads that radiate out from the center at peak drive time (rush hour). Determine how long it is possible to drive for 5 minutes/miles, 10 minutes/miles, and so on up to 30 or 45 minutes/miles. Record the location, for example, a crossroad, where you were at each time frame or mileage point. With this information, a GIS, and existing data, call center managers can begin using a powerful tool for their centers.

GIS software contains a variety of base maps based on different geographical units. For purpose of example, this book will use a zip code boundary map of Lafayette, LA (Figure 3-2). If a center is located in Lafayette, the manager of the center must first discern how many people are within the greater Lafayette area. By clicking on various zip codes surrounding the center and sorting them by higher and lower populated zip codes, a general map of the population of Lafayette is created.

Adding another map layer will offer a view of major roads, enabling the manager to see overlap areas of high population and transportation access (see Figure 3-3). Next, the manager can use the buffer function of a GIS to set up time and distance zones around an existing center or a potential site to place a new call center. These zones can be in different increments. Figure 3-4 demonstrates five concentric circles of 5 miles each.

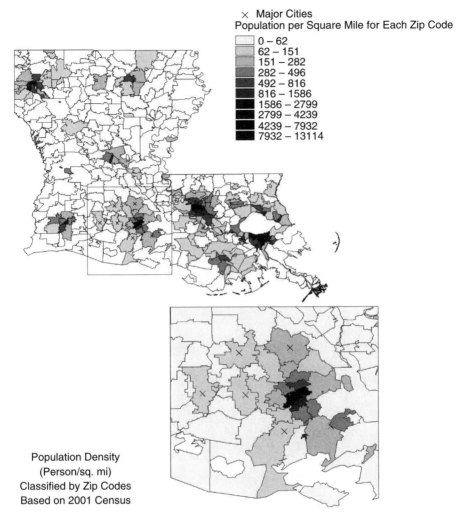

Figure 3-2. Population density of Lafayette classified by zip codes.

Once these zones are created, it is possible to query the census database for the type(s) of employees you are seeking. For example, if you are interested in unemployed people, you can choose that option. If you are seeking students, that can be chosen as well. What about women? Men? Married? Single? Within a specific age range or household income? All of these individually or grouped can be queried and placed on the map, enabling the manager to determine the potential labor pool within a given commute distance/time from the existing or future site of a call center (see Figure 3-5).

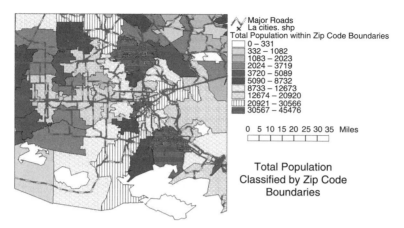

Figure 3-3. Major roads and corresponding population areas in Lafayette. (Courtesy of George Roedl, The University of Southern Mississippi, Hattiesburg, MS.)

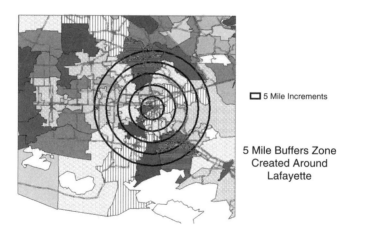

Figure 3-4. Five-mile buffer zone around Lafayette. (Courtesy of George Roedl, The University of Southern Mississippi, Hattiesburg, MS.)

GIS technology, when used expertly with good data, offers a powerful tool to help managers determine what exists within a delimited labor shed. Since most call center managers are strapped for time, it is recommend that the GIS labor shed project be outsourced to an expert, consulting

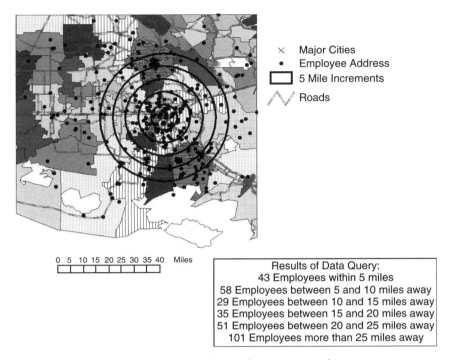

Results of Data Query:
43 Employees within 5 miles
58 Employees between 5 and 10 miles away
29 Employees between 10 and 15 miles away
35 Employees between 15 and 20 miles away
51 Employees between 20 and 25 miles away
101 Employees more than 25 miles away

Figure 3-5. Location of potential employees in Lafayette. (Courtesy of George Roedl, The University of Southern Mississippi, Hattiesburg, MS.)

company, university, or organization that specializes in GIS technologies and data for analysis and model building.

FINAL THOUGHTS

This chapter demonstrates that the labor and location of call centers are intricately interwoven. Because of this direct connection, any and all decisions of managers of calls center in terms of hiring practices, recruitment, retention, change of location, expansion prospects, and a host of other decisions must take both the labor and the location processes into account. Furthermore, research and logic indicate that the manager with the largest amount of reliable data on his/her call center and labor shed has the opportunity to make the most informed decisions possible in the pursuit of a high ROI for the call center and continued advancement within the organization. Given this reality, every manager should have an effective and frequently updated database of the center's labor shed and should examine it frequently before making tactical or strategic decisions for the call center.

REFERENCES

Dawson, K. *The Call Center Handbook,* 4th ed. Gilroy, CA: CMP Books, 2001.

Levin, G. "College Call Center Programs Help to Fill Shallow Labor Pool." *Call Center Recruiting and New-Hire Training.* Annapolis, MD: Call Center Press, 2001.

Read, B. B. *Designing the Best Call Center for Your Business: A Complete Guide for Location, Services, Staffing, and Outsourcing.* Gilroy, CA: CMP Books, 2000.

FURTHER READING

Bocklund, L. and D. Bengston. *Call Center Technology Demystified: The No-Nonsense Guide to Bridging Customer Contact Technology, Operations and Strategy.* Annapolis, MD: Call Center Press, 2002.

Phillips J. J. (Series Ed.), and N. L. Petouhoff, (Ed.). *In Action: Recruiting and Retaining Call Center Employees.* Alexandria, VA: American Society for Training and Development, 2001.

Waites, A. J. *A Practical Guide to Call Center Technology.* Gilroy, CA: CMP Books, 2001.

CHAPTER 4

Hiring

> *"To know exactly whom you should hire, you must first understand the skills, attitudes, interests and motivations that make an agent successful in your center. This involves more than just writing a job description with job requirements. It includes understanding the type of work that is done, the skills and motivations it takes to complete this work, the expectations that are set for agents and the cultural aspects of the company that are critical for success"*
> *(Cline, 2002, pp. 27–30).*

What are the basic and essential skills required of reps which would enable a manager to successfully operate a call center? How does a manager determine if he/she has the right mix of people in his/her center? Are all of the sub-managers, supervisors, and front-line reps the right people for the jobs given the focus of the center? Every manager should be able to answer these simple questions with easy and quantifiable answers. If a manager cannot answer these questions easily, then he/she needs to step back, reflect on the goals and missions of the call center, and begin to rebuild the employees of the center based on a set of clearly defined goals and associated attitudes, skills, and level of training for the representatives for the center. Let's begin this process.

HIRING

There is an abundance of advice in books and articles on how to hire and/or train the "best" or "right" employee for a call center. A key reason this is such an important and seemingly ubiquitous topic is that

1. Call centers use a large input of labor.
2. Turnover rates at call centers have been very high.
3. Competition for call center-type labor is increasing.

4. Call centers pay a lot of money to hire and train employees only to lose most of these reps to other employers within 2 years.

In short, lists on how to select the right person to work at a call center are all motivated by the same factors: to save money and/or increase revenue for the center. If you can hire the right person for the center with the necessary skills already in hand, then potential training costs will be less for this person; thus, the center will be able to recoup the money spent on hiring and training this employee in a shorter period of time. Likewise, since training time will be less, the center can reap the benefits of this employee's production faster.

An examination of the many lists of qualities, skills, attributes, etc. in hiring and training a call center employee shows that each list is as diverse as the people who create them. As stated previously, Cline (2002, p. 27) suggests that you must first understand the skills, attitudes, interests, and motivations that make an agent successful in your call center before hiring a new agent. She argues that there are four success factors in the call center environment. The factors and associated categories are:

1. Cognitive ability (can do)
   Apply information = productivity
   Examples: problem solving, learning, and applying information

2. Planning (can do)
   Organizing ability = efficiency
   Examples: planning ability, organizing ability, adherence to policies, following rules, accuracy

3. Interpersonal (can do)
   Persuasion = upselling
   Examples: customer service, persuasion, getting along with others, teamwork, coaching ability

4. Motivation (will do)
   Attitude toward work = turnover
   Examples: attitude toward work, attendance, flexibility, going above and beyond, energy

Anita O'Hara (2001, p. 21) states that there are six fundamental steps in the recruitment and selection process that a manager should consider before making a hire for a center. These include:

1. Analyze job tasks.
2. Identify specific skills and competencies required.

3. Describe the performance required by the job.
4. Develop a job description.
5. Identify source pools and a recruitment plan.
6. Define and implement your selection process (O'Hara, 2001, p. 21).

Ann Smith (2001), taking a different approach than the previous two authors, has delimited a full list of skills/knowledge analysis for potential supervisors in a call center. The skills/knowledge consist of the following:

1. Call center mission, vision, values
2. Call center objectives
3. Supervisor's role in meeting objectives
4. Team as a business unit
5. Time management
6. Delegation
7. Managing meetings
8. Conflict management
9. Performance evaluation
10. Applicant interviewing and selection
11. Diversity training
12. Career development (their own/employees)
13. Analytical skills
14. Customer service skills
15. Sales skills
16. Leadership skills
17. Negotiation skills
18. Listening skills
19. Presentation skills
20. Employee management skills
21. Quality monitoring
22. Coaching and feedback
23. Product knowledge
24. ACD report analysis

Brendan Read (2000, p. 251) recommends that each manager of a center have a set of parameters or profiles of what type of agent would fit each type of position available. Furthermore, Read argues that there are some common characteristics that call center agents must have and that should be in all profiles when seeking employees. Read uses Kathryn Jackson's list of "What Makes a Good Agent" as the set of competencies for successful agents working in a medical services call center. The list includes:

1. Oral communication
2. Customer service orientation
3. Tolerance for stress
4. Sensitivity. Agents must be advocates for the customer.
5. Teamwork/cooperation. Agents must be able to cooperate with their team members and understand internal customers.
6. Analysis. Agents must be able to analyze the patient information and identify the type of problem the customer is facing to provide a quick solution. Agents must also be able to analyze customer billing statements and understand the best way for customers to use their prescription benefits.
7. High work standards/work ethic
8. Motivational fit
9. Ability to learn. The insurance business is complicated and agents must understand its nuances.
10. Resilience. If agents are discouraged by an interaction with a customer, they must recover quickly and go on.

There are also skills and attitudes that separate the senior-level reps and specialists, according to Susan Hash (2002, p. 78). Hash articulates that these skills are:

1. Change management
2. Problem identification and resolution
3. Interaction with peers
4. Conflict resolution
5. Group leadership abilities

Noel Bruton (2002, pp. 309–310), examining call centers from a technical help desk point of view, conveys that many managers find a specific set of attributes and skills in ideal support reps. The skills include:

1. Patience—the ability to be able to listen to a user describe a situation you have encountered many times before, yet still be able to patiently explain the solution and to painstakingly go through the diagnostic process in search of the cause of a problem.
2. Assertiveness—the ability to give the user confidence in your ability to solve the problem; to be able to deal with a user whose expectations are unrealistic.

3. Thoroughness—the ability to make sure the job is complete, that the problem is truly solved, the user is satisfied, and the paperwork is filled out.
4. Enthusiasm—the ability to enjoy the job and stay motivated; to remain positive in a challenging situation.
5. Responsibility—the ability to be able to take on the burden of a task, set oneself an objective, and maturely follow it through to a successful conclusion without unnecessarily involving others.
6. Technical knowledge—the ability to have acquired and to continue to acquire naturally the sort of technical knowledge the job requires.
7. Empathy—the ability to put oneself in the user's position so as to understand the real nature of the difficulties.
8. Communication—the ability to use language well enough to convey confidence, to ask the right sort of questions to solicit information about the nature of the user's problem.
9. Ability to work well under pressure—this can range all the way from staying amusing and positive when the office gets noisy to being able to handle quite dangerous levels of stress.

Each of these authors makes abundantly clear the specific skills, attitudes, behaviors, and motivations centers would ideally like to see in applicants that would enable both the employee and the center to be successful. Furthermore, each of these authors suggests that these are the core skills and attributes; however, few researchers quantify or rank the importance of each item on the list. Is patience as important as empathy to a center? Is problem identification as important as problem resolution? Furthermore, most lists such as these just outlined highlight the skills and abilities of a person as the most important aspect of a rep, often overlooking deeper characteristics about employees such as outlook on life, work ethic, motivation, and attitude, which help determine the success or failure of a person no matter the existing skill set.

SKILLS

Given the goals of the call center, what skill should employees have before applying for a job? The skills for each center should be abundantly clear to the manager. Furthermore, the manager should also be able to discern the importance/weight of each of the skills desired and have these in priority order. Likewise, the manger should know how much he/she is willing to train a particular employee. If a center has an intensive training program, it is sometimes more desirable to have a person that is teachable with few or none of the skills necessary to perform the job than it is to hire someone who has worked in a similar center in the past with a specific set of skills designed for another center. This way the "blank slate" employee will learn the processes of the center the "correct" way, while employees with call center experience may have to unlearn before they can relearn the processes in the new center.

COMPETENCY MODEL

Each manager, in association with his/her staff, should create a working competency model uniquely designed for the culture and operations of his/her center. This model should be dynamic, allowing flexibility over time to meet the demands of the center (growth, expansion, contraction, new products, etc.). According to Gaudet, Annulis, and Carr (2002), competency modeling "is an attempt to describe work and jobs in a broader, more comprehensive way." Traditional job and task analyses are not flexible enough and often become obsolete quickly due to the nature of maturing information technologies. The most effective approach to develop the workforce for your center is to focus more on identifying work-related competencies and less on specific tasks and duties. Competencies include behaviors, beliefs, and values and generally represent the tasks and activities needed to accomplish a specific job. Besides an effective means of performance measurement, competency models are also great because they can be easily translated into training and development programs (Gaudet, Annulis, and Carr, 2002). Until the call center industry is recognized as a leading industry, a competency model for reps will most likely not be developed on a national or international scale. With this in mind, it is up to each call center manager to create his/her own competency model which can be used for hiring, evaluation, and training.

ATTITUDE

Attitude is critical in helping to determine the success or failure of a call center and should be an integral part of any competency model. Attitude refers not only to that of the employees of a center, but also to that of the company and upper management as well. Both of these groups, the upper management who represents the face and decision-making process of a company and the employees who ensure that the company continues to produce on a daily basis, must have a positive and mutually reinforcing attitude. If either of these groups is not aligned, then the benefits will not accrue. If one of these groups has a "bad attitude," then this will bleed into the other group and vice versa. For example, if a company has a great attitude in the headquarters and believes in their mission, goals, and success, but has a poor call center manager who has created an environment that is producing low morale in a center, no matter how much of a positive attitude exists at headquarters, if it does not trickle down and is seen and reinforced through the manager to the employees then the excitement over a good attitude is never manifested in work at the center. Similarly, a call center manager may be great at having created a positive culture where employees are loyal, happy, and with good attitudes that can field great feedback from customers. Even in this center of nirvana, bad attitudes and bad policies from headquarters cannot be stayed and will trickle in. Obvious questions that will emerge in the heads of the reps are, "Why am I busting my butt to deliver a great attitude to our customers when the big shots in headquarters seem to hate everything and cause us to work harder because of their attitudes?" In order for success to be real and lasting, both the upper management in headquarters and the manager of the call center must have a positive attitude. This alignment, like with goals, can have a positive amplification effect for the whole organization. It is a manager's duty to ensure that each is aligned with a positive attitude, outlook, and focus.

How important is attitude to a call center's productivity on a scale of 1–10, with 1 being the lowest and 10 being the highest? The answer is somewhere between a 9 and a 10.

Attitude is an essential element; in fact, attitude is so important to an organization in recruiting and retaining employees that attitudes are built into the cultural fabric of most organizations. It is quite common for people in one organization to be able to identify the culture, positive or negative, of other organizations based on personal experience or from their network of associates. Some of these businesses are known to be aggressive and savvy, and others are known for their laziness and lack of trust. Hiring for attitude is not to suggest that employees with critical skills are not important; they are, but an employee with a poor attitude and skills will become a net negative drain on an organization, where a positive employee who is trainable will stay with an organization for years to come and will become a positive value-added asset. Another example can be found in Wal-Mart. Many communities have multiple Wal-Mart stores, and each store carries mostly the same goods all at the same price and in a similar environment. However, one Wal-Mart can "feel" significantly different from another one. These differences are usually reflections of the particular store manager's style. One may be friendlier since the employees say "hi" and smile all the time. The other may have dirty restrooms, unhelpful reps, and clusters of employees chatting while customers are seeking assistance to find an item. In one store, the manager hired a specific attitude and expected the attitude to be positively reflected on a daily basis by the employees at the store. The attitude emerges in a positive manner, not only in customer–employee interactions, but in the cleanliness of the store and the willingness of all of the employees to actively seek out customers to help. The other store feels dark, dingy, and actively discourages people to shop there due to the unfriendly environment. The same example can be used for call centers.

Many call centers contain a similar basic setup, including technology and location in a city, and they serve a common customer service function; however, each center can have a positive or negative environment depending upon the tone set by the manager.

Employee attitude and call center culture go hand-in-hand; however, most employees do not enter a call center with an existing culture, but all enter with a specific attitude toward work. If the culture of the center is sufficiently positive, chances are that the center will hire the correct employees for the job. However, if by accident, an employee with a bad attitude is hired, the employee will either have to change his/her attitude to conform to the existing culture or will choose to leave quickly with the realization that he/she does not fit in.

Southwest Airlines, a company known for having a positive and unique culture, has a long waiting list of people wanting to become a member of the company. Once someone is hired at Southwest, that person seldom leaves, thus vacancies are rare and cherished. In the book *NUTS! Southwest Airlines' Crazy Recipe for Business and Personal Success,* Kevin Freiberg and Jackie Freiberg (1996) explore the unique culture of Southwest Airlines and the reasons this company has remained successful and profitable over time. The authors suggest that much of the success of Southwest is due to the culture initiated early on by Herb Kelleher and his management team. However, the culture of Southwest has been developed for many years, and it no longer requires the leadership of the company to maintain the great culture. The employees police themselves and the company to ensure that the basic principles are in place that makes their job so enjoyable. The Freibergs summarize the cultural philosophy of Southwest Airlines in charts, called "Success in a Nutshell," at the end of sections in their book. Two such tables, combined into the following list, hold specific values that should ring true to call center managers.

"Success in a Nutshell

- ☐ Hire people with a sense of humor.
- ☐ Quit pretending. Give yourself the freedom to be yourself.
- ☐ Train for skill. Hire for spirit, spunk, and enthusiasm.
- ☐ Be religious about hiring the right people. If you make the wrong hiring decision, within the first 90 days make the tough decision to say goodbye.
- ☐ Treat family members as best friends; do not take them for granted.
- ☐ Do whatever it takes. Remember, there is very little traffic in the extra mile.
- ☐ Define your own standard of professionalism.
- ☐ Treat everyone with kindness and equal respect; you never know to whom you are talking to.
- ☐ Do what you ask others to do.
- ☐ Inform your people. It teaches them to care.
- ☐ Make living legends out of your service heroes. Real examples may inspire others to offer legendary service too.
- ☐ Show people what legendary service looks like, then trust them to do the right thing.
- ☐ Publish stories of extraordinary service in your newsletter. If you do not have one, write them up in a letter to employees.
- ☐ Make it a practice to give everyone—customers, co-workers, friends, family—more than they expect."

Though at first this list may seem both unrealistic and impractical, it is neither. If you are still not convinced, then go online and look up the history of the New York Stock Exchange ticker symbol LUV. Read the financial history of the company. Not only is this culture real, active, and self-perpetuating, it is by its very nature profitable. Remember, Southwest not only talks a good game, it walks the walk as well. For example, post-September 11, 2001, most airlines laid off large percentages of their workforce. Southwest Airlines chose not to lay off employees and instead tightened the company's purse strings as much as possible. It is difficult to imagine the loyalty that the company created by refusing to get rid of what it considers its most important asset—its employees. However, they were able to not only prove that they mean what they say about culture, but a few years later as airline traffic volume is increasing, Southwest has retained its experienced and extremely loyal workforce, giving it a competitive advantage in experience and loyalty, as well as an intact workforce for expansion as air travel increases.

A positive culture and work environment not only make good values sense, it makes economic sense as well. The question of every call center manager should not be, "Should I try to adopt a positive culture in my center?" The question all managers should be asked is, "How can you not have a positive culture in place since it benefits everyone and the bottom line?"

RECOMMENDATIONS FOR FILTERING

To ensure that the people hired have the correct attitude for the center, managers should initiate two layers of filters. Layer one is pretesting, and layer two is to create an interesting and unexpected interview atmosphere.

Pretesting is an effective means to filter out of the existing applicant pool a new, more concentrated pool of candidates. Do not forget that the goal of pretesting and an interview is to find a person that best matches the culture, vision, and goals of your call center. Pretesting should not ask only the basic questions of

1. How many words per minute can you type?
2. Do you consider yourself a follower or a leader?
3. Why do you want to work for this call center?

These types of questions, like letters of recommendation, are expected to be answered in a positive and uplifting manner. Anyone answering them any other way is naturally selecting themselves out of most employment pools. Because most rational people will answer all questions in the affirmative, most pretests will not help to allow specific uniquely qualified people to rise to the level of an interview. Instead, a manager should create an interesting pretest that will bring out personality, attitude, work ethic, and other characteristics. This can come in many forms. You can ask a person to write out a reality television show about a call center, to place themselves as the lead character in their favorite book, to write out a manual for interviewing and pretesting candidates for call center jobs, or even to write their own obituary. Ask existing employees for suggestions on scenarios, you will be surprised at the level of creativity you already have on staff. These types of questions allow the more creative, bright, and effective communicators in the applicant pool to rise above the others. Depending upon the quality of the essays, the manager and staff can then select out potential interviewees.

It is vitally important to create interesting interview questions for potential employees. Ask questions other than the old and predictable questions of

1. What is your strongest point?
2. What is your weakest point?
3. Why did you apply for this job?
4. Who do you consider to be a role model?

These questions, and many others, are considered to be classic or standard interview questions. Managers should break the mold and try something new. They should ask candidates what their favorite words are or ask them to pick from a set of five words to best describe their working style. Put the employees in a scenario and have them walk you through their resolution to the problem. Ask them to act out a scene in their favorite television show or to impersonate a famous person and have the interviewer guess who the impersonation is of. Maybe ask them to be a call center manager who has to fire an employee who is not performing. These types of questions do not have a correct and incorrect answer schema; instead, they give insight into the employee's personality and attitude. Furthermore, this innovative interviewing style will broadcast to potential employees that this is an interesting place to work, especially since the management has taken the time to carefully select the right people for the job as indicated by the interesting questions asked during the interview process. Besides attitude, skills are also an important process of interviewing and hiring decisions.

Southwest Airlines has a policy to make interviews interesting. During one interview, recounted in Freiberg and Freiberg (1996), a group of applicants for pilot positions showed up for interviews in the classic dark suit and tie. Each was offered Bermuda shorts and a tropical shirt to change into for the remainder of the interview to reflect Southwest Airline's casual working atmosphere. Most of the candidates chose to change clothes, but a few insisted on staying in suits. Can you guess which group of pilots got the job? This does not mean that a call center manager must have a closet with 100 sets of casual wear for group interviews and pretesting, but each manager can come up with unique and insightful ideas on how to reflect their image and center during the interview processes.

Bruton (2002, p. 317) states that "let us not forget that the attitude comes first. The key . . . is the attitude of the staff—not your efforts to motivate, but to do anything the company, the job, the weather, or the users may throw at them. Do they shrug off the pressures, even enjoy them, or do they let the pressures add to one another? And, what do you do as a manager to help them to survive those pressures? For only if your support staff can automatically and subconsciously survive the pressure of the user support job can they hope to retain a positive attitude to both the good and bad of the job they do and who they do it for."

There are certain essential technical skills necessary for all call center employees, all of which can be trained into a new hire. In fact, most call centers are not highly technical anyway. As software continues to develop, the level of skill required for the rep is declining. Given this reality, most hires (and thus interviews) should be based on the attitude of the employee given the goals of the company. This is especially true since most people are trainable, even if they enter with few or no skills.

EMPLOYEES COME FIRST

Yes, this statement is phrased correctly. The old adage "customers come first" is both trite and incorrect. "When systems, structure, policies, procedures, and practices of an organization are designed and lived out so that employees genuinely feel they come first, trust is the result" (Freiberg and Freiberg, 1996, p. 282). If the customer comes first, then by default if there is a potential disagreement between a rep and a customer, the employee will always be wrong. If the employee is always wrong, inherently a conflicting environment will be set up between not only the customer and the employee, but also the employee and the manager. If, however, the employee comes first, then the employee, feeling loyalty and trust from the management, can act in a way that he/she believes to be in the best interest of the company and feels a sense of empowerment, ownership, and control of his/her decisions. This is a powerful tool and should be implemented and fully understood by all in each call center.

While Freiberg and Freiberg (1996) insist that employees come first, Bruton suggests that hiring the right people for the job will influence a company's relationship with its customers. He states that "because they are customers, they are consuming something we produce. They may not be consuming what we want them to, or they may have a distorted impression of our output, but it is still our output. Customers will always form an impression of the product they receive. If we do nothing to influence that impression, it will be formed by default—and it may or may not be accurate, indeed it may or may not be rational. This is why we must always strive to manage our relationships with our customer, so that the impressions they have is a favourable one" (Bruton, 2002, p. 74).

Therefore, it becomes essential that the right people are hired to manage the customers, to set the tone, the image, and the culture of the center. The impression that the customer shall leave the phone call with is not hard data, but instead is a feeling of a customer-driven company who made the call enjoyable for them.

FINAL THOUGHTS

There are a plethora of published ideas concerning who to hire for a call center and the expected skills, talents, and abilities the ideal or best employee will have. Though all of these authors have insights as to why their lists are correct, it appears as if the focus is in the wrong place. A call center should not be hiring for skills. Skills are acquired over time with experience. Managers in a center should create the right environment of positive culture, great work environment, and superior service. With this environment and necessary expectations in place, the manager should then hire the people with the correct attitude and outlook on life to fit this culture. Once employees have been hired, they will be trained to the tasks and technologies required to complete the job successfully. However, training attitude is nearly impossible; thus without the right attitude to help build and reinforce a productive employee-first environment, it does not matter much what skills someone comes to an interview with. Colleen Barrett, the current CEO of Southwest Airlines, summarizes thoroughly in Freiberg and Freiberg when she said, "We are not an airline with great customer service. We are a great customer service organization that happens to be in the airline business" (1996, p. 295). The same should hold true for all call centers.

REFERENCES

Bruton, N. *How to Manage the IT Helpdesk: A Guide for User Support and Call Centre Managers*, 2nd ed. Woburn, MA: Butterworth-Heinmann, 2002.

Cline, M. "Cut Agent Turnover by Hiring Motivational Fit." *Call Center Agent Turnover and Retention*, Annapolis, MD: Call Center Press, 2002, pp. 27–29.

Freiberg, K., and J. Freiberg. *NUTS! Southwest Airlines' Crazy Recipe for Business and Personal Success*. New York: Bard Press, 1996.

Gaudet, C., H. Annulis, and J. Carr. "Building the Geospatial Workforce." Urban and Regional Informational Systems Association Special Education Issue, no. 15, 2002, pp. 21–30.

Hash, S. "Effective Career Progression Programs Balance Both Staff and Business Needs." *Call Center Agent Motivation and Compensation*. Annapolis, MD: Call Center Press, 2002, pp. 77–85.

O'Hara, A. "How to Develop a Retention-Oriented Agent Recruiting and Selection Process." *Call Center Recruiting and New Hire Training.* Annapolis, MD: Call Center Press, 2001, pp. 21–25.

Read, B. B. *Designing the Best Call Center for Your Business.* New York: CMP Press, 2000.

Smith, A. "Developing Super Reps into Supervisors." *Call Center Recruiting and New Hire Training.* Annapolis, MD: Call Center Press, 2001, pp. 109–111.

FURTHER READING

Bohlander, G., S. Scott, and A. Sherman. "Training and Development." *Managing Human Resources*, 12th ed. Cincinnati, OH: South-Western College Publishing, 2001.

Gaudet, C., H. Annulis, and J. Carr. *Workforce Development Models for Geospatial Technology.* The University of Southern Mississippi, Hattiesburg, MS: Geospatial Workforce Development Center, 2001.

Gilley, J., and A. Maycunich. *Performance Consulting, Organizational Learning, Performance and Change.* Cambridge, MA: Perseus Publishing, 2002.

Mathis, R., and J. Jackson. "Job Analysis and the Changing Nature of Jobs." *Human Resource Management*, 12th ed. Cincinnati, OH: South-Western College Publishing, 2000.

Zemke, R., and S. Zemke. "Putting Competencies to Work." *Training and Development Yearbook*, Paramus, NJ: Prentice-Hall, 2000.

CHAPTER 5

Your Reps

*"The immense responsibility of improving customer satis-
faction and loyalty as well as increasing profits must come
from employee empowerment. Customers want empowered
reps capable of making important decisions and resolving
problems quickly. You want empowered reps capable of
building customer relationships and/or upselling or cross-
selling products and services"*
(Call Center Operations, 2000, p. 30).

As the statement above illustrates, for an organization to offer superb service, it is fully dependent on the call center reps. Therefore, for employees
to deliver the highest quality service possible, they must be empowered
to make decisions and serve the customer to the best of their ability.

The focus of this chapter is to build upon the concepts examined in
Chapter 4 on hiring, training, and creating the best culture possible for
a center to ensure low turnover and high profitability. Chapter 4 stated
the employee comes first! This chapter examines how managers can focus
directly on the call center's best asset—its employees, the customer service
representative.

WHY DO YOUR REPS WORK AT YOUR CENTER?

In order to fully understand and empower employees of an organization,
it is necessary to examine in detail what they expect to get from their
employment. In this way, both the manager and the employee will be
clear about what they desire from the workplace and they can then agree
upon expectations. Only with this understanding can both parties work
to move the organization in a positive direction.

This researcher asked reps in numerous centers what their motivation
was for working at their present job in a call center and whether they

Table 5-1. Do You Find Your Work Challenging?

Answer	Number	Percentage
Yes	267	76.3
No	83	23.7
	$n = 350$	

Source: David L. Butler

found their job challenging. Table 5-1 shows that most of the reps found that working in a call center environment was challenging, which is not too surprising considering the call volume, expected level of service, and minimum time for calls in queue at most centers. Since three of every four employees at a call center considered their job challenging, what does this say about the employee?

Employees who are challenged in their jobs can follow one of two paths. On path one, an employee feels challenged, has difficulty meeting expectations in the center, and becomes increasingly frustrated, which leads to high levels of stress, thus driving down the productivity of this employee. An employee following this path will within a few months leave the center after he/she finds alternative employment.

On path two, the employee feels challenged. The manager recognizes through efficient communication that an employee feels challenged and spends time helping that employee through the challenges, rewarding positive work done well, and assisting when the rep does not do well. The manager will also help set the tone, keeping the level of stress low and fun and keeping excitement and active engagement with the customers at the forefront of the employee. Remember, employees come first. Only when this concept is fully absorbed by the employees (believed) can they then act to give the customers the best service possible. Putting employees first produces the best customer service possible. If an employee is having difficulties in an area and knows that he/she can approach management, that employee will actively seek out help to overcome the difficulty because

☐ The environment of employees first allows it.
☐ The employee is interested in serving the customer and realizes that the difficulty he/she is having is hampering this service.

In summary, employees who find their work challenging can be either a positive or a negative factor, depending upon the culture in place and the

Table 5-2. Why Did You Choose to Work at This Call Center?

Answer	Number	Percentage	Total Respondants
Good benefits	267	76.3	350
Good pay	217	62.0	350
Job hours	172	49.3	349
Possibilities for advancement	160	45.7	350
The type of work	138	39.5	349
Close to home	102	29.3	348
Fit with partner's schedule	36	10.3	350
Close to children's school or daycare	9	2.6	350
Access to public transportation	3	0.9	350

Source: David L. Butler

active nature of the manager to assist the employees to improve themselves in their customer service function.

A recent survey conducted by this author asked customer service reps why they chose to work at their particular call center. The findings from this question were quite interesting. Table 5-2 presents the answers to all of the answers (except answer "J. Other").

The top two reasons for working at their particular call centers were good benefits and good pay. Number three was job hours, and number four was possibilities for advancement. The bottom five factors listed on the table, "type of work," "close to home," "fit with partner's schedule," "close to children's school or daycare," and "access to public transportation," represent less than 40% of the total respondents and so will not be explored in detail in this chapter.

Good benefits and good pay make rational sense as a response. Most people do not work because they love to sell their time to a company. Instead, most people work to pay bills and have the ability to earn enough money to live a particular lifestyle, which includes specific benefits associated with employment explained in Chapter 9. Number three, job hours, is very interesting, with almost 50% of the people responding with this answer. What should a manager learn from this response?

If over one-half of the employees state that part of the attraction of their job at the call center is flexible hours, this means that the manager should sit up and take note. Flexible hours mean different things to different people. Some common desires for flexible hours include:

1. Time to take care of school-age children without the need for daycare.

2. Time to work with or on alternating schedules with a spouse/partner.
3. Maximize the time allowed to take care of a family member.
4. To have flexibility to complete projects outside of a 8/9 am to 5 pm job.

What this list indicates is that people's personal life and work life intersect and strongly influence each other. This means that any alterations in the flexibility of scheduling at a center need to be examined thoroughly before implementation. If a less flexible work schedule is introduced, it is likely that a significant number of the 50% of the employees who answered this question as a motivation for working at the center would seek employment where they could still have the flexible schedule. On the flip side, a call center manager could potentially alter the work schedule of a center to make it more flexible and thus attract a larger segment of employees that were not attracted in the past due to the more rigid schedule of the center.

The easiest and simplest way to alter a work schedule framework is to close the office door, get out a blank sheet of paper and a pen, and begin writing and diagramming or better yet, use a scheduling software package. The problem with this approach is that it allows zero input from the employees who the work schedule that will be imposed upon. Empowerment of the employees is zero, and clearly, the employees are not coming first in the mind of the center manager. Instead, a slower, less easy, but solid method that will pay dividends for years is to constitute a committee of reps to draw up a workable and flexible work plan for the center. The committee should include not more than eight and no fewer than three reps. These reps will be charged with soliciting feedback from all center reps, ensuring that EVERY employee has a voice. The committee then draws up a plan of the new work schedule that is centered on flexibility, simplicity, and profitability. The committee will then present its proposal to the manager for discussion and evaluation. The full processes will be transparent throughout so that each employee can follow the full deliberation, creation processes, and eventual implementation if they wish, ensuring that the processes is not biased toward a particular person or group.

Table 5-2 clearly indicates that almost 46% of the reps surveyed stated that they worked at this call center because of the chance for promotion. This means that nearly 50% of the center's total customer service reps are interested in promotion at some time in the future. What is the likelihood that even 5% of the employees will be promoted from within to a supervisor role? What about promotion to manager or director? What is the likelihood that a center manager or director will be promoted within the organization to another division or will become an executive of the company for that matter? What about from call center rep to CEO?

CHOOSING A CALL CENTER MANAGER

Ann Smith (2001, pp. 109–110), in her chapter "Developing Super Reps into Supervisors," outlines problems of filling a supervisory role with a great agent, but one with little or no leadership or management experience. Smith suggests that the center manager should determine needs before jumping to fill an empty position too fast. The needs assessment should include:

1. Prior to filling the position, review the supervisory position summary. Assure that the expectations are clear. Include specific duties and responsibilities.
2. Define the position requirements. Include skills, traits, attitude, competencies, abilities, etc.
3. Translate the job requirements into a specific needs analysis.
4. Assess the new supervisor's capabilities. Determine the gap between the job requirements and the new supervisor's skills and knowledge.
5. Design a training program to fill the gap. The plan should be specific with goals and time tables and a method for determining proficiency.

Dan Lowe (2001, p. 115) also cautions call center managers to avoid filling a supervisory position too quickly with a good rep. Instead, Lowe suggests that a training program modeled after the training program for front-line reps should be used for training supervisors. These phases include:

1. Orientation. New supervisors should be given some kind of introduction to the position. This can be formatted in different ways, but the main objective is to clearly identify the roles and responsibilities of the front-line supervisor.
2. Training. The actual training process for supervisors should be conducted using a variety of methods (i.e., classroom, seminars, self-paced, mentors, etc.). The focus of the training should be to identify knowledge and skill areas that are outside of the front-line agents' knowledge and skill set.

3. Nesting/shadowing. Many call centers find that providing new supervisors with a "nesting" opportunity by having the person shadow or "co-manage" a team for a period of time can help to ensure the individual's success as a leader. Nesting gives new supervisors a chance to observe an experienced supervisor's work flow.

4. Coaching and/or mentoring. Every new supervisor should be assigned a mentor. This may be his/her immediate manager, but it does not need to be. The role of the mentor is to meet with new supervisors on a regular basis for the first several months in the position, as well as to make themselves available on an as-needed basis.

Though the first two authors examined supervisors in call centers, Mark Craig (2001, p. 117) highlights hiring call center managers. He argues that manager positions "can often be filled by in-house employees, but not always. Sometimes it is necessary to look beyond the walls of your company to find the person best suited to maximize the potential of your center." The author brings up an interesting point of looking for new perspectives from outside the center. This is common practice in business, to reorganize periodically to shake things up, create new teams, and get rid of some old blood and bring in some new blood. If this is the path a company chooses, and a call center adopts, is this communicated to the employees of the center? Remember that almost 50% of the employees in the centers examined expected to have a chance of promotion within the organization. If the company adopts a policy of recruiting and hiring from outside, then avenues of promotion for these reps and supervisors are closed. If this is the case, the following actions should be considered.

☐ The fact that the path to leadership is closed to the employees at the center must be made abundantly clear to everyone from the initial stages of hiring.

☐ If there is a promising rep that has management potential, then the center needs to communicate to this employee that they cannot be promoted from within, and thus, if they are interested in a leadership position in the organization, they must go to another center and work for a while to gain both more experience and new experiences that can then be brought back into the organization when the time is right.

If, however, the center chooses to promote from within, then the process of choosing supervisors and management must be made clear to all employees. Once again, do not forget that about 50% of the employees indicated that one of the reasons they work at this center is the opportunities for promotion. Even at a high turnover rate for supervisors and managers in a call center, a 500-seat center could not promote 250 of the reps in a reasonable time period. This means that a selection process must occur to determine who is most qualified for promotion. This process must be transparent for everyone in the center for two main reasons. One, employees wishing to promote know that there is a clear set of requirements necessary to be considered for promotion, allowing them to seek to meet these expectations. Two, since not every employee will be promoted, hurt feelings will emerge. To prevent the hurt feelings which can cause a stir and potentially a bad culture in a center, the process of promotion needs to be clear at each stage. In this way, when an employee complains about being overlooked for a promotion, this person's colleagues in the center will know full well that he/she was not selected because the person was not the best person for the position, truncating any potential problems and rumblings in the call center that could emerge. Everyone must play by the same set of rules—no exceptions!

Cleveland and Mayben (1997) examine what a call center manager should convey to their managers or executives about his/her center. "A prerequisite to getting good support from senior management, and from managers in other key areas, such as marketing, information systems, telecommunications, and human resources, is that they have a basic working knowledge of how incoming call centers tick." They list ten items that all of the upper support management should know about a center:

1. Calls bunch up. Calls arrive randomly. Senior management needs to know that planning for a workload that arrives randomly is different from planning for working in other parts of the organization.
2. There is a direct link between resources and results. You may need 36 people on the phones to achieve a service level of 90% answers in 20 seconds, given your call load. But if you have 25 people and are told to hit 90/20, that is not going to work.
3. Staffing on the cheap is expensive. If you provide toll-free service for callers, you are paying for the time they spend in queue. Further, average handling time will increase as more callers comment about the long wait and as reps need more "breather" breaks because there is no time between calls.
4. There is generally no industry standard for service level. No one service level makes sense for every call center.

Different organizations place different values on customer service, and each will have different staffing costs, network costs, and numbers and types of callers.

5. When service level improves, productivity declines. Senior management should understand that the better the service level you provide, the more time your reps will spend waiting for calls to arrive.

6. You will need to schedule more staff than base staff required. Senior management needs to recognize that schedules should realistically reflect the many things that can keep reps from taking calls.

7. Staffing and telecommunications budgets should be integrated. Staffing and trunking issues are inextricably associated. Call center budgets should consider both staffing and telecommunications costs and their impact on one another.

8. Buy the best systems you can afford. Senior managers should be aware that equipment and software generally make up less than 15% of a call center's budget over time. These are valuable tools, and it makes sense to buy the system that has more capacity, better reports, and more advanced features.

9. Telecom and Information Systems (IS) people should support call centers, not manage them. When they wield too much control, it usually stems from the assumption that call centers are "technology operations." Indeed, call centers are laden with systems, but senior management should understand that the systems must be managed from within, with the support of telecommunications and IS.

10. Summary Automatic Call Distribution (ACD) reports do not give the real picture. Interpret summary ACD reports with caution. They can be very misleading.

Though Cleveland and Mayben bring up some interesting points, their list and focus strike at the core of a central issue with call centers in larger organizations—their value and place in the organization. The fact that there has to be a top ten list to explain call center operations to senior managers/executives in a company suggests that most senior-level people in an organization have no understanding of call center operations. The reasons for this are too numerous to list, but one item stands out clearly: too few call center managers promote into executive-level positions.

Traditionally, if a person wants to promote within an organization, he/she joins a company with a degree in hand and starts out as a researcher or something similar in a specific unit, department, or division. If this person performs well, he/she will be promoted a few times within his/her unit. After a few years in that unit, if he/she is pegged as someone with potential for a top executive position, he/she will be encouraged to apply for a lateral move or promotion from his/her current unit to another unit or division, for example, from operations to marketing. In this way, the future executive is cross trained on as many functions of the business as possible, making for a well rounded and very knowledgeable executive of the company in the future. If managers have to go out of their way to educate senior management or executives on call center operations, the impression is left that a call center manager is not a slot that people are promoted into or out of in business. This means that managers of call centers may have little promotion potential to upper management. Likewise, it also means that call center managers must fight an uphill battle to educate upper management and executives about call centers without the executive having any experience in a center to draw upon.

This dilemma for some call centers necessitates action. Action must come from both the top levels of businesses as well as from the call center managers. Business leaders must not exclude call center operations from their full understanding. What better way to understand a call center than to work in one? Call centers, because they are often the only conduit to customers, must be a part of the flow of education of future leaders of companies. Call center managers, likewise, not only need to educate senior management about call center operations, but they need to learn more about other divisions, units, and departments in the organization as well. Instead of just explaining to an executive that call centers are unique and thus should not be responsible for fluctuating labor costs and little or no revenue generation, call center managers need to learn the tools of the various units to be able to deliver reports in a manner that upper management, who may have never set foot in a call center, can fully understand. This is why regular data collection is critical to a call center. Managers of call centers will likely find many similarities and possibly some good ideas to implement in their center from other managers of the other units and vice versa.

Another interesting set of data emerged from the survey of the call center reps when they were asked to write in other reasons why they choose to work in this particular call center. Approximately 21% that answered the question responded that the company's good reputation was a motivating factor (Table 5-3).

What exactly does this mean to the employee, and what is the expectation of the call center manager to ensure that this continues? Many companies are considered great places to work; some of these are

Table 5-3. What Other Reasons Do You Have for Working in Your Call Center?

Answer	Number	Percent
The company's reputation	14	21.2
Benefits of the company	13	19.7
Other	12	18.2
Money/needed a job	10	15.2
Flexible schedule	8	12.1
Fun/friends/co-workers	4	6.1
Relocation	2	3.0
Working with people	2	3.0
Find work challenging	1	1.5
Total	*66*	*100.0*

Source: David L. Butler

highlighted in this book. What makes these companies great places to work? In three words: a great culture! Notice it is not as easy to list the top 12 best-paying companies or the top companies for the fastest promotion. What is remembered is the culture of the company as a great place to work, which is something to look forward to when the alarm goes off at 6:30 am. A place that allows people to be themselves, that utilizes their best assets toward a collective goal, and where everyone in an organization is working hard for the same reason is a place people want to be.

EMPOWERING EMPLOYEES

A manager needs to empower his/her employees not because it sounds like a nice thing to do, but because it can generate a strong financial return. Empowerment begins with "a respect for employees and an organization-wide understanding of the value of the call center rep's critical role within the context of your business strategy. This must be reflected in your organization's culture—most often starting with senior-level commitment. It begins with educating employees on their role in the business and entrusting them with the power and the knowledge to make a difference" (*Call Center Operations*, 2000, p. 31).

As the quote above suggests, employees in an organization must be educated in the workings of the business and be trusted with making decisions, both individually and collectively, to move the business into the future. Empowerment serves the company positively in two ways. One, it utilizes the existing workforce, who are already a labor cost, to generate new ideas and solve existing problems in a center without having to hire a new person or outsource the job, which would increase costs to the center. Two, empowered employees who see that their decisions are implemented start connecting their own success to that of the organization. This connection means that the reps know that by doing the best job possible, they are positively influencing the center's business operations, which is good for their employment—a positive feedback loop.

For example, flexibility in scheduling was a major attraction to over 50% of the call center reps examined (Tables 5-2 and 5-3). If a center did not currently have a flexible scheduling system, the manager or director could appoint a team of employees to draft a plan. This is exactly what occurred at one call center. The solution was an exchange board. Each rep was assigned their work schedule every two weeks. If a rep needed a day off for vacation, a birthday party, or some other event, the rep posted a specific colored card with that time slot on the board. If there was a rep in the center that was not working that particular shift, he/she could take those hours and work them. If the employee did not get any takers to work his/her shift, he/she could attach $1, $5, or $10 to the card as an incentive for someone to work the shift. Once a taker was found, both signed the card as an agreement.

On the flip side, if an employee was seeking to work more hours because he/she needed to earn more money for a vacation or for a present, he/she could post a different colored card stating that he/she was seeking hours. An employee could see this request and could offer hours if he/she was interested. Both parties would sign the card indicating agreement. This e-Bay-like system accomplishes many tasks, including:

1. It is built on a system of supply and demand, the most efficient system in place to date.
2. Employees are in charge of their shift, selling and acquiring open shifts.
3. The process is transparent for all to see and participate in.
4. Managers do not have to act as arbiter or auctioneer with people changing shifts and schedules.
5. The exchange system ensures that if an employee needs a day off, the time can be shifted to another person instead of the employee potentially not showing up for a shift because of an important engagement during his/her schedule.

This is a perfect example of how empowering employees can accomplish something positive in a call center that benefits everyone involved and in the end produces a higher attendance rate (lower absenteeism) and productivity that help produce a strong bottom line. Other committees can be formed to handle other issues such as training, improvement in customer service, and new technology implementation.

THE WHOLE PERSON

When an organization hires a person, an exchange is taking place—the person for a limited time in exchange for monetary compensation. That said, just because a call center may hire someone because of their work ethic, telephone skills, tireless energy, or speed and accuracy in typing does not mean that the center should ignore the person's other skills and abilities which could be used to help add value to the work environment and the company. The company should have an environment that allows employees to bring their full selves to work and incorporates their abilities into the organization.

For example, imagine you have an employee with a great voice at singing, an employee who knows many great jokes, and another employee who is just full of trivia. When calls are in queue, why not have your employees be the recording the customers hear and not some elevator music? Having actual employees describe what is going on in their center while people are on hold, telling the customers a joke, singing a song, or offering trivia would help pass the time and offer a human side to the center for both the employees and the customers alike. Other talents could be used on center projects, joint projects between multiple centers, or even the center sponsoring to help volunteer to serve the community on a project. Whatever the multiple talents of the individual employees, a center would benefit greatly from using these assets to the fullest extent possible. A stale, boring, cold, and sterile call center is interesting to no one. Customers are quite savvy and can quite often pick up on the level of satisfaction of an employee in their workplace in just a few minutes. A sterile workplace comes through to the customer. If it is a fun place to work, this is apparent as well. And as Bruton (1995, p. 74) notes, "customers will always form an impression of the product they receive. If we do nothing to influence that impression, it will be formed by default—and it may or may not be accurate, indeed it may or may not be rational. This is why we must always strive to manage our relationships with our customers, so that the impression they have is a favourable one."

Financial Transparency

Too often in business mistrust begins and spreads in a vacuum of knowledge where the specter of distrust can grow. Many times distrust can float around the concept of money—who has it, who does not, where it is being spent, etc. To truncate any potential problems associated with money and budgets, managers can open their books to the employees, if they wish to see them. Managers can post the center's financials and show each person's pay, including the management's. Show how much is spent in long distance contracts, electricity, benefits, equipment, building leases, landscaping, and more. This transparency will accomplish several goals:

1. Any distrust due to money will be eliminated. The numbers are there for all to see.
2. If a manager has to make a decision based on an increase or decrease in budget, the employees can see how the decision process was made given the current financial statements.
3. Employees can also offer suggestions to increase productivity and decrease costs in the center now that they are familiar with the breakdown of the center's budget.
4. The manager can initiate a goal of reducing the phone budget. The employees can track the increase or decrease of the budget through the postings and see if the labor costs actually increased in proportion to decreasing the time in queue, which enabled savings in long distance.

Employee Satisfaction

Two fundamental themes need to be reiterated. One, employees come first. Two, the manager should develop the best environment and culture possible at his/her center. If these two themes are realities, employees should be very pleased with their work and work environment. Besides the manager spending time communicating to all of the reps (one-third of the time is often cited as a necessity), the manager needs to measure the level of (dis)satisfaction within the center with the goal of consistently improving the level of employee satisfaction. Remember, employee satisfaction parallels that of customer satisfaction. The happier the employees, the happier the customer; therefore, it is in the manager's best interest to keep the employees happy with their work environment (*Call Center Operations*, 2000).

e satisfaction surveys come in many flavors, colors, and sizes. may want to outsource this project to an independent consulting firm so that the level of potential bias is reduced on the part of the manager. However, when an employee satisfaction survey is completed, the results must be anonymous to the individual, but, in aggregate, transparent to the employees who participated. Likewise, the manager must acknowledge if there are problems in the center and actively seek workable solutions to these problems, ideally in the form of empowered employee teams. The only means to ensure that potential problems are corrected and no new problems have arisen is through continued measurement, possibly every quarter or half year.

MEASURING JOB SATISFACTION

To have a successful center, the level of employee job satisfaction must be measured. Measuring will not only help set new and higher goals for the center, but it also gives the manager some ammunition to articulate to the executives in the parent organization why this center is hands down the best center in the businesses. How can this data be obtained?

As stated before, metrics on call rates are accessible to most managers through improvements in technology. However, other measures such as employee satisfaction, reason for turnover, cost of training, and a return on investment for each of these is often not collected at centers. However, if a call center manager has never worked with surveys, interview instruments, data collection, coding, or analysis directly, a professional consultant can be hired to assess the center. There are consultants who have this type of expertise such as Butler and Associates, Inc., Hattiesburg, MS 39401, USA, The Chelsea Group, Inc., Chelsea, AL, USA, and a host of others who specialize in this type of data collection and analysis. Hiring an outside consultant arms a manager in two different ways. One, the consultant is an expert. With an expert comes years of experience, including successes and failures, which the manager may not have. Many managers who try to do an assessment of their own without prior experience make repeated mistakes that are common in assessments but could have easily been avoided by hiring an expert. Think of the analogy of home improvement. Imagine a homeowner has a leak in a pipe. Instead of calling a professional and experienced plumber, the homeowner chooses to fix the pipe himself. He goes to the home improvement store, purchases materials and tools, reads the directions, and jumps in. Hours, if not days later, he believes he has corrected the problem, assuming he made it this far. However, he may have replaced a hot water line with PVC or

Happy employees result in happy clients. ✗

combined a galvanized pipe with copper, both of which are no-nos that will eventually cause more damage than what was there before. Now, imagine instead the homeowner called a plumbing expert. The job was done professionally, in only a few hours, and the cost was close to what he would have paid for the tools and materials he had to get. Now if he calculated in the cost of his time and the problems that could eventually reemerge, then the professional plumber becomes a bargain. The same is true for an expert consultant. Though the cost may seem steep at first, the cost is actually a bargain compared to someone without experience trying to do the same job and making error after error, eventually having to call a professional in the long run to fix or complete the project.

The second reason to hire an expert consultant is to ensure that biases are not interjected into the data collection. To successfully collect data, questions must be written in such a way that will eliminate as much bias as possible from the data collected. Quite often this is very difficult for someone who is so close to the subject under examination. For example, imagine a manager asking his/her reps a question on a survey instrument about the work environment. Because the manager knows the environment and helped to create it, he/she may ask something such as the following:

"How would you describe your work environment?"

A. No problems
B. Pretty good
C. Good
D. Great
E. Excellent

Because the manager knows that the environment is good, especially since he/she has seen the environment in other centers, he/she scales the answers from pretty good to excellent. This way the manager can determine what employees think of the environment he/she worked hard to create. However, the manager just stepped into several common problems associated with novices collecting data that they are close to. First, he/she never defined "work environment." This means that each person will define this differently. One employee may think this is his/her cubicle, while another will think it is the cleanliness of the restroom, the color of the paint on the walls, or possibly the number of windows in the building. This means that no matter the answer to the question, the manager cannot really know what the employees are thinking since work environment was never collectively defined. Second, the answers on the survey are all positive. Though the manager knows the work environment is good, because he/she know what he/she means by work environment and thinks it is good, there may be some employees that do not like the work conditions and do not have an option from the choices to answer the question honestly. Questions asked in evaluations must be scaled correctly, which means that there must be an equal number of positive and negative answers and even a possibility for a neutral and/or no answer. Third, what if none of the descriptions fit the employees' view of the work environment? How are these employees supposed to answer the question? Are they to just guess? Mark the closest one? Circle two of them? Don't answer it? All of these are common responses to poorly written questions. Each creates an obstacle for the employee in answering the question as well as eventually producing poor data that cannot be effectively used for evaluation. Once again, this is why a manager would want to hire an expert for evaluation. An expert research consultant will ensure that these common problems do not occur and can truly evaluate the center in an unbiased manner. This allows for good data to be produced and effective management strategies and tactics to be formed based on reliable data. No matter what the measurement may be, an expert can set the right direction. Now when the manager goes before the executives and makes the bold statement that he/she has the best center in the organization, he/she can show the final report to prove that the statement is not only true, but also that a third-party independent evaluation shows this to be true.

A case study of a call center in New York (Harps, 2002) shows that when good and reliable data are collected, a center can increase performance through representative feedback. In this case, the center's manager realized that the work environment produced low morale. After obtaining the data on employee satisfaction, the center took a number of steps, including:

1. Enhancing work spaces with new paint and furniture.
2. Creating teams and increasing team interaction so that all persons in the center could interact with each other.
3. Creating an organization-wide event that allows agents to meet and see other workers in other divisions, which enables the workers to fully understand their contribution to and where they fit in to the overall structure of the organization.

Without the measurement, feedback, and regular data collection, these types of workplace/performance improvements could not have occurred.

HOW TO HIRE A CONSULTANT

Consultants come in a variety of sizes, flavors, and costs. Finding the quality of consultant needed for the services in a particular call center is similar to purchasing any other business product. Books such as *The Consultant's Scorecard* (Phillips, 2000) and others have been written for either consultants or people who need to hire a consultant for a project. Besides having years of experience working in a particular area and becoming an expert, consultants with advanced academic degrees often bring much to the table in terms of their own research, other research contacts, and easy access to published material on a particular topic the manager seeks consultation on. Furthermore, the researcher consultant may have worked on a similar project elsewhere, and thus, the data in one center may be comparable to other centers, allowing a greater return for the center than the manager had originally counted on.

PERFORMANCE MEASURES

Managers must have a set of clearly articulated performance measurements for each rep in the call center. A clearly defined set of measurable expectations is valuable to a center for several reasons. One, it clearly tells the reps what the expected level of performance is, and then the rep can work toward that expectation. Two, the manager can align the performance expectations of the employees with that of the center's and overall organizational goals to ensure the goals are met. Three, performance measures are quantifiable so the center manager can deliver reports with numbers and graphics demonstrating that the center is improving performance over time.

What does a performance measure look like? How is it used? What should be measured and how? When a manager is creating a new performance measure or modifying an existing one, the big picture must be kept in mind. What is the goal of the center and organization? If revenue growth is the goal, then a specific set of measures should be in place to help ensure revenue growth. If bringing back customers is the goal, a different set of measurements are needed. "Every call center is challenged with keeping its reps' eyes focused on the corporate mission. One of the most important aspects of that challenge is to ensure that the linkage from rep behavior to the corporate vision is transparent" (Hack et al., 2000, p. 56). It is often too easy just to measure a simple metric such as calls per hour. Fortunately, according to Cleveland and Mayben (1997), this trend is fading. Calls per hour measures output, and that is all. It does not measure levels of satisfaction or repeat calls, nor does it maximize the use of an employee's skills and personality. If a call center uses calls per hour as a major metric of success, then it is in the employee's best interest to get the call completed as fast as possible, no matter the level of service. This type of motivation will always lead to poor quality, diminishing returns, and customers that will opt for another business or organization with better service. Instead, a manager needs to examine the goals of the center and then create a metric that reflects this goal(s). For instance, if customer loyalty is a goal, then a metric of performance should be first resolution issues and the number of times a person compliments a rep or makes positive statements about an employee. Whatever the measure the manager and staff create, it needs to be clear that the rep's performance will change the variables. A rep cannot directly control time in queue for a call; queue times are a staffing issue which is on the shoulders of management. Once the power of control is in the hands of the rep, the rep will do everything in their power to excel. As noted by Cleveland and Mayben (1997, p. 201), "as call centers handle increasingly complex transactions, 'calls per hour' as an individual productivity measure is fading, while qualitative measures continue to gain acceptance."

In their chapter "Performance Evaluations: A Practical Guide and Examples for Call Center Employees," Koons and Pettway (2001, p.44) outline a generic performance evaluation. Up front the authors state that "it is important to create a methodology for evaluations that is based on the employee demographics and company culture." To write an effective evaluation of an employee, the manager must know the full participation of an employee to the center. Likewise, the method by which the evaluator delivers the evaluation, and the tone set, makes a difference on how the performance evaluation is received and responded to by the employee. Remember, not only is this a tool to keep the center on focus toward a goal and a method to collect data for numerous justifications, it is also a strong tool to help modify or reinforce the performance of an employee. Consistency is critical in evaluations to ensure that they are as objective as possible. For example, if one employee is evaluated and needs improvement in a specific area, then this should hold true for all employees with similar challenges. On the flip side, if an employee is congratulated on surpassing expectations in a particular area, then all employees who surpass expectations in a given area need to be congratulated. This consistency is important since employees gossip, and they will find out very quickly if the metrics and parameters are not consistently applied, potentially undermining the call center's culture.

Common elements in an employee performance evaluation include (adapted from Koons and Pettway, 2001):

1. Customer service skills/communication—Ability to listen effectively and properly respond to service enquiries while communicating policy and processes to internal and external customers.
2. Telephone etiquette—Consistently implements company standards in regard to scripting and observer checklist guidelines.
3. Knowledge—Maintains an understanding of the clients; utilizes all of the assets available for continued training and development.
4. Interpersonal skills—Values other's contribution and is open to constructive feedback.
5. Quality-quantity—Meets quality and accuracy objectives against output goals.
6. Judgment—Has the ability to properly identify, analyze, and make reasonable decisions on behalf of the employee, the client, and the company.
7. Initiative—Empowers him/herself to resolve issues and problems; possesses the ability to actively participate, volunteer, and accept new challenges on his/her own with minimal direction.
8. Technology—The ability to integrate technology into the daily work routine; maintains a basic understanding of company/client technology.
9. Team development—Participation in building team morale, unity, and flexibility.
10. Attendance—Timely and reliable.
11. Appearance and habits—Personal habits, clothing, and grooming.
12. Adaptability—Ability to quickly understand new information, situations, and environment.

Though clearly this is not an exhaustive list of what can be included in a performance evaluation, it does cover a spectrum. A manager must also decide if he/she will weigh one category over another or not. For example, does appearance carry the same weight as attendance or initiative? If not, then this needs to be made clear to all reps.

FINAL THOUGHTS

Reps are the single most important asset to a center. They are the face (voice) of the company/organization. Because of this importance, a manager needs to know as much about his/her reps as possible. This includes knowing why they are working at the center, what their future aspirations are, and their likes and dislikes. Once this knowledge is in hand, a manager needs to use the full range of skills and abilities of the rep to meet the center's goals. Employees should come first in the company. Once this policy is in place, the employees will naturally pass on this positive attitude to the customers. To ensure that a manager is fully in tune with the employees, the center's finances and metrics need to be transparent to the whole center. This way no potential miscommunication can happen. This said, employees also need to be held accountable for meeting the goals of the center, and therefore, a solid and well thought out employee performance evaluation needs to be constructed that allows each rep to strive to meet the center's goal(s) call by call and day by day until success is reached.

REFERENCES

Bruton, N. *How to Manage the IT Helpdesk: A Guide for User Support and Call Centre Managers*, 2nd ed. Woburn, MA: Butterworth-Heinemann, 1995.

Hack, B., Newton, P., and Wyckoff, T. *Call Center Operations*. Houston: American Productivity and Quality Center, 2000.

Cleveland, B., and J. Mayben. *Call Center Management on Fast Forward: Succeeding in Today's Dynamic Inbound Environment*. Annapolis, MD: Call Center Press, 1997.

Craig, M. "Tips on Recruiting Top-Quality Call Center Managers." *Call Center Recruiting and New-Hire Training*. Annapolis, MD: Call Center Press, 2001, pp. 117–120.

Harps, L.H. "Government Call Centers Share Tips for Improving Moral Motivation." In *Call Center Agent Motivation and Compensation*. Annapolis, MD: Call Center Press, 2002, pp. 5–9.

Koons, T., and J. Pettway. "Performance Evaluations: A Practical Guide and Examples for Call Center Employees." *In Action: Recruiting and Retaining Call Center Employees*, Jack Phillips, J. (Series Ed.), and N.L. Petouhoff, (Ed.). Alexandria, VA: American Society for Training and Development Press, 2001, pp. 41–80.

Lowe, D. "Training and Support for Frontline Supervisors." *Call Center Recruiting and New-Hire Training*. Annapolis, MD: Call Center Press, 2001, pp. 113–116.

Phillips, J. *The Consultant's Scorecard*. New York: McGraw Hill, 2000.

Smith, A. "Developing Super Reps into Supervisors." *Call Center Recruiting and New-Hire Training*. Annapolis, MD: Call Center Press, 2001, pp. 109–111.

CHAPTER 6

Pay, Benefits, and the Dreaded Labor Unions

Considering the high level of turnover in call centers (about 18 months average) and the associated costs of hiring and training employees, it is quite natural that call center managers first look at call center wages to see if a higher pay within the industry would slow the rate of turnover. Not surprisingly, many authors have their own points of view on call center rep pay, benefits, recruitment, and retention. A few will be explored here.

Barbara Bauer (2002, p. 31), in her chapter titled "Build Long-Term Loyalty from the Agent's Perspective," states that good employees expect to be paid a salary that is perceived to be above the market standard. She continues that it does not matter if the rate is above the market standard only that the employees perceive that it is. Bauer continues, "While building agent loyalty starts with salary, it doesn't end there. While some employees leave for more money, most people change jobs for other reasons."

In his chapter "Call Center Managers Share Secrets at Human Resource Roundtable," Greg Levin (2001, p. 3) states that while "centers approach turnover in different ways due to a diverse range of factors specific to each company, including job complexity, career paths and local competition, all agree that call centers that struggle the least always seem to have one thing in common: employees who are involved in decision-making processes." Levin uses Sylvania's incentive program as an example of how this company was able to curb turnover. "In addition to paying a pay-for performance plan to determine employee raises, Sylvania sponsors a Perfect Attendance Award. For each year a rep has a perfect attendance record, he or she receives $500. Since implementing the attendance award three years ago, tardiness is down 40.5 percent and absenteeism is down 25.6 percent" (Levin, 2001, p. 8).

In a separate chapter, Levin examines the key aspects of a successful agent retention process (2002b). The author suggests that though money can be a motivator, it is only one piece of a larger process that agents respond to in a complicated and challenging call center environment. Successful retention and incentive programs necessarily must include call center employees as part of the process. This not only builds trust between the call center manager and employees, but the employees will inherently know more about what motivates employees than the manager. "One of the best- and easiest-ways to enhance the overall image of the agent position and improve retention is to actively involve agents in a variety of important projects, processes, and decisions in the call center" (Levin, 2001, p. 6).

Levin continues his examination of call center agent pay and turnover in the chapter titled "Call Center Professionals Speak Up for Underpaid Agents" (2002a). This chapter quotes many managers who appear frustrated with low agent pay and high expectations. Many suggest that executives in companies with call centers do not fully understand the call center agent's impact on revenue. Levin continues, "While many managers acknowledge that low pay isn't the only cause of attrition, they claim it is the reason most commonly cited by agents leaving the center" (2002a, p. 35).

Noel Bruton responds to claims like those by Levin by suggesting, "this begs a big question straight away, that of money-because since when did money do any inspiring or aiming? I subscribe to the school of thought that in the non-incentivized professions like user support and customer service, money is not a motivator. It may work in the greed-based professions, but even there it depends upon what you are trying to achieve. Let us test the money theory: When was the last time you bounded from your bed screaming 'Look out world, here I come' just because you had remembered you were going to be paid... on Thursday? Rather than waiting for and being driven by the same old salary you will be getting whatever happens, is it not more rewarding to have your work recognized and appreciated by those you do it for?" (2002, pp.316–317).

Dan Coen (2002, pp. 39–41), in his chapter "Agent Compensation: Motivating Staff without Burying Budgets," suggests that there are seven principles of agent compensation. The seven principles include:

1. The compensation plan must be centered upon a company's ability to pay. Every company is different when assigning a certain percentage of pay to its agents. Management must be cognizant of how much money and investment the company can make in the call center.
2. The compensation plan must be centered upon demand. Developing a compensation plan in the heart of a large city is quite different from coordinating a plan for a small-town center.
3. The compensation plan must be centered upon job requirements. While the basic concept of an agent position is the same, the job duties are always different. This means that the management cannot mimic other compensation plans because each company has different objectives.
4. The bond between the management and the agent must be based on trust. The more confusion about pay, the weaker the bond.
5. A compensation agreement must be based on appropriate performance objectives. If an established agreement leaves open any doubt about measurements or objectives, the compensation plan will falter.
6. Pay agents based on what you want them to make, regardless of industry averages. I encourage management to create their standards for a position. The needs of one company may not work for another.
7. Do not be afraid to play with BIG NUMBERS or to create a unique standard. This opens the door to creative compensation. Agents feel motivated when presented with the opportunity to strive for something unique.

Many of these authors' points overlap, and other points are far apart. Before examining what research indicates about these issues, it is important to understand what exactly a wage is and what it represents.

WHAT DO YOU PAY?

Because labor is a major component of call center costs, a manager should always be fully aware of what the center is paying all of its employees. Most centers have a set wage scale that determines the per-hour rate of reps based on one or more factors. Likewise, most centers have in place a pay raise plan based on both time at the center and an expected level of performance. Let us say for sake of argument that a given center pays reps $12 an hour, a rough national average for call center reps in the United States. An important question to ask is why pay $12 an hour? Why not pay minimum wage? Why not pay $20 an hour? The obvious answers from the manager to these questions are:

1. "I could not get good workers for minimum wage."
2. "Twenty dollars is too much, I can't afford it with my budget."

What about paying your employees $14 an hour, just $2 over the national average? What about $10 per hour, $2 under the national average?

Assumed in a wage, hourly or otherwise, is the idea that someone is exchanging their labor time and skills for a specified price. For instance, when a new employee is hired, a manager hires not only a warm body to work the phones, but also the person's skills, existing abilities, and potential of the employee after training and the expectation that the employee will work at a consistent level over time within a particular window of time (say, for instance, 9 am to 6 pm CST, 6 days a week). Before 9 am, the employee is on his/her own time; the same is true after 6 pm. This relationship between the manager and the employee is symbolized in the production of a payroll check to the employee from the call center account, signed by the manager. The payroll check is the final act in the employees' bartering themselves (abilities, skills, and time) to the manager. In this contractual relationship, the employee can leave and seek higher employment. Likewise, if the employee does not meet the standards set forth in the agreement, the manager can let the employee know that he/she has not fulfilled his/her obligation and can remove that rep from employment (firing).

In this relationship of labor exchange, it is assumed that the higher the wage paid the more education/skills a manager will receive in return for the increased wage and associated benefits. Similarly, the fewer skills offered by the employee, the less a manager has to pay for the employee's time. Parallel to the skill set wage driving mechanism is also the law of supply and demand of these skills in the marketplace. Generally, there are more people with no or few skills than there are people with advanced education and skills. Therefore, everything else being equal, the few people with advanced skills and education will command higher wages since there are fewer of them than those with no or few skills (see Table 6-1). The large number of people with few or no skills are all competing for fewer jobs, many of which are becoming automated, thus driving down

Table 6-1. Supply and Demand of Wages Generalization

Group	Skills	Highest Education Level	% Workers in Group	Wage Demand
Worker A	None	High school	65	$7.50
Worker B	Few	Some college	25	$12.00
Worker C	Many	College graduate	10	$25.00

the demand for lower wages due to the great supply and limited demand of these workers. Given the bartering system of a person's time for work and the law of supply and demand for workers with specific skills and education levels, how much should a manager pay per hour on average for workers? Why that wage?

After examining the information in Table 6-1, a manager can begin to answer what his/her center pays employees and why? Though Table 6-1 conveys the general processes of supply and demand of workers based on level of education and skills, readers should immediately realize that this scenario is based on an ideal world where information flows are pure and all information is reliable and available (i.e., it is not real). In reality, all centers have a limited number of potential call center workers within a specific area of a center. This means the center's location will help influence how the center's wages are determined. For example, if a center is in a rural location, the majority of the labor shed population may have similar education, skills, and demographic profile, and the center may also be the only employer of this type in the area. If a center is in a more urban or suburban location, the manager is more likely to have a greater variety of potential workers to choose from with strong variations in demographics, education, and skills. Though the urban or suburban location has a larger pool of potential employees, and thus a higher level of flexibility in choosing workers, the location comes with an immediate drawback. Other businesses will be competing for the same people, potentially hiring away or out-bidding call center managers for employees. However, if a center is in a more rural location, the possibilities of competition are fewer, and thus the chance of other options of competition are reduced, suggesting that a center can offer lower wages for higher skill levels (if available) than it could in a city or suburb. In short, in a rural location, the options for employment are few for people who live there. In a city, the options are more numerous. Therefore, as the location flexibility for centers increases in more urban areas (more choices), the flexibility for the worker simultaneously increases, thus potentially driving up wages. Furthermore, the more rural the location, the fewer the options for employers, but also the fewer choices for the workers as well, thus holding down labor costs.

Most businesses, without knowing it, walk through the exact process outlined above to determine wage levels for the employees. In fact, many centers probably do a quick assessment of the current wage level from other centers then choose to meet or increase the wage slightly in an attempt to attract any existing unemployment base, underemployed group, and those workers at other centers who are not content with their current employment options.

What Does Your Competition Pay?

Before determining a compensation plan for employees, a call center manager should consider the answer to the following questions. How many call centers are within 100 miles of your center? How much do they pay their starting reps? What is included in their benefits package? Can you compete head to head with this center in terms of wages? Some managers might argue that pay should be independent of the local wage and should reflect more of the value of the service to the company. Though the motivation for such a scenario is understandable, the reality is that businesses are in business to make a profit. Therefore, a business should maximize the work from an employee in exchange for the lowest compensation possible, yielding the highest profit possible for the company. The challenge is to set the wage at a pricing point that will attract people to the position and be substantial enough to keep employees from vacating the position in a short period of time (turnover). Therefore, before a manager sets the wage and benefit package and creates a strategy to decrease turnover and increase retention, it is absolutely necessary to find out what types of pull mechanisms exist that can attract his/her employees away from the center.

If there are not many call centers in close proximity, do not be fooled into believing that there is no competition for the employees in your center. Competition for your center may be companies such as Wal-Mart, food establishments, and other small- to medium-sized businesses. Besides taking an inventory of other call centers in your area, be sure to include other companies that hire the same type of employee you attempt to recruit and retain.

What Is Culture Worth?

The critical balance the call center manager must maintain is to keep wages, incentives, and benefits at the level necessary to attract and retain employees without pushing them so high that it threatens to take too much away from the company's bottom line. If the manager cannot retain employees and the cost associated with turnover and training becomes too high, higher management will look askance at the call center manager. Likewise, if the manager pays a wage that is well above the going rate for the job within the region, the executives will also cry foul that the manager is overspending and hurting the company's bottom line. If the manager chooses to pay the going rate in the region or less, then the total labor cost of the center will be low; however, the turnover rate will be such that the cost will be driven up anyway, creating a vicious cycle for call center managers. So, what can a call center manager do to keep total labor costs low while at the same time keeping turnover low? The answer to this question is building a strong positive culture within the center where people would want to work even at a lower wage. The idea of a positive culture as a great ROI is explored in more detail in Chapter 9.

SPATIAL FIX

According to the FAQ at www.incoming.com, one way to combat staff turnover is to examine a center's pay structure. "Pay could be a problem if you're not keeping pace with the market. As the call center environment becomes more complex, I think a lot of organizations are going to have to do some soul-searching on the importance and commensurate enumeration associated with these jobs" (2000, p. 2). The reality is that the soul-searching has occurred, and decisions have been made. The solution being implemented is what academics call the "spatial fix." In short, as labor costs increase due to competitive pressures for the same labor force (which is limited), prices are often pushed up. If a company does not want to pay increasing costs for labor, which eventually must be passed onto the customer, increasing the costs of the service and product against the competition, then at some point the company has to make a decision on how to resolve the increasing labor costs. An increasingly common solution is to simply move the call center to a location where labor is less expensive—the spatial fix. This may be from a more urban location to a rural location; it could mean moving from a more unionized state to a non-union state. More frequently, this means moving the call center from the United States or Britain to other parts of the world where English is a prominent language, but labor costs are low, such as India, The Philippines, South Africa, and more. The spatial fix, as history has indicated, is only a temporary solution. As many more companies relocate businesses to these areas, the wages are once again bid up, eventually creating the same problem that existed in the original country. A longer lasting solution is what I will call the cultural fix. This solution begins with re-visioning the call center as an important piece to a company, a value-added conduit to the customer and not a drain on capital. This requires a sea change in how many executives view call centers as well as the expectations of a call center and call center management. Instead of a call center being a reluctant requirement of servicing a product that a company offers, a call center should be seen as a means or mechanism to promote the company and as an extension of both the sales and the marketing arm. Remember, often the only interaction a customer may have with a company outside the use of a product is through a call center. This is the one opportunity to sell the company and its brand image to create a lifelong customer. Most executives understand the value of a lifelong customer to the bottom line. Therefore, another option to the spatial fix is to create a cultural fix which allows a center to create a positive atmosphere internally where people are willing and desire to work there, thus keeping wages in check since demands for these jobs exceed the supply. Furthermore, as the culture is created internally as a great place to work and make a career, this same positive atmosphere is translated to the customers through the phones. A customer remembers when they call (or are called by) a center where people like to work and love their company or organization, mainly because it so rarely occurs and the experience is very positive for both parties. The question for the executives in the company/organization is not whether creating a positive culture is a right path; it is the right path. The question is where will this culture be created, in a center that still exists domestically or that now exists overseas?

UNIONS YIKES!

"There is one word that is guaranteed to frighten many businesses, especially those with call centers: unions. To many firms, unions raise the frightening specter of high wages and benefits costs, grievances, and strikes, and, underlying them, the biggest evil of them all, another powerful force telling them how to run their business" (Read, 2000, p. 261).

Unionization issues have permeated the global call center industry in the past decade. As more centers come online, there are more pressures for managers to show performance in their centers and a corresponding higher expectation level of reps, creating a higher level of pressure and stress in these centers. These indicators correspond to rumblings of union activity and, in some instances, strikes at call centers throughout the United States and Britain. Paralleling speculative and actual union activity has been the movement of a large number of existing centers, and a corresponding number of new centers, to developing countries with a large labor pool of English-speaking workers and/or little unionization (*The Economist*, 2003).

This chapter will examine union activity generally and the manner in which this activity influences call center management and the bottom line.

BY THE NUMBERS

The U.S. Bureau of Labor Statistics (BLS) collects data on labor union representation by age, sex, demographics, ethnicity/race, state, and other identifiers. The most recent data indicates that 13.2% of wage and salary workers were union members in 2002, down from a high of 20.1% in 1983 (BLS, 2002). Men (14.7%) were more likely to unionize than women (11.6%), and African-Americans were more likely to unionize than Whites and Hispanics, respectively. African-American men had the highest unionization rate (18.2%) among all groups, and Hispanic and White women had the lowest rates at 9.8 and 10.9%, respectively. Union membership rates were highest among workers between the ages of 45–54 years. Full-time workers were more than twice as likely as part-time workers to be union members, and the South had lower rates of unionization than other locations within the United States (see Figures 6-1, 6-2, 6-3, and 6-4).

As the data indicate, the most likely profile of someone to unionize is an African-American male, 45–54 years in age, working full-time, and living in the Northeastern United States or the West Coast. The person least likely to unionize in 2002 was a Hispanic woman, 16–24 years in age, working part-time in the South. Interestingly, when examining the movement and growth of new centers within the United States over the past decade and a half, there appears to be an interesting parallel between emerging centers in Texas, Florida, New Mexico, and Arizona and the demographic population less likely to unionize.

UNION AVOIDANCE

When most managers hear the words "labor union," small hairs on the back of their necks usually stand up because they understand there is a

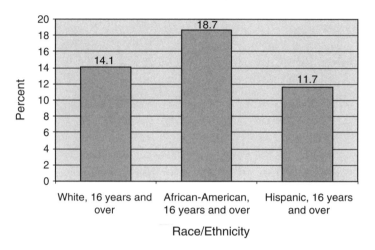

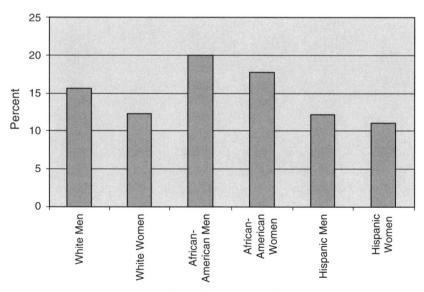

Figure 6-1. Percent of total employment represented in 2002 by unions by race/ethnicity and gender. (Source: U.S. Bureau of Labor Statistics.)

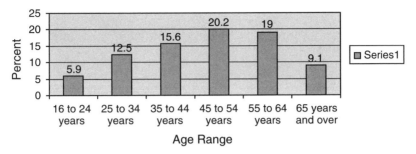

Figure 6-2. Percent of total employed in 2002 represented by unions by age. (Source: U.S. Bureau of Labor Statistics.)

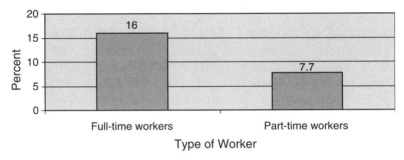

Figure 6-3. Percent of full-time versus part-time workers represented by unions in 2002 in the United States. (Source: U.S. Bureau of Labor Statistics.)

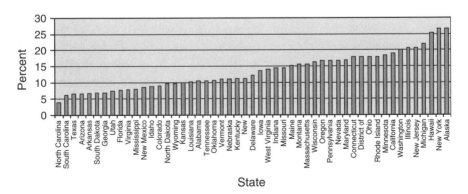

Figure 6-4. Percent represented by unions of total employment in 2002 by state. (Source: U.S. Bureau of Labor Statistics.)

potential threat to their center. The last thing managers want to report to executives in a company is that their center has voted to go union and there is nothing to be done about it. As a general principle, it is best for an organization to avoid labor unions as much as possible. The reasons for this are many, but here are just a few:

1. Wages usually increase for workers, driving up labor costs for the company.
2. Benefits usually increase for workers, driving up labor costs for the company.
3. Labor union representation usually occurs when there is a distrust between the workers and management, thus indicating strong inefficiencies in the organization to begin with.
4. Labor unions like to interject themselves between the management and unions, thus slowing down the communication process and effectiveness.
5. Management must take on a new level of scrutiny of the employees and vice versa, creating increased tensions and downgrading performance in the organization.
6. The specter of a strike is real!
7. Labor unions are notoriously conservative organizations that resist change. This resistance does not enable an organization to rapidly respond to fast-moving market forces in many industries, causing the potential loss of market share and an overall decline in the company.

Given the myriad of problems that emerge with labor unions in an organization, avoiding union activities as much as possible is the most effective and sensible route. Interestingly, many companies train their managers on how to handle any potential union organizing events in centers in an attempt to stop potential activities before they begin. However, the most effective repulsion mechanism for any organization against unionization is to have an already established culture and positive environment that would not encourage, and should discourage, any movements toward unionization. The best and most effective anti-union practice is actually a well-managed call center.

UNIONIZATION! NOW WHAT?

If you are a manager at a union center, or a manager at a center that has become unionized, the only option is to make the best of the situation.

Always keep in mind that the number one goal or focus of any business is to make as much profit as possible. This requires that all managers keep the bottom line in sight at all times. A center manager wants to either produce the highest revenue possible with the least expenditures or, if a non-revenue producing center, to maximize the return on investment for the expenditures, ideally in a measurable way. Remember, no matter the personal feelings about unions and union activity, the focus is on the ROI for the company. Given this endgame, the question becomes: What can a manager positively accomplish for the bottom line if they manage a unionized center?

National Contract

Some industries have been unionized for many decades and have unions as a part of their organizational culture. These include many manufacturing industries such as automobile and steel located traditionally in the North and Northeastern United States. Airlines are likewise unionized with pilots, flight attendants, mechanics, and others often being represented by separate unions with different agendas. Government is the most recent organization to undergo mass unionization with approximately 42% of all government workforces unionized in 2002 (see Figure 6-5).

When these historically unionized organizations choose to create call centers for sales and customer service, unions are often eager to ensure that any new unit of the company becomes a union shop. In fact, some collective bargaining agreements contain provision stating that the company must allow unionization as expansion of the organization takes place.

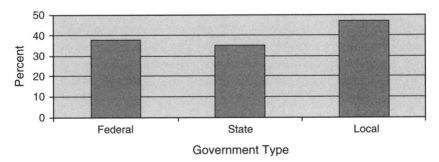

Figure 6-5. Government workers represented by unions in 2002. (Source: U.S. Bureau of Labor Statistics.)

If a company faces this level of unionization, how can a manager use this to the advantage of the bottom line?

The answer to the question is in simple economics. If labor union representation exists in an organization that has multiple centers, the goal is to negotiate a single union contract across the board for all centers at the lowest possible rate (salary plus benefits). In short, this creates a single national contract that gives an organization a fixed labor cost structure throughout all centers for the contract period. With a national labor contract in place, the company can successfully estimate labor costs over the multiple years of the contract and plan revenue streams accordingly.

EXAMPLE

There are two organizations, each with five call centers, located in the same cities throughout the United States. Because costs of living and labor differ from city to city and region to region, the cost structure for an organization with five call centers will differ from one center to the next, that is, labor costs on the East and West coasts are substantially higher than those in the Midwest and the South.

Differential labor costs at five centers throughout the United States:

Organization 1	
Number	Average Wage Per Hour
Center 1	$10.00
Center 2	$9.50
Center 3	$7.80
Center 4	$11.00
Center 5	$10.65
Total	$48.95
Avg. wage	$9.79

The average wage of Organization 1 is $9.79 per hour, with a high of $11.00 in Center 4 and a low of $7.80 in Center 3. Therefore, if this organization is unionized, the best tactic for the bottom line would be to negotiate a national contract for all of its centers that would cost on average less than $9.79 per hour. For example, let say that Organization 2, which has centers in all the same locations as Organization 1, has just that type of national labor contract.

Organization 2

Number	Average Wage Per Hour
Center 1	$9.00
Center 2	$9.00
Center 3	$9.00
Center 4	$9.00
Center 5	$9.00
Total	$45.00
Avg. Wage	$9.00

What is the long-term value difference between Organization 1 at $9.79 per hour and Organization 2 at $9.00 an hour?

Assuming that each center is an above-average size, with 250 employees, and the average number of hours worked by each worker is 35 per week:

	Per Hour Wage	# of Hours Avg. Per Week	# Employees	Total Cost Per Week
Organization 1	$9.79	35	250	$85,662.50
Organization 2	$9.00	35	250	$78,750.00
Difference				$6,912.50 per week

If there was a national union contract that set the wages as a fixed priced, then Organization 2 would save approximately $6,912.50 per week over Organization 1. Extrapolated, the labor savings per month and per quarter can be

	Cost Per Week	Cost Per Month	Cost Per Quarter
Organization 1	$85,662.50	$342,650.00	$1,027,950.00
Organization 2	$78,750.00	$315,000.00	$945,000.00
Difference	$6,912.50	$27,650.00	$82,950.00

Therefore, over one month, labor savings would reach $27,650, and in one quarter, labor savings would reach $82,950.00. Once again, the point of these examples is not to advocate unionization or anti-collective bargaining. The point of this exercise is to suggest a rationalization of labor costs nationally if an organization has multiple centers in different locations and a large number of the centers are already unionized.

Furthermore, besides potential labor costs savings, a fixed national contract in call centers can offer a predicable, measurable, and stable labor cost over time. Often, stability is preferred in an organization over uncertainty, even if the uncertainty has the potential to have cost savings. Why? Because companies price their products and services taking into account expected costs. If these costs are known, then a company can safely and accurately predict the cost of production of the product and service, then they can add on their expected level of profit for the anticipated sales, with a good estimate of revenues and profit per quarter and year. If labor cost are fluctuating, and doing so as a major cost of operations in multiple centers in different regions within a country, then the ability to predict production and service costs (and by extrapolation the cost of the product on the market) becomes more difficult and time consuming to manage on a daily basis, leaving the level of profitability unknown from quarter to quarter. This uncertainty causes instability, and instability is generally an indicator of a poor organization and can slow investments in the organization.

EXAMPLE

Labor cost fluctuations versus fixed

Organization 1: labor cost in flux

Center 1	$9.25–10.50
Center 2	$8.90–10.00
Center 3	$7.20–8.30
Center 4	$10.05–11.50
Center 5	$9.45–11.15
Avg.	$8.97–10.29

Organization 2: labor costs fixed

Center 1	$9.00
Center 2	$9.00
Center 3	$9.00
Center 4	$9.00
Center 5	$9.00
Avg.	$9.00

In Organization 1, average labor cost per hour could be as low as $8.97 to as high as $10.29. In Organization 2, the labor costs are known upfront due to the national union contract, thus there will be no change in labor cost. If in Organization 1 all labor prices for all five centers' averages hit the lowest mark, then this model would come out at $8.97 per hour, lower than the fixed national union contract in Organization 2. However, if just a few of the centers averaged in the middle to the high end of the average wage cost per hour, then the total average wage could be as much as a $1 or more per hour per employee. Therefore, in terms of monthly and quarterly labor costs, the organizations are left with the following two scenarios.

SCENARIO 1

250-seat center, avg. 35 hours per week

Organization 1	Per Month	Per Quarter	Per Year
Lowest cost	$313,950	$941,850	$3,767,400
Highest cost	$360,150	$1,080,450	$4,321,800

SCENARIO 2

250-seat center, avg. 35 hours per week

Organization 2	Per Month	Per Quarter	Per Year
Cost	$315,000	$945,000	$3,780,000

Given these two scenarios, the ideal scenario is Organization 1, lowest cost, since it is the lowest labor cost option. However, there is no certainty of the low range. Because of the large need for labor and labor cost fluctuation, the difference between low cost and high cost in Scenario 1 is $554,500 per year. The question the manager faces is: What is the cost of uncertainty? If everything goes as expected in Organization 1, then the lowest cost becomes a reality. If, however, some of the variables influencing labor costs are out of the organization's control, Organization 1's highest cost could be the reality. Therefore, what is the risk tolerance for Organization 1? If they choose to go with Scenario 1, they could save the $554,500 in labor cost from the low to the high per year. However, if a manager had the option for a fixed price contract across all call centers, the actual potential savings between Scenario 1 low cost and Scenario 2 is only $12,600 per year. Furthermore, the real risk is not in saving $12,600 per year, but paying higher costs in Scenario 1 versus fixed costs in Scenario 2. The difference between these two annual figures is $541,800. Therefore, the question for a call center organization is the risk tolerance that could save a center up to $12,600 per year, but could likewise cost a center up to $541,800 per year more than necessary. Given the conservative nature of many corporations and the desire for continuous profitability, most organizations would not take the risk and would go with the fixed price contract because the potential for loss is much greater than the potential for gain. The risk in Scenario 1 would be worthwhile for an organization only if the payoff were very high and the risks could be managed or minimized to the maximum extent possible.

If the organization has a significant number of unionized centers, it may behoove the management to have them all fall under a single large umbrella national collective bargaining agreement. Similarly, if a center has no union activity, it would clearly be in the organization's best interests to stave off union activity to ensure direct access to employees in terms of hiring, promotion, pay scale, discipline, and flexibility in plans.

The European Model: Outsourced Operations

The only other way to change unionization from a negative to a positive would be to adopt the European model of unions. In many European nations, the unions act less as a wedge between the workers and management and, instead, often manage the workers themselves. This has two benefits:

1. The union does not spend time interfering with communication channels between management and employees; they are the management and thus are part of the communication channel.
2. By having the unions manage a part of the business function, a business can eliminate that labor cost from it books.

In action, a company can negotiate a reasonable rate for production with the union. The union is then responsible for meeting the contractual agreement and absorbs all of the responsibility for labor. This is almost like outsourcing the project. With this model, a company can rationalize labor costs over time, while at the same time removing the problems associated with labor unions interfering with business activities. However, once again, the ideal situation would be not to have labor unions as part of the business, but if they do arrive, the European model of unionization is an effective way to ensure that the focus remains on the bottom line of the organization.

FINAL THOUGHTS

There are many schools of thought about pay and benefits for call center reps. This chapter explains that call center pay is a function of both the education and the skill level of the employee applying, the location of the call center and its available labor shed, and the regional market for the collective skills of this category of employees. Because there is ample pressure on call center managers to keep budgets down while turnover is high and to move higher wages in the opposite direction, managers need to examine (re)creating a positive call center culture (cultural fix) that allows lower-than-average market wages and keeps turnover low, thus creating a positive spiral and positive ROI for the center.

This chapter also briefly examines the most recent data about unionization in the United States. It also appears as if the recent location patterns of call center development parallel those of the demographic groups who are less likely to unionize. The best choice for a call center is to avoid unionization efforts, ideally by creating a great place for the employees to work and to help in making the organization successful. If unions already exist, the best management plans are to keep the focus on the bottom line, potentially adopting a low fixed national contract for all centers or adopting a European model of unionization where the union becomes a partner rather than a distraction from the business process.

REFERENCES

Bauer, B. "Build Long-Term Loyalty from the Agent's Perspective." *Call Center Agent Turnover and Retention*. Annapolis, MD: Call Center Press, 2002, pp. 31–39.

Bruton, N. *How to Manage the IT Helpdesk: A Guide for User Support and Call Centre Managers*, 2nd ed. Woburn, MA: Butterworth Heinemann, 2002.

Butler, D. L. "Culture Matters! Retaining Employees and Increasing Profitability." *In Action: Retaining Your Best Employees*, Phillips, Jack J. (Series Ed.), and P. P. Phillips (Ed.). Arlington, VA: American Society for Training and Development, 2002, pp. 135–150.

Coen, D. "Agent Compensation: Motivating Staff without Burying Budgets." *Call Center Agent Motivation and Compensation*. Annapolis, MD: Call Center Press, 2002, pp. 39–42.

Incoming.com. Frequently asked questions. April, 14th, p. 2. www.incoming.com, 2002.

Levin, G. "Call Center Professionals Speak Up for Underpaid Agents."

Call Center Agent Motivation and Compensation. Annapolis, MD: Call Center Press, 2002a, pp. 33–38.

Levin, G. "Key Aspects of Successful Agent Retention Process." *Call Center Agent Turnover and Retention.* Annapolis, MD: Call Center Press, 2002b, pp. 3–10.

Levin, G. "Call Center Managers Share Secrets at Human Resources Roundtable." *Call Center Recruiting and New Hire Training.* Annapolis, MD: Call Center Press, 2001, pp. 3–16.

Read, B. B. *Designing the Best Call Center for Your Business.* Gilroy, CA: CMP Books, 2000.

The Economist. "Growing Pains: Outsourcing to India," Aug. 23, 2003, pp. 51–52.

U.S. Bureau of Labor Statistics. "BLS Releases 2000–2010 Employment Projections." www.bls.gov. 2003.

CHAPTER 7

The People and the Technology

To have an operationally successful call center, a manager needs a good balance of technology and reps, or to put it another way, physical and human capital have to be in harmony. The question is how to achieve this harmony, which will produce an effective return on investment and influence the bottom line positively.

There are a number of books on call center technology on the market at present. Each of these texts gives advice on which technology to choose given the nature of a center and the current and expected demands and, of course, suggests that a manager be prepared for changes in his/her call center when available technologies allow the center multiple channels to access customers and vice versa (see suggesting readings at the end of this chapter). There are also other books which examine technical support call center help desks specifically. Each of these books is good for the specific markets and reader they address. This chapter will cite several references from these books, but the majority of this chapter has a different focus than these books. Instead of focusing on the technology as a centerpiece, this chapter instead focuses on the people in the call center and how technology can be adopted, or not adopted, to improve call center performance influencing the bottom line.

This chapter is not about how to upgrade your center with the newest whiz-bang technology. Instead, it argues that technology is only a means through which your reps can interact with the customer and vice versa. Therefore, the focus of a center should be neither on the technology itself nor the way to get customers to use technology and avoid your reps. Instead, it should be on how to effectively manage the interactions of your reps with customers through technology to improve the quality of customer service. "[T]echnology is the tool, not the solution to a successful call center. The tool must integrate with your company's vision to be effective" (*Call Center Operations,* 2000, p. 49). "Remember people by and large prefer talking to people. They hate, but to differing degrees tolerate, talking to machines, especially ones that don't let them talk to live people. Especially stupid live people" (Read, 2000, p. 155). Customer service is NOT an interaction of a customer with a machine/technology. Every time I purchase a cold beverage or snack out of a vending machine, I do not thank the local vending owner or beverage distributor for their customer service. If a call center articulates that they are a customer support/service center, then by golly a customer/client should be able to reach a human being very fast and efficiently. This is not to say that there is not a market for, or demand from customers for, automated information systems; there clearly are. But managers should not deceive themselves and call this customer service. It is not. It is information retrieval and exchange only.

TECHNOLOGY AS A PANACEA

Technology within the call center industry is too often considered a panacea. It is critical to success in this business and can help in routing and switching calls more effectively, data analysis, storage, retrieval, and measuring the metrics of your organization. Likewise, specific technologies can offer advice on when to staff for peak and off peak windows. However, it must be clear that technology is only a tool, and this tool is only as effective as your least effective rep in a call center. No level of technology can make a poor employee into a good employee, just as a good employee is good no matter the level of technology available to him/her. Therefore, if a manager spends a considerable amount of money and time on technologies (physical capital) and disregards the reps (human capital), the ideal balance between these two and the center's goals will never reach the level of potential rewards to the bottom line. Bocklund and Bengtson (2002, p. 8) restate this alignment of goals and human and physical capital, suggesting that "companies need to align three elements, business strategy, call center strategy, and technology strategy."

Different technology packages offer different solutions to a call center. And be assured, the hardware and software salesperson will make it clear that by purchasing their NEW technology that a center will enter nirvana on its own. Do not buy this argument. A center would be much more efficient using older technology with a highly trained and motivated workforce than spanking new technology with an employee base that was neither motivated nor properly trained to take maximum advantage of the technology. Remember, the name of the game is the bottom line, not the newest technology! Do not get caught in the trap Read describes where a salesperson allows a manager to become "mesmerized with their alleged benefits to the point where you forget what the call centers are for: the customers" (Read, 2000, p. 155).

ADOPTING NEW TECHNOLOGIES

Before even beginning the first step towards embarking on a new technology acquisition, the manager of the center must know all there is to know about the current status of the center and the value-added nature of the current technology. Only then can a full and sincere effort be put forth in looking for a technology(ies) that will surpass the current level in the center. All managers want to avoid the pitfall Cusak (2002) describes as "[s]tagnating budgets, crumbling infrastructures, rampant attrition, and nasty stains on the carpets are a growing hallmark of call centers across America as management resigns itself to the fact that (big surprise) installing the latest customer interaction technology doesn't mean that you can fire everyone and still delight the customer." According to *Call Center Operations*, technology affects call centers in three major ways. You can use technology to:

1. Reduce Costs. Technology products or systems are justified on how much they will save the company. Most call centers do this.
2. Generate Revenue. Fewer call centers look for newer technologies to generate revenue. Return on investment for this technology systems is harder to demonstrate.
3. Reduce costs while generating revenue. Only the most effective call centers focus on ways to both generate sales and reduce costs (2000, pp. 47–48).

All progressive call center managers should only adopt new technologies if they fit category three. Anything short of reducing costs and generating revenue will cause his/her center to be behind the competition, thus not maximizing the potential mix of human and physical capital available to them. Given the complex interactions between the human and physical capital of a center, this section will outline a six-step plan for any manager who is thinking about new technologies for his/her center.

Step 1: Assessment

Managers need to assess the current level of technology in their center. What is the value-added nature of the technology? One mechanism to find out the positive or negative impacts of the current technology is to imagine the productivity of the center if the technology was turned off. Another question to ask is what type of multiplier does the current technology add to the employees in your center? Does it save them one-forth of the time per call? Does it save any time at all? Does it help generate revenue? If no, why not? If yes, how much revenue and how often? Can a different system, not necessarily more advanced, accomplish this revenue generation and cost savings more effectively? Or as Read asks, "When sorting new technology, ask yourself, is it something truly of value...or a seemingly valuable but, in reality, worthless tool. Do you have a true use for it, or do you have to engineer your life around it, in unacceptable ways?" (2000, p. 147). Each of these facets of the technology the manager should know like the back of his/her hand. The manager should also know what type of technology and services he/she would need to operate more efficiently by decreasing cost (time = money) and increasing revenue. This "ideal" technology should be written down, and then the manager should move on to Step 2.

Step 2: Evaluation

Once the manager knows what he/she needs to be more effective in a center, it is now time to examine the technologies offered by various vendors. By walking in with a written evaluation and needs statement from Step 1, the manager is less likely to be gee whizzed into buying something he/she does not need. The goal of the manager in Step 2 is to seek out a technology that will multiply the current strengths and offer an ability to nullify the weaknesses in his/her center. If this technology does not exist, then stay out of the market, period. That said, listen, learn, and ask hard and penetrating questions to the vendors. They may, and I stress may, have come up with a technological system that will accomplish the goals and value added in a manner you had not thought of before. However, make sure this is a genuine value added by revising Step 1. If it does not meet the needs, pass on the new technologies. If technologies exist to serve your evaluated needs, then proceed to Step 3.

Step 3: Testing

If a manager believes he/she has found several technologies that fit the bill described in Steps 1 and 2, then a test drive is needed to see if the technology actually delivers what the salesperson says. Remember, no vendor will tell you the problems inherent in the technology, and there are always problems and trade-offs. It is just like buying a new car. Yes it is new, and yes it is more clean that the old car; however, this one requires more maintenance and at a higher cost. It also handles differently, so it will take some getting used to and there will be a break-in period. And finally, the old car was paid off; this new car will have to be paid for. Is it worth the cost in terms of value provided? To answer this question, it is time to have these technologies demonstrated head-to-head in the center by both the management and the reps that will have to use the technology.

Keep the technology in the center for a week or two trying it out. This serves multiple purposes. One, it tells the reps that you care what they think about the new technology. Two, since they are not purchasing the new technology (it is not their car), they may actually be more resistant than a manager to the pressures of a salesperson. At the test-drive stage, one or more of the technologies will show their weakness and problems and will be eliminated. If there is one technology still left and the value added is still clear, the move to Step 4. If the technologies show their obvious weaknesses, have high price tags, and do not pass the test drive the reps put them through, then exit the market and re-examine technologies again next year.

To determine the potential cost effectiveness of the new technology, a manager should be able to quickly calculate a break even point where the technology will pay for itself with savings and revenue generation. This time frame should be fast. If it is long, then a manager should wait because (1) the price of the technology will drop over time and (2) a newer technology will arrive, making the best system today look outdated within a few years. So, the technology you adopt must pay for itself within the time frame that a new technology enters the market that can replace it. If not, then waiting the year or two for the newer technology, or for the price of the older technology to drop, may be the best choice for the center.

STEP 4: IMPLEMENTATION

Once a new technology has been adopted, then it needs to be quickly implemented so the center can gain the maximum advantage of the technology as soon as possible. This means that the center needs to have in place a new technology training session. Adapt to the new technology quickly. Since the reps have already test driven the new technology and have agreed that it is a more valuable tool for the center and their performance, resistance to the technology will be minimal, increasing the chances that the benefits from the new technology will be seen sooner rather than later. Make sure that all of the functionalities of the technol-ogy are being used to the maximum. Only maximum use will allow the most efficient use of the technology. For example, if an airline purchases a new Boeing airplane to carry passengers and cargo, the most efficient use of the plane will be to have it in flight as often as possible hauling people and goods. The most inefficient use of the plane would be to use it sparingly so that it does not get dirty or too many miles on its engines. Why? Because when in use, this transportation technology is generating revenue and decreasing costs over the older model of airplane. The same is true with technology in a center. The goal should be to maximize out the functionality of the technology, push the limits. If this cannot be done in the center, then it is possible that too much, or not the right type of, technology was purchased.

Step 5: Reevaluation

With the new technology in place, within a year the manager needs to complete a new assessment of the new technology. This reassessment serves to allow the manager to indicate what the return on investment the new technology is delivering to the center, including clear evidence that the technology is generating more revenue per person than before and an increase in savings either directly or through time.

Step 6: Annual Assessment

Step 6 is an annual assessment of the existing technology and a loop back to Step 1. Though it may seem a bit premature, it is not. If a short pay-off period can be justified through increasing revenue generation and cost savings, then it is seldom too early to adopt a new technology. Let me give you an example. Andrew Carnegie was a famous steel producer who helped to mature this industry within the United States and made billions of dollars doing it. In a famously recounted story, Carnegie had just finished building a brand new steel plant with the most modern furnaces available. A few days before the plant was to go operational, Carnegie's leading technology man informed him that a new furnace design had just been developed which was more efficient and effective than the new ones they just installed. Instead of opening the plant, to everyone's surprise, Carnegie scrapped the furnaces in the plant that was about to be opened and instead spent the time and money to purchase and install the new furnaces Carnegie's man had informed him about. Why did Carnegie do this? The answer is because he new the value of the newest design of the furnace would allow him to recoup the costs of the furnaces he had just built in a short period of time and to keep his industry on the cutting edge against the competition. Call center mangers need to be knowledgeable enough about their current level of technology to be able to determine if such an opportunity comes along as it did for Carnegie. With this knowledge they can make the correct decision for their center.

TECHNOLOGICAL CHANGE AND RESISTANCE

Before a manager searches for a new suite of technologies for his/her center, the reps of the center need to be queried. Do the reps want new technology or are they happy with the current system? Has the level of adoption or resistance by the reps been examined? If not, why not?

Most people are conservative by nature. People are conservative in the sense that many people dislike change and will go to great means to avoid change. Since you have taken the initiative to read this book, you may not fall into this category, but you must be aware that most employees in a call center will fit this description. Because most employees are weary of change, if a manager is pondering an adoption of a new technology for a center, it is recommended that he/she allow the reps to evaluate the new technologies in a collective manner, which brings the employees into the process early and often. After all, the reps will be using the technology many hours a day. Imagine the following two scenarios.

SCENARIO 1

As a manager of your call center, you make a general meeting announcement that next month new hardware and software will be installed in the center. Each rep will be required to attend a mandatory 10 hours of training on the new system and will be given a test after the training where they must make at least an 85% to be considered competent on the new system. If they do not pass the exam with an 85%, they must retake the 10 hours of instruction again and test once again. After this announcement, the employees will become entrenched, fearful, and the quality of their work will decline. Comments such as these will be common.

> "I have just gotten the hang of the system we have now, and now we have to change?"
> "I bet they are going to make us produce more with this new system and that is why they are using it, to make us work harder for the same money."

"I will do the training and test, but I am going to keep doing what I
normally do. I don't care what the management says."

"I am going to quit before they make me learn a new system."

"This is the 3rd system I have had to learn since I have been here.
I wish they would give me a pay raise rather than buying all this
new tech!"

"The old system didn't work well. Why do they think this new one
will?"

You have probably heard these or similar sentiments which emerge
when new technologies, processes, and practices are adopted in an organization. Though it is easier for the manager to work directly with the
vendors and make a rational decision and then tell the employees, the
most productive path would be to include the employees in the full
process.

SCENARIO 2

As the manager, you believe that you can be more productive by adopting
a new system. However, before you move forward with this decision, you
need to communicate to your reps that you believe that there are opportunities to become more efficient in the center with a new system, but before
you make a final decision, you would like a committee of employees to
undertake an evaluation of the need of new technology. This committee of
volunteers will be charged with evaluating the current technology system
and the thoughts/beliefs of the current reps about potential new technologies. Their final report will help shape the final decision on whether to
adopt a new system or not. Furthermore, if a new system is needed, then
the employees will have an input in the type of system that is adopted and
the type and length of training that is needed. Since employees are part
of the process, comments such as these will be expected.

"I think we need a new system. If the system is faster, then we can
complete more calls faster and meet our quotas easier."

"I have a friend who works at Butler and Associates, Inc. and they
have the latest Zyrog system. It's cool. It takes them only two clicks
to have all of the information where our system takes about five. I
would love to have that system here."

"Look, I think the system we have now is fine. It works, we know
how to get the information and it doesn't crash. What if we ask to
use the money for a new system for a nicer lunchroom instead?"

"I can't believe the manager has asked our opinion on the new system. In my other jobs, the management didn't ask our opinion on any-thing. We were told what to do, how to do it, and when to do it."

The difference between the comments in Scenarios 1 and 2 are striking. In Scenario 1, fear and resentment are the two major emotions driving the opinions expressed. Scenario 2 has employees discussing and debating among themselves the choice to adopt or not to adopt and even offering an alternate suggestion for the use of the money if the new system is not adopted this year. The fear and uneasiness is now replaced with a "buy in," the feeling of inclusion and a voice in matters that are important. This empowerment of the employees, if sustained through a positive culture, will pay handsome dividends in the future.

To expand on Scenario 2, let us imagine that the recommendation of the committee was to adopt new equipment and you concur with this recommendation. Now what? You have a decision to either unilaterally make a decision on the new technology or continue to develop a positive culture in your center through the inclusion of employees in the centers decision-making process. Instead of the new technology vendors showing only you the new systems, why not allow a committee of employees to test drive the new systems for a few days? After all, they will be using the system more than you and will be the ones to make the necessary adjustments to adapt to the new system. Why not have the top three vendors showcase their technologies and let the reps use the systems head-to-head for a few days to determine which one is best suited to their needs. Then the employee-led committee will make a final decision and communicate it to the manager. This type of employee governance will accomplish many positive items for your center.

1. The sales vendors will be confused since they will not only have to convince you of their product, but a whole committee of employees. This will keep the salesperson off your back long enough to get some work done as they are trying to sell to the committee.
2. The employee buy in will show the employees the value you have for their opinion and thus increase the likelihood of retaining these employees over time.
3. Since it was a committee of employees that helped decide that new technology was needed and which one to choose, their resistance to change will be minimized, since each employee will be aware that this was, in part, a bottom up effort. Since the perception will not be that this was imposed on them, there are more likely to help

each other out collectively to learn about the new system and thus adoption will occur faster and more efficiently.

4. If employees had a chance to test drive the new technologies, they realized that the new systems have specific functionalities that they can use to do their job better and faster and to make their job easier. Therefore, they are more likely to use the full functionality of the new system rather than just the necessary parts, making the system more cost effective over time.

Measuring Technology Change Success

Once a manager has opted to purchase/lease the new technology, at considerable expense of course, how will he/she know it will pay for itself over time? The only way to effectively measure the new technology and increased production will be to have a pre- and post-evaluation holding all other variables constant except the technological change. The manager has already run some numbers of potential productivity from item number 2 above. If not, the new technology would not have been purchased. Now it is time to see if the numbers actually work. As stated in previous chapters, this measurement can probably be most efficiently and effectively accomplished by outsourcing to an experienced consultant. The consultant will offer both a third party less biased point of view and an independent factor to the analysis which lend more credibility to the reports a manager will generate for headquarters justifying the equipment/technology expense.

An ROI of Technological Change

There are many different measures for return on investment (ROI). A simple and quick measure on the potential ROI for new technology would follow the five general broad measures below. Interestingly, as the examples below will indicate, a major variable, which can lead to success or failure of a technology, is the level or resistance and/or quick adoption of the technology by the employees. A technology is only as efficient as the employees use or utilization of that technology. If an employee chooses to work slower, not using the new flexibility of a new technology, or keep old and inefficient practices, then the technology investment will take longer or, worse, never achieve the necessary ROI. Using the airline and airplane analogy, an airline can buy the new plane with all of its efficiencies and force this technology on pilots, flight attendants, mechanics, baggage handlers, etc. However, a pilot can fly faster or slower, burn more or less fuel, and use other tactics that can wipe clean the expected savings and efficiencies with the new airplane. The same is true for the other groups as well. So, employee buy in and adoption of the new technology is critical.

Without Employee Input

Measure I:	Average daily effort of employees measured on a Likert scale from 1–10, with 10 being the highest. The employees are about 80% efficient, clearly indicating room for improvement.	8
Measure II:	Average daily effort of employees measured after the announcement that a new technology will be implemented in the center (without their input). An expected degradation of production by 1 Likert point. Depending upon the level of resistance, this could be higher, but the desire is to keep the number conservative for this example.	−1
Measure III:	Without employee input on the new technology, employees will be slow to adopt and learn the new technology, frustration level will be high, and there will be a general lack of personal motivation for the employee to embrace the technology quickly and with vigor. An expected degradation of productivity during the transition period by two Likert points.	−2
Measure IV:	The expected level of new efficiencies offered by the new technology system. A positive on Likert points scale.	2
Measure V:	New expected level of production based on original production level, subtracting resistance to adoption and degradation of performance, and adding the expected level of improvements with the new technology yields the new average daily effort number.	7

With Employee Input

Measure I:	Average daily effort of employees measured on a Likert scale from 1–10, with 10 being the highest.	8
Measure II:	Average daily effort of employees measured after the employees are notified that they will be an actively important part of the new technology assessment and adoption process. An expected increase in production by 1 Likert point due to the employee's enthusiasm for the management choosing to involve them in the new technology decision-making process.	1
Measure III:	With employee input on the new technology, employees will be quick to adopt and learn the new technology, frustration level will be low, and there will be a general positive personal motivation for the employee to embrace the technology quickly and with vigor. No expected degradation of productivity during the transition period.	0
Measure IV:	The expected level of new efficiencies offered by the new technology system. A positive on the Likert point scale. Similarly, with employee involvement, there is the potential to have this efficiency number increase as reps learn more about the new technology and how to best maximize their performance.	2
Measure V:	New expected level of production based on original production level, subtracting resistance to adoption and degradation of performance, and adding the expected level of improvements with the new technology yields the new average daily effort number.	11

To gain the full productive capacity of a new technology, the human capital part of your center must be willing and able to actively and enthusiastically adopt the new system. As demonstrated in the example without employee input, the new technology adoption can actually lead to a degradation of production (from an 8 to a 7 on the Likert scale). Often, managers are left scratching their heads as to why this new technology with all of its bells, whistles, and promises has led to a decrease in performance versus the old system in place. It can become quite problematic if a manager acquires a new and expensive piece of technology only to be able to demonstrate that the equipment has a negative ROI. However, with employee buy in, the productivity number goes from an 8 to an 11, even though the efficiency number of the technology is a 2 and the expected outcome would be a 10. This is because with buy in, the efficiency of the workers themselves will increase, and with the added increase enabled by the technology, there is a stronger multiplier for the center than originally expected, creating a stronger ROI.

WHO CONTROLS THE TECHNOLOGY?

Depending upon the center, the purchase, lease, upgrade, and/or maintenance of the call center equipment and technology may or may not be in the hands of the manager. In many organizations, the manager is there to "manage" the reps and customers but a completely different division or department is in charge of all of the information technology (IT) of the organization. If this is the case the manager has two options. Option 1 is to change this relationship. Gain control of your technology from the other division or department. The on-site manager should be the controlling force (daily) for the technology in the center. Purchasing new equipment may need to be vetted through the chief information officer (CIO) or similar executive, but day-to-day operations, technology, and equipment needs to be in the hands of the manager. If this is not feasible, use option 2: get to know the person in charge of the technology and buy this person a lunch or two. Take this person out, explain your needs, invite them to the center to visit, take a tour, and maybe even answer the phone in a cubicle for half a day. Whatever it takes, create a positive working relationship with this person. If not, the ideal balance between human and physical capital for a center can never be achieved if 50% of the equation is out of the control of the call center manager which will directly influence and impact the productivity of the center.

There is also the other extreme as described by Dawson (2001), where a manager is hired because of his/her technology skills and the interviewers appear to forget that this person will be managing more than just technology and will have possibly hundreds of people working for them.

"[W]e need to admit, once and for all, that knowledge of technology and its structures are an imperfect and outdated selection criterion for a call center manager. Admit it to yourselves now: it's all about people skills" (Dawson, 2001, p. 262).

TECHNOLOGY AS AN ENABLER OR A WALL?

Call center technology, depending upon the philosophy behind the architecture and adoption, can be used in one of two ways. The first way is to help enable the rep to service the customer better with access to much information, assistance networks, and decision-making systems seamlessly, quickly, and timely. The second way to use technology is as a type of gate-keeper to put a wall of technology between the customer and the service support, ensuring that it is difficult if not impossible for a customer to reach as rep.

Here are a few real-life examples of these. A transportation company has a policy of one ring in their center. This one-ring policy means that the phone should be answered by a rep within one ring; any more than one ring is unacceptable. Occasionally, during discounted sales, call volume increases beyond expectations and customers are placed in a queue, but this is rare. This company uses its technology to drive the customers to the reps directly so that they speak to a person first, not last. The second example is from a music company. This company used to have multiple call centers for customer support throughout the states. Now, there is one toll-free number to call for all services. Everything at the toll-free number is fully automated; no human can be found, and pressing zero is not an option. If a customer is not satisfied with the options on the phone, they can go to the website or write a letter using snail mail at the address the recording offers. Because the answer to the question could not be found in the phone menu choices, the website was examined. The website referenced the toll-free number and an e-mail address for customer support. After e-mailing customer support, an automated response was generated. This scanned the e-mail for word choice and content to determine which of the hundreds of automated e-mail responses should be sent. The question was still not answered. The researcher has chosen not to make purchases at this company again due to their lack of desire to have interaction with the customer.

Peter Lewis (2003), writing in *Fortune*, had a similar experience with a package company. Lewis states, "Companies all over the world are installing automated telephone support systems as a way to save money. Human beings are expensive, and each time a customer calls to ask a question it comes out of the company's bottom line. The crucial difference is this: some voice systems are designed to help the customer get service faster. Some are designed to help the business save money by doing everything possible to keep the caller from speaking to a human."

Though the business plan that calls for this type of full automation will surely pay a handsome ROI for the first few years since labor costs have been drastically reduced, the reality is that many customers will make the choice of this researcher and will choose not to make purchases from this company. Thus, the long-term strategy of a technological wall between the customer and customer service will eventually cause a decline in revenues as well as leave an opening for a competitor with a strong customer service commitment to fill the vacuum. Managers of call centers need to assess their technological plans and strategy and determine if their technology is being used as an enabling mechanism or to stave off customers by keeping electronic gatekeepers between the customer and the high labor costs of reps.

Consider what Bocklund and Bengtson have found. "Is business strategy relevant to call centers? Absolutely! Your call center is a vital link to one of your company's most important strategic assets—your customers" (2002, p. 5). The authors continue and state that successful executives "understand the influence of the call center on customer acquisition, retention, satisfaction and growth. They know that all call center excellence translates into increased profitability" (2002, p. 6). The authors continue with four examples which are interesting in light of the transportation and music example above.

EXAMPLES

- ☐ "Decreasing the customer defection rate by 5% translates into profitability increases of 25–100%, depending on the industry.
- ☐ When customers leave a company, 75% of the time it has nothing to do with the product.
- ☐ The number one reason for customer defection is poor service.
- ☐ Numerous studies have determined that it is significantly more expensive to acquire new customers than to retain existing ones (three times to ten times or more)" (Bocklund and Bengtson, 2002, p. 6)."

Which company above, the transportation or music, is mostly likely to grow customers and which is more likely to lose customers?

FINAL THOUGHTS

The main thrust of this chapter is to argue that the call center's main focus is about the people working there and the people being served, not the technology. Only after the employees are fully engaged in a positive culture within a center should a manager begin to examine new technologies. Though new technologies are neat and fun, if they do not improve production substantially and in a measurable way, then avoid them. All investments in new technologies must include input from the employees who will utilize the technologies. If not, the employees themselves can deliberately or subconsciously slow total production and efficiency in the center, erasing all potential gains from the new technologies. Remember, the physical capital and the human capital must be in harmony to produce the value added expected from new technology acquisitions. Also, when a manager is considering the five-step model for technology acquisition, he/she must also keep in mind whether this technology will enable customers to access customer service faster or whether the technology will throw up walls between the customers and customer service. The larger the wall between the customers and customer service people, the more dissatisfied customers will become, potentially causing a loss of a customer base which in the long term will destroy a company or organization.

REFERENCES

Hack, B., Newton, P., and Wyckoff, T. *Call Center Operations: A Guide for your Journey to Best-Practice Processes.* Houston, TX: American Productivity & Quality Center, 2000.

Cusack, M. "The (Changeable) Call Center." www.crmguru.com, January 31, 2002.

Lewis, P. "So Much for Customer Service." *Fortune.* August 28, 2003; www.fortune.com.

Read, B. *Designing the Best Call Center for Your Business: A Complete Guide for Location, Services, Staffing, and Outsourcing.* New York: CMP Books, 2000.

Dawson, K. *The Call Center Handbook, 4th ed.* New York: CMP Book, 2001.

FURTHER READING

Bocklund, L. and D. Bengtson. *Call Center Technology Demystified: The No-Nonsense Guide to Bridging Customer Contact Technology, Operations and Strategy.* Annapolis, MD: Call Center Press, 2002.

Phillips, P. P. *The Bottomline on ROI: Basics, Benefits, and Barriers to Measuring Training and Performance Improvement.* Atlanta, GA: CEP Press, 2002.

Phillips, J. J., R. D. Stone, and P. P. Phillips. *The Human Resources Scorecard: Measuring the Return on Investment.* Boston, MA: Butterworth-Heinemann, 2001.

Waite, A. J. *A Practical Guide to Call Center Technology: Select the Right Systems for Total Customer Satisfaction.* New York: CMP Books, 2001.

CHAPTER 8

Return on Investment (ROI)

This chapter gives a brief overview of a common use of ROI for evaluating change within a corporation or organization. The model reviewed and utilized for this chapter is adopted from Jack Phillips (Phillips, Stone, and Phillips, 2001). The Phillip's model is widely used in both the private and the public sector for evaluating the ROI for many programs, most recently as an evaluation of training programs and their contribution to overall growth of an existing business or organization.

BY THE NUMBERS ACCOUNTABILITY

For a manager to make an argument for his/her center's solid performance, he/she must demonstrate this to the boss in a report, which has some form of logical and rational numerical support and measurement. Stating that "My center is great. My employees are happy and the customers seem to like us" without any support will only serve to have a domestic center move faster along the cycle to overseas outsourcing and the manager seeking other employment opportunities. Wise executives in a company/organization will seek hard and fast numbers to justify the performance of a call center. Now, most call centers with the latest technology will be able to produce reports ad nauseam. However, what do these reports mean? What value does that add to the center? What do they communicate to the executive on how the budget was spent most effectively or revenue stream per person generated? Remember, the rule about running a business is to bring in more money than you spend. This is called profit. The higher the profit the better because the profit can be reinvested into new opportunities and human capital to generate even more profit. Though governments and non-profits do not have the same profit reporting functions as do for-profit companies, this does not mean that these organizations are not concerned with the most efficient means of production possible—a strong ROI. Though the goal is not the same as a for-profit company, the logic behind the efficiency remains the same. To make the best sell possible to the leaders of the company or organization, a manager must be armed at all times with data to justify the centers' existence and value added to the company/organization. If this cannot be established, the center will eventually disappear.

RETURN ON INVESTMENT

Brief History

ROI has been around since before the 1920s. In recent years, ROI has expanded to a wide range of investments, including human resources, training, education, change initiatives, and technology. Today, hundreds of ROI calculations have been created or are under development for programs. "As long as there is a need for accountability of ... resource expenditures and as long as the concept of an investment payoff is desired, the ROI process will be used to evaluate major ... investments" (Phillips, Stone, and Phillips, 2001, pp. 2–3).

WHY ROI?

Developing a strong and balanced set of measures, including measuring ROI, has gained a strong position in many fields. The topic of ROI appears through conference proceedings, on the cover of newsletters, and as the focus point of journals, both trade and academic. Clients are requesting that ROI calculations be conducted for various programs and initiatives within their division or unit, both in private and in public sector organizations. Even top executives in major companies have increased their knowledge and interest in ROI related information (Phillips, Stone, and Phillips, 2001, p. 12).

Though it may seem obvious to the reader why measuring ROI is a value-added tool that all call center managers should pursue, it helps to examine why the time is ripe for call center managers globally to adopt the ROI calculations. The main reasons include:

1. Client demands. More clients than ever before are requesting evaluation data, including measuring the ROI. Many call center managers, in these times of center expansion, consolidation, and outsourcing overseas, are asking, "How do I know a particular

program, decision, or technology will be a good return on my investment?" Though accountability has existed in the past, the expected level of accountability, and the recourse for not being accountable, is at an all time high. When a client demands a process, then it must be examined and delivered in a credible fashion so the client can believe and use the results.

2. Competitive advantage. Call center managers must fight for scarce resources both internally within an organization and externally for labor between existing call centers and organizations that employ a similar labor pool. Because of this environment, a manager must be able to measure an ROI to meet or beat the existing competitive forces for scarce resources. Many leading call centers are beginning to develop the ROI around projects and programs in order to stay competitive or even stay ahead of the competition for resources.

3. Resource allocation. When a call center manager can show a contribution in clear monetary terms, an excellent case can be made for additional resources for his/her center. Some organizations are actually using the ROI process to drive additional funding and increasing budgets. For example, if a minimum threshold is reached, the budget remains the same. If an ROI is exceeded, then additional resources are allocated to that unit (call center) from the unit that performed under the ROI threshold. Though ROI cannot be used for all units and every program and should not be used for individual performance, it can shed a bright light on those functions that contribute (or do not contribute) to the bottom line of an organization.

4. Case study database. Developing a case study history of ROI applications builds a history of credible results for a call center and call center manager. The database can show executives in organizations success with previous programs, as well as indicate trends and patterns within the organization. A portfolio of projects using a credible and acceptable process can offer a critical advantage to a call center manager pursuing new growth opportunities and initiatives.

5. Self-satisfaction. Most motivated and dedicated workers in an organization want to know that the work they do is making a difference. Showing the ROI can become one of the most self-satisfying parts for a call center manager, staff, and reps. When completing an initiative on schedule, within or under budget, and with positive customer feedback, the actual value-added benefits in monetary

terms for the center with an impressive ROI adds the final touch to a major project.

6. Consequences of improper or ineffective practices. Many call center projects have not lived up to the expected promises. These centers have not delivered the results the company expected, at least in terms executives understand, mainly the bottom-line contribution. As more and more call centers are opened, consuming the limited resources of an organization, the expectations of the call centers have not always materialized. Reports from many call center managers are viewed with skepticism and concern, and often the credibility and objectivity of the data is challenged. This has caused many executives in organizations to rethink the role and value of a call center and to place more constraints and demands on call center managers, including more justifications, ROI, for call center operations.

7. The need for balanced measures. Throughout the trade literature a debate has ensued on what should and should not be measured and how. Different people recommend different measures, number of calls, calls per hours, employee and customer satisfaction surveys, first time call success, and the list goes on. There exists a critical need to examine data from a variety of groups and point of views, from different time frames, and for different purposes. This mix of data is often referred to as a balanced approach and is driving the need for the ROI process outlined in this chapter.

8. Top executive requirements for call center contribution. ROI is now enjoying an increased level of interest from executives in organizations. Top executives have watched as the call center budgets have steadily increased over time without the appropriate accountability measures and are now demanding an ROI for call centers. Measuring the ROI for call centers is a global issue because executives in companies with call centers understand that the call center market, like their organization, is global in scope. Whether an organization is mature or developing, the competitive economic pressures of running a business with a global scope make accountability of call centers an important issue.

THE APPROACH

For an ROI process to succeed in a call center, it must balance many issues including feasibility, simplicity, credibility, and soundness. The call center managers and supervisors who use this process often find that long formulas, complicated equations, and complex models appear confusing and complex, causing them to give up due to frustration. Because of these concerns, a simple, clear, and easy to understand process is a necessity for call centers. Furthermore, since call centers are very busy places, the process cannot take an excessive amount of time to implement. Finally, the ROI process should not be too expensive, given the competition for resources in call centers; the process should not command a significant portion of a manager's budget.

The ROI process must meet certain criteria to be accepted and correctly implemented in an organization. These criteria include:

1. Simplicity. The ROI process must be simple and must avoid too detailed or complex formulas, lengthy equations, or complicated methodologies. Most ROI models to date have failed in this regard, since many seek statistical perfection and theories more akin to a university than a business operation.

2. Economic. The ROI process must be economical and be able to be implemented easily within a call center. The process should be adaptable, enabling it to become a routine part of the functioning of the center without requiring a significant input of additional resources.

3. Credible. The assumptions built into the process, the methodology, and the outcomes must be credible to both the manager and the staff of the center, as well as to the executives of the company or organization who control the center.

4. Theoretically sound. From a research point of view, the ROI process must be theoretically sound and based on generally accepted principles and practices. Ideally, the process should strive to strike a balance between maintaining a practical and sensible approach while not compromising the sound theoretical basis for the procedures.

5. Account for other factors. An ROI process must be able to account for other factors that influence the output variables. Isolating variables that are tangential to the program is necessary to build credibility and accuracy within the process.

6. Appropriate. The ROI process must be appropriate for a variety of call center programs. Some models may apply to only a limited number of programs, while others will apply to a full spectrum. Ideally, the process should be applicable to all types of initiatives.

7. Flexible. The ROI process must have the flexibility to be applied on both a pre- and post-program basis. Ideally, the process should be able to adjust to a range of time frames for calculating the ROI of a given program or programs.

8. Applicable. The ROI process must be applicable to all types of data, both hard (output, quality, costs, time, etc.) and soft (job satisfaction, customer satisfaction, turnover, etc.).

9. Inclusive of costs. The ROI process must include the costs of the program. The highest level of evaluation compares the benefits with the costs. An acceptable ROI formula must include costs because omitting or understating costs will destroy the credibility of the ROI values.

10. Successful track record. Finally, the ROI must have a successful track record in a variety of programs and applications. Too often, models that are created are never successfully applied. An effective ROI process should withstand the wear and tear of implementation and prove valuable to users.

These ten criteria are considered both critical and essential, so any ROI processes should incorporate as many of the criteria as possible, if not all.

THE ROI MODEL

The ROI process model outlined in this chapter was developed several years ago and has been applied to hundreds of programs in multiple industries. Since that time, the process has been refined and modified and is represented in Figure 8-1.

The model comprises eight major phases that include:

1. Evaluation planning. The first two parts of the ROI model focus on planning, a critical issue. First, objectives must be developed appropriate to the initiatives within the call center.

2. Collecting data. Data collected at call centers measure reaction, satisfaction, and learning. Collecting this data during a program ensures that adjustments are made during the process and that any alterations necessary can be made to keep the assignment on track. Satisfaction and learning data are critical for immediate feedback and necessary to make any project successful.

   After program implementation, post-program data are collected to compare and contrast to pre-program data, including control

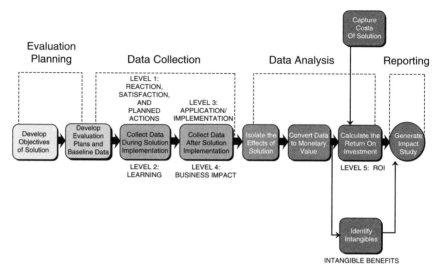

Figure 8-1. The ROI process model (Phillips and Connell, 2003).

group differences and expectations. Both hard and soft data are collected through a variety of means, including:

    a. Follow-up surveys and questionnaires

    b. On-the-job observation captures

    c. Tests and assessments

    d. Interviews

    e. Focus groups

    f. Action plans

    g. Performance contracts

    i. Business performance monitoring

    The biggest challenge in most data collection is using the best methodology appropriate for the specific program and call center within the necessary time and budgetary constraints.

3. Isolating the effects of the call center program. Too often in evaluations the process of isolating the effects of a given program is overlooked. Isolating these effects are critical to determine the level of performance improvements directly related to the call center program. Strategies in this step help to pinpoint the amount of improvement directly related to the intervention. The results enable an increase in both the accuracy and the credibility of the ROI calculation. Several strategies used to ensure isolation of the

data include:

  a. A pilot group compared to a control group
  b. Trendlines
  c. Forecasting models
  d. Participant and stakeholder estimates
  e. Supervisor's and manager's estimates
  f. External studies
  g. Independent experts
  h. Other influencing variables are identified and isolated
  i. Customers provide feedback

In total, these nine strategies prove a set of tools for the evaluator to help isolate the effects of the call center program.

4. Converting data to monetary values. To calculate the ROI for any given project, business impact data are converted to monetary values and compared to the costs of intervention. To accomplish this, each unit of data collected for the program must have a specific monetary value assigned to it. There are multiple strategies available to convert data variables to monetary values, including:

  a. Output data are converted to profit contribution or cost savings and are then reported as a standard value.
  b. The cost and quality of measures, such as number of accidents, are calculated and reported as a standard value.
  c. Employee/rep time saved is converted to wages and benefits.
  d. Historical costs of preventing a measurement, such as customer complaints, are used when available.
  e. Internal and external experts estimate a value of a measure based on extensive experience.
  f. External databases contain an approximate value of the data item.
  g. Supervisors or managers provide estimates of costs or value when they are both willing and capable of doing so.
  h. The call center staff estimates a value of a data item.
  i. The measure is linked to other similar or connected measures for which the costs are easily developed.

The conversion from data to monetary values is one of the most important processes of a program since it helps to determine the monetary benefits to a call center from such a program. The process of conversion is challenging, especially when using soft data, but can be accomplished using one or more of the nine strategies delimited above.

5. Tabulating the costs of the call center program. The other side of a benefits/cost call center program is the costs. Quantifying the costs involves constantly monitoring or developing early on the costs related to the program. A fully loaded cost approach is recommended where all direct and indirect costs are tabulated. A more conservative approach to costs ensures both the rigor of the formula and the methodology as well as the benefits of the program to the call center. The following seven cost components should be included in all calculations.

    a. The cost of initial analysis and assessment, possibly prorated over the expected life of the program

    b. The costs to develop solutions

    c. The cost to acquire solutions

    d. The cost for application and implementation of the program(s)

    e. The cost of maintaining and monitoring the program(s)

    f. The cost of evaluating and reporting

    g. The costs of administration and overhead for the program, allocated in some convenient way

6. Calculating the ROI. The ROI is calculated using benefits and costs. The benefit/cost ratio is the benefits of the call center program or intervention divided by the costs. The basic formula is

Benefits/Costs Ratio = BCR

BCR = Call Center Program Benefits/Call Center Costs

Sometimes this ratio is stated as an ROI; however, the ROI uses the net benefits divided by the total costs. The net benefits include the program benefits minus the costs. The ROI formula is

ROI% = Net Call Center Benefits/Call Center Costs × 100

This is the same basic formula used for evaluating other investments in which the ROI is historically reported as earnings divided by investments.

The BCR and ROI offer the same basic information, but with slightly different perspectives. The following two examples illustrate the relationship. Assuming a call center program produced benefits of $581,000 and costs of $229,000, the BCR would be

$$BCR = \$581,000/\$229,000 = 2.54 \text{ or } 2.5:1$$

This calculation shows that for every $1 invested, $2.50 in benefits was returned. In this example total net benefits are $581,000 − $229,000 = $352,000. Based on the BCR, the ROI would be

$$ROI\% = \$352,000/\$229,000 \times 100 = 154\%$$

This means that each $1 invested in the call center program returned $1.50 in net benefits after covering all expenses. The benefits are usually expressed for 1 year beyond implementation of the program. Though the benefits may continue after one year, the impact usually diminishes over time. For long-term projects, benefits would be spread over multiple years. This conservative approach is used in all ROI calculations throughout this book.

7. Identifying intangible benefits. Most programs will produce not only monetary tangible benefits, but also intangible, non-monetary ones, as well. During data collection and analysis, every attempt is made to calculate all variables to monetary data. All hard data can easily be converted to monetary values; however, soft data is more difficult. If the process of converting soft data is too subjective or inaccurate, the resulting values lose credibility. For some projects, intangible, non-monetary variables have extreme value, often commanding as much influence as hard data items. Intangible benefits can include
   a. Improved public impact
   b. Increased job satisfaction
   c. Increased organizational commitment
   d. Enhanced technology leadership
   e. Reduced stress
   f. Improved teamwork
   g. Improved customer service
   h. Reduced customer-response time
   The seven intangible benefits listed above are commonly found in call center projects, but the list is in no way comprehensive.

8. Reporting with an impact study. The final step of the operational ROI process is to generate an impact study to document the results achieved by the call center program and to report them to the various interested parties. The impact study shows the basic process

used to generate the measures and data. The methodology, assumptions, key concepts, and guiding principles are all delimited before the final results are presented. Next, the different categories of data, including hard, soft, tangible, and intangible data, are presented in a rational and logical process, indicating the steps to success for the study. This becomes the final official document that presents the complete assessment of the success of the program. Its length generally ranges from 20–30 pages for a smaller project and up to 200–300 pages for a larger, long-term impact study.

Due to the fact that there are possibly multiple audiences for a given study, different reports may need to be generated.

Barriers to Implementation

Though much progress has been made over recent years in the implementation of ROI, barriers still exist than can inhibit the implementation of the project. Some barriers are real, while others are hyperbole or myths based on false information. The six most common barriers include:

1. Costs and time. The ROI process will add some additional time and costs to existing programs within the call center; however, this amount is not excessive. Most ROI projects do not add more than 3–5% to the total call center budget. The additional investment in an ROI project is often offset by the additional value achieved from these projects and the reduction or elimination or prevention of unproductive or unprofitable programs and processes.
2. Lack of skills and orientation of staff. Many call center managers do not understand ROI. Also, the typical call center manager does not focus on ROI data and instead focuses on very narrow individual performance metrics of each employee. Consequently, a tremendous barrier to implementation is the change needed for the overall orientation, attitude, and skills of the whole call center staff.
3. Faulty initial analysis. Many call center programs do not have an adequate initial analysis or assessment. Some of these programs have been implemented for the wrong reasons and are based on requests from other departments, divisions, or executives in headquarters chasing a popular fad or trend in the industry. If a program is not needed, the program will not produce enough benefits to overcome the costs. An ROI calculation on such a program will likely produce a negative value. This is a realistic, and needed, barrier/filter for many programs.

4. Fear. Fear is an overwhelming factor in decision making. Often, managers will not pursue ROI because of fear of failure or fear of the unknown (xenophobia). Fear of failure manifests itself in many ways. Managers may have concerns about the consequences of a negative ROI. A fully comprehensive evaluation program can stir up the traditional fear of change. Fear of change, though mostly based on unrealistic assumptions and false information on the process, is so strong that it becomes a major barrier to many ROI implementations.

5. Discipline and planning. A successful ROI implementation project requires much planning and discipline to the approach to ensure the project stays on track. At a minimum, the project will necessarily include implementation schedules, evaluation targets, ROI analysis plans, measurement and evaluation policies, and follow-up schedules. Some practitioners may not have enough discipline to stay the course. This becomes a barrier when there are no pressures to measure the ROI of a project or a full center. Given the reality of outsourcing and off-shoring of centers, this barrier is melting away quickly.

6. False assumptions. Many people have false assumptions about the ROI process. False assumptions commonly include:
   a. ROI can only be applied to narrowly focused projects.
   b. Senior management/executives do not want to see results expressed in monetary values.
   c. If a call center manager does not ask for ROI, it should not be pursued.
   d. If the CEO does not ask for ROI, then he/she does not expect it.

These false assumptions form realistic barriers that impede the successful progress and implementation of ROI in too many call centers.

BENEFITS TO IMPLEMENTATION

The benefits of adopting a comprehensive measurement and evaluation processes (including ROI) are elucidated in many previous chapters. Important benefits can be derived from the routine use of the ROI process. Some examples of the benefits include:

☐ Show the contributions of selected call center programs. With the ROI process, the call center manager, staff, and executives in the company/organization will know the contribution of the call center programs in terms that were not previously articulated or understood by the stakeholders. The ROI will show the actual benefits versus the costs of a given program (or center), elevating the evaluation data to the highest level of analysis. The process presents indisputable evidence that the program succeeded, reducing the need to make multiple justifications to upper management.

☐ Earn the respect of senior management. Measuring (and reporting) the ROI of a call center program is one of the best ways to earn the respect, support, and positive attention of senior executives in an organization or business. Executives will respect the processes that add bottom-line value to the center and thus the whole organization in monetary terms they understand. The result of this analysis is comprehensive, and when applied consistently and comprehensively to all center projects, it can convince executives that the call center function is an important investment for the company and not just an expense. This is a critical step toward building an appropriate partnership with the senior executives and getting the call center positively noticed.

☐ Gain the confidence of the client. In a third-party call center, an ROI will now allow a center to provide the client with a complete set of data to show the overall success of the process in place. Not hampered by a lack of data (qualitative or quantitative), this information provides a complete profile from different sources, at different time frames, and with different types of data for the manager, executives, and potential clients.

☐ Improve the call center performance. With a variety of feedback data collected during the ROI program, a comprehensive analysis provides data to drive changes in the center and to make adjustments during a program. It also provides data that helps improve call center performance when certain processes are revealed as non-productive (or under-productive) while others add value. Thus, the ROI process is an important process (value-added) improvement tool.

☐ Develop a results-focused approach. The communication of data at different time frames and with the detailed planning that is involved with the ROI process focuses the entire call center (and organization) on bottom-line results. This focusing effort often enhances the results that can be achieved because the ultimate goals are clearly in mind to all parties and stakeholders. In essence, the process begins with the end in mind, a type of goal alignment examined in Chapter 2. All the processes, activities, and steps are clearly focused on the ultimate outcomes and goals. As the call center program demonstrates success, confidence in using the process grows, which enhances the results of future programs and initiatives (a positive spiral).

☐ Alter or enhance existing call center programs. This benefit is multifold. First, if a program or strategy is not working effectively, and the results are not materializing as expected, the ROI processes will prompt changes or modifications to move the program back on track. On rare occasions, the strategy may have to be halted if it is not adding the appropriate value. Although stopping an existing program that may not be working will take courage from the call center manager, it will reap critical benefits from the staff, the employees, the executives, and the clients and/or customers if it is clearly evident that it will not produce results. The other part of this benefit is that if a new program/strategy succeeds greatly, the same type of processes can be applied to other areas of the corporation. It makes a convincing argument that if one division has a successful program and another division (or call center) has the same needs, the program may add the same value and enhance the overall success and reputation of the call center within the organization or company.

In the end, the expectation is for everyone in the organization from the top down to be working toward the same set of goals and working at maximum performance toward those goals with efficiency. This means any activities that distract from production, cease or slow down production, or do not allow for maximum production need to found, corrected, and modified to free up the potential for efficiency.

ROI CANDIDATE?

Figure 8-2 presents a call center ROI evaluation checklist. The checklist is designed as a self-assessment tool for the call center manager to determine if a particular center is a strong or weak candidate for an ROI evaluation plan. Read each question and check off the appropriate level of agreement (1 = Disagree; 5 = Total Agreement). The higher the total score, the better candidate your center is for ROI.

	Disagree			Agree	
	1	2	3	4	5
1. My organization is considered a larger organization with numerous call centers within the total organization.	☐	☐	☐	☐	☐
2. We have a large call center budget that reflects the interests of senior executives.	☐	☐	☐	☐	☐
3. Our organization measures consistently and has as a focus to establish a variety of measures for the call center.	☐	☐	☐	☐	☐
4. My call center (organization) is undergoing significant change.	☐	☐	☐	☐	☐
5. There is pressure from senior executives/upper management to measure and justify results.	☐	☐	☐	☐	☐
6. The call center, at present, has a low investment in measurement and evaluation.	☐	☐	☐	☐	☐
7. My call center has suffered more than one budget/evaluation/project disaster in the past.	☐	☐	☐	☐	☐
8. My organization has some new leadership.	☐	☐	☐	☐	☐
9. My staff and reps would like to be the leading call center in measurement, evaluation, and ROI.	☐	☐	☐	☐	☐
10. The image of our call center is less than satisfactory.	☐	☐	☐	☐	☐
11. My clients and/or senior management are demanding that we show bottom-line results.	☐	☐	☐	☐	☐
12. My call center/customer support function competes with other functions within our organization for resources.	☐	☐	☐	☐	☐
13. My organization has increased its focus on linking processes to the strategic direction of the company.	☐	☐	☐	☐	☐
14. My call center is a key player in change initiatives currently taking place in my organization.	☐	☐	☐	☐	☐
15. Our overall call center budget is growing and we are required to prove the bottom-line value of our processes.	☐	☐	☐	☐	☐

TOTAL SCORE _____

Figure 8-2. Call center evaluation checklist.

EXAMPLE

Below is an example of the power of an ROI evaluation (modified from Petouhoff, 2001, p. 3):

Manager A spends much of his/her time running around fixing problems of various natures in the center most of the day. He/she is able to spend only an average of 2 hours of his/her time working on positive developments that move the center forward. Thus, 6 hours of his/her time is unproductive in that it is not adding anything to the center. He/she realizes that if a solid positive culture was in place, most of the center could run itself since individual responsibility would be the norm, not the exception.

Manager B has the correct culture in place so that if a problem did arise that the reps could not handle, supervisors, who are likewise empowered, could tackle the issue. This frees up more time for him/her to promote the center and guide it in the correct direction. Manager B spends 6 hours of the time promoting the center in the right direction (this includes face and communication time with the reps). Only 2 hours of this manager's time could be counted as unproductive. Therefore, the following are the productivity calculations for Managers A and B.

$$\text{Manager A: } 2/8 \text{ hours} = 0.25 \times 100 = 25\% \text{ productive}$$
$$\text{Manager B: } 6/8 \text{ hours} = 0.75 \times 100 = 75\% \text{ productive}$$

The question is how to turnaround Manager A so that he/she is more productive in the center. The cost associated with the turnaround cannot cost more than the 75% inefficiency over time. Therefore, the cost of a training solution formula would be the following assuming a $100,000 base wage.

Productive work
$$\text{Manager A: } 0.25 \times \$100,000 = \$25,000$$
$$\text{Manager B: } 0.75 \times \$100,000 = \$75,000$$

Inefficient work
$$\text{Manager A: } 0.75 \times \$100,000 = \$75,000$$
$$\text{Manager B: } 0.25 \times \$100,000 = \$25,000$$

The cost of the solution needs to be examined for Manager A. An average management training course is estimated at $2000 for one day.

Assume that the increased benefit of efficiency after training is 80%, or $60,000 of the inefficient work,

$$0.8 \times \$75,000 = \$60,000$$

The cost of the solution to the problem of inefficiency is calculated as the cost of the one-day training session at $2000. To calculate the ROI, subtract the cost of the solution from the benefit of the solution and divide that amount by the cost of the solution. Then multiply the answer by 100.

ROI = Benefit of the Solution − Cost of Solution/Cost of Solution × 100

ROI = $60,000 − $2000/$2000 × 100

ROI = $58,000/$2000 × 100

ROI = 29 × 100

ROI = 2900%

As this ROI formula clearly demonstrates, the actual monetary benefits to the center from improving management are real and measurable. Now imagine the other multipliers (hard and soft data, tangible and intangible benefits) that will result from better management throughout the whole center. This is a number that executives can understand.

FINAL THOUGHTS

This chapter methodically walks the reader through the ROI process, its justification, how it works, barriers to implementation, and reasons why a call center manager should adopt this tool for his/her call center. The chapter ends with a self-assessment tool to determine how strong a candidate a particular call center may be for an ROI evaluation and a simple example of previously published call center ROI work. One item that should be abundantly clear is that all of the necessary items outlined in Chapters 1–8, such as building a strong culture, keeping your reps front and center, measure, measure, measure, goal alignment, and more, are all embedded within the ROI process. Chapter 9 examines the ROI process utilizing data collected by the author at selected call centers within the United States.

REFERENCES

Petouhoff, N. L. "Tools to Increase Human Potential and Bottom Line." *Recruiting and Retaining Call Center Employees*, Phillips J. J. (Series Ed.), Petouhoff N. L. (Ed.). Alexandria, VA: American Society for Training and Development Press, 2001, pp. 1–26.

Phillips, J. J., and A. O. Connell. *Managing Employee Retention: A Strategic Accountability Approach*. Boston, MA: Butterworth-Heinemann, 2003.

Phillips, J. J., R. D. Stone, and P. P. Phillips. *The Human Resources Scorecard: Measuring the Return on Investment*. Boston, MA: Butterworth-Heinemann, 2001.

FURTHER READING

Phillips, P. P. *Bottomline on ROI: Basics, Benefits, and Barriers to Measuring Training and Performance Improvements*, Atlanta, GA: CEP Press, 2002.

Phillips, J. J., and P. P. Phillips. "Using an Internal Degree Program to Reduce the Turnover of Technical Specialist: An ROI Approach." *Retaining Your Best Employees*, Phillips, J. J. (Series Ed.), and Phillips, P. P. (Ed.). Alexandria, VA: American Society for Training and Development Press, 2002, pp. 151–174.

CHAPTER 9

ROI Case Study at Happy Airways[1]

CULTURE MATTERS! RETAINING EMPLOYEES AND SHOWING A STRONG ROI

Background

Imagine that you walk into an ordinary brown brick building near an airport. Letters over the building's entrance announce that this structure belongs to Happy Airways. The bland building could easily be used for storage or any nondescript purpose. The building and its facade do not give away the activity of the people within. Walking inside you are overwhelmed with the friendliness of the busy people inside. Seeing people walking, talking, and chatting in groups is common. "How are you doing today?" and similar phrases, said with smiles, abound. "Friendly" is the feeling that permeates the air. Hanging on the walls are framed posters mirroring the atmosphere and culture within the building. One particular sentence on a poster catches your eye:

It wouldn't kill you to laugh: Don't be afraid to laugh at yourself.

The concept behind this sentence can be seen in actions throughout the organization and epitomizes the culture created within the walls of this call center. Figure 9-1 presents the organization's key values.

---

[1] Based on a case study by David L. Butler, previously published in *In Action: Retaining Your Best Employees*. Phillips, J. J. (Series Ed.), and P. P. Phillips (Ed.), Alexandria, VA: American Society for Training and Development, 2002, pp.135–150. With permission.

ACT WITH INTEGRITY: "Walk Our Talk" ... our actions ought to reflect what we deeply believe. Be who you are. HONESTY. A person with integrity has one face, not two or three. Allow others to be themselves – the freedom to be themselves. Integrity inspires trust, confidence and loyalty. LEAD BY EXAMPLE.

RESPECT, GRATITUDE, AND APPRECIATION: Maintain the self-esteem of others. Refuse to participate in the belittling of others. Engage in building people up, rather than tearing them down.

IT WOULDN'T KILL YOU TO LAUGH: Don't be afraid to laugh at yourself. Spread goodwill and create an atmosphere of relaxation and FUN!! Lighten up. Be who you are!!!!!

COMMUNICATE CLEARLY: Develop a comfort level for open communication, be a good listener, and follow through. Speak the truth in loving ways. BE RESPONSIVE.

BE ACCOUNTABLE: Be willing to be part of the solution, not part of the problem. Recognize you have the opportunity to create your own experience, the outcome of the situation. Before blaming something on someone else, try to see what your role might be!! Accountability is a two way street. Take constructive feedback openly and with emotional maturity.

ACT WITH COMPASSION: Be vulnerable, trust, and be willing to give the benefit of the doubt. Be consistently fair.

ENJOY DIFFERENCES: Be open to other's ideas. Be conscious. Be accepting of other's leadership styles. Celebrate differences and diversity

Figure 9-1. Airline reservation center key values.

Organizational Profile

Happy Airways is a leading airline in terms of the number of passengers served. It has more than 33,000 employees and makes more than 2700 flights a day. The company has total annual operating revenues of more than $5 billion. In 2001, Happy Airways received 194,821 résumés and hired 6406 people. Many companies discourage both spouses working for the organization, but Happy Airways promotes its employee couples on its Web page, stating that there are 928 married couples within the organization. This means that 1856 Happy Airways employees have a spouse who works for the airline. The airline was one of the first in the U.S. airline industry to offer a profit-sharing plan, and, to date, employees own about 10% of the company's stock. The company is approximately 81% unionized and has nine call centers located throughout the United States.

The focus of the research presented in this case study was a 500-seat center located in a southwestern U.S. city.

The Survey Process

In 2000, a research and data collection project was conducted at Happy Airways to examine the relationships between site location and labor needs at call centers within the United Sates. The surveys that formed the basis for this project were the first steps in creating the necessary national research database on call centers that would allow companies to make educated decisions on call centers.

The survey used at the Happy Airways reservations call center was created by examining existing research on back-office labor. This allowed the findings from the survey to be compared and contrasted with existing research results and allowed hypotheses to be corroborated or refuted. The survey included such basic demographic information as age, sex, race and ethnicity, and marital status. It also included targeted questions based on commuting patterns, past work experience at call centers, and employees' reasons for taking a job at a call center.

The four-page, self-administered survey was voluntary and anonymous. Happy Airways' reps filling out the survey were required to read and sign a release form. To increase turnout for the survey, a table in the employee break room offered free drinks and cookies. As reservation agents (reps) took breaks on their shifts, they could come into the break room, see the sign announcing the free refreshments, and ask about the survey. Most reps that entered the break room filled out a survey. The director of the center encouraged turnout by asking his supervisors to let the reps know that the survey was being given in the break room, which increased the turnout and the sample size. The surveys were set up for approximately 12 hours to ensure that employees in all three shifts had the opportunity to participate. Approximately 110 surveys were completed during the 12-hour period. The surveys were coded and statistically analyzed for comparison with similar data at nearby call centers where data was also collected.

What Was Different at Happy Airways

When the more than 100 surveys completed at Happy Airways were coded and statistically examined, some interesting findings emerged. One of the many reasons why the Happy Airways call center was chosen as the focus of this case study was its remarkably low turnover: 3%.

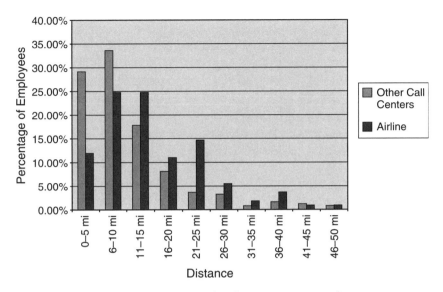

Figure 9-2. Length of journey to work.

This information was divulged by the call center director during a one-on-one interview in June 2000 (the Happy Airways' reservations director said that 3% was still the turnover rate as of late February 2002). The Happy Airways reservation center survey data was compared to data from five other call centers in the same city to determine if the answers of the employees in the airline's reservation center deviated in any way from the other centers and, if so, if this deviation could, in part, explain its low turnover.

Figure 9-2 shows the time reps spent traveling from their homes to the airline's call center. Most employees (62.75%) at the other call centers lived within 10 miles of their offices, but only 36.7% of Happy Airways employees lived within 10 miles of their call center. Almost 15% of the Happy Airways employees traveled from 21 to 25 miles to work; only 3.64% of the other centers' employees traveled the same distance. Research suggests that people who travel farther to work have better opportunities to command higher wages, thus the reason to have a tight labor shed around a call center. However, in the case of Happy Airways, its labor shed was significantly larger than the norm, allowing it to draw labor from distant areas and allowing more flexibility in location for the reservation center. The hypothesis that the farther people travel, the higher the wages they command did not hold when the data shown in Figure 9-2 was examined.

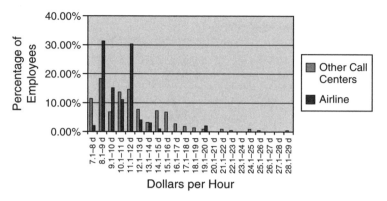

Figure 9-3. Wage levels.

The average wage in the other call centers in the area was $11.85 per hour, compared to the Happy Airways wage of $10.44 per hour. This meant that employees at the Happy Airways center were driving farther for less money per hour, which not only ran counter to the existing research, but also to common sense.

Tracking the data shown in Figure 9-3 from left to right reveals that the Happy Airways call center reps' pay clustered around two large peaks: one at $8.10–$9.00 and the other at $11.10–$12.00 per hour. Each peak reflects two events: first, an expansion of the center from a 200-seat facility to a 500- to 600-seat facility; and second, a hiring class (employees hired at the same time) and the retention of those same employees through time and promotions. Happy Airways center also was working under a national union contract that dictated a starting wage of $8.50 per hour for all call center employees. The other call centers in the area had the standard high turnover wage curve, with many employees starting at a lower wage and the number of employees dropping off dramatically once they reached $11.10–$12.00 per hour because few stayed long enough to earn pay increases above this range.

Retention at the call centers is not only seen in these figures, but also in Figure 9-4, which shows how many years employees had been at their call centers. The bar that first commands attention is the large one that represents employees who had a year or less of service at their call centers. This clearly reflects the high turnover of the centers, especially when you consider that more than 40% of the total employees had been in their jobs 1 year or less, but fewer than 10% had been in their jobs between 1 and 2 years. This meant that costs associated with hiring and training were eating up much of a center's budget.

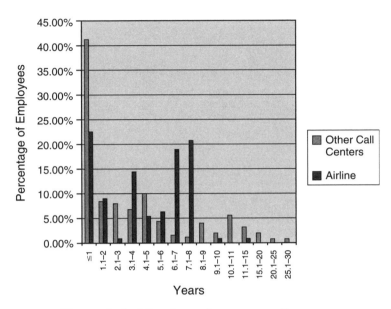

Figure 9-4. Number of years at call center.

Happy Airways shows four peaks, which perfectly mirror the growth of the Happy Airways reservation center. The center had been opened 7.5 years before the time of the survey, which is reflected in the peak at 7.1 to 8 years of employment. This meant that the first group of reservation agents hired made up more than 20% of the existing workforce at the time of the survey, enabling Happy Airways to mine the experience of its veterans and to give new recruits a sense of stability and strength within the organization.

Figure 9-5 shows the responses when employees were asked if they found their work challenging. Most of the employees at other call centers did find their work a challenge, which may be partially a reflection of the large number of new employees at these centers. Only a little more than 60% of the Happy Airways employees found their work challenging, suggesting that they did not work at the center because of its intellectual demands.

Figure 9-6 shows the answers to the question, "Did you choose call center work because of the wages?" The answers do not shed light on why so many Happy Airways reps remained on the job. Almost 70% of the employees at the other centers stated that monetary rewards were important, but only 50% of the Happy Airways employees suggested that this was important. One can assume that the Happy Airways employees

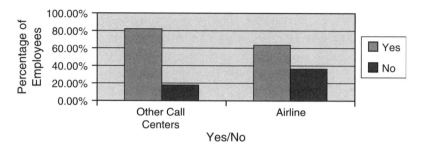

Figure 9-5. Do you find your work challenging?

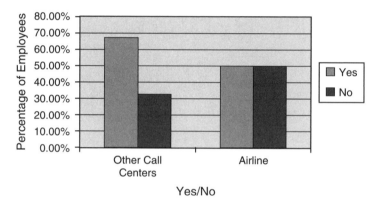

Figure 9-6. Did you choose call center work because of the wages?

are not dumb and realize that their wages are lower than the local industry standard.

Figure 9-7 shows the responses to the question, "Did you choose call center work because of the benefits?" In the other centers in the area the reps responded with about 70% saying "yes"; at Happy Airways, 91% responded "yes." This meant that many call centers originally attracted their employees with wages and benefits, but at Happy Airways, because of the lower average wage, benefits were very important.

Table 9-1 shows the answers reps gave when asked, "Why else did you choose call center work? Please list." Two items emerged from the answers to this open-ended question. First, most employees at other nearby centers initially accepted their jobs because they were the first they could find or because their jobs offered something specific that they wanted, such as sitting in a chair all day, security, or freebees. In contrast,

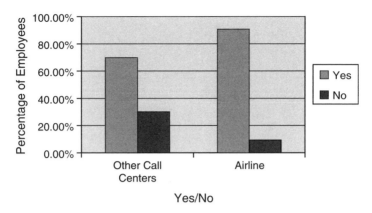

Figure 9-7. Did you choose call center work because of the benefits?

Table 9-1. A Sample of Other Reasons Employees Listed for Choosing Call Center Work

Other Call Centers	Happy Airways
Get to sit in a chair	Very flexible scheduling
Government job equals security	Stable company
Holidays off	The company's track record for 30 years
Incentives, lunches, freebees	The people in the company
Job location, moved from Chicago	The company itself
Money	The flying benefits (free flights)
Money until I find a job in my field	Benefits of the company
Needed a job, laid off	Company's reputation
Quick temp job	

the two reasons reps at Happy Airways consistently repeated for choosing call center work were their overall positive view of the company as a great place to work and the free flight benefits, which allowed employees to fly on the company's aircraft for free. Many people mentioned this benefit as important to them.

Corporate Cultures Can Spiral Up or Down

If a major goal of your call center is to reduce turnover, retain your experienced employees, reduce training and recruiting costs, and eventually increase the profitability (and ROI) of your call center, it is an

> - 1 Unhappy employee – tells 6 colleagues – 3 choose to leave as well
> - 3 Unhappy employees – tell 18 colleagues – 9 choose to leave
> - 9 Unhappy employee – tell 54 colleagues – 27 choose to leave and so on

Figure 9-8. Negative retention spiral.

> - 1 happy employee – tells 6 friends – 3 friends choose to apply for jobs
> - 3 happy employees – tell 18 friends – 9 choose to apply for jobs
> - 9 happy employees – tell 54 friends – 27 choose to apply for jobs and so on

Figure 9-9. Positive retention spiral.

absolute necessity that you examine the culture of not only your individual call center, but also the whole corporate organization. If the culture of the organization creates a productive work atmosphere that gives positive reinforcement to employees, not only are they more likely to stay, but they are also more likely to voice their contentment to their friends and family. This produces a strong recruitment tool. Imagine the scenarios depicted in Figures 9-8 and 9-9.

As Figure 9-8 suggests, eventually a high number of resignations lead to high turnover and a negative work atmosphere within a company. As each person who resigns tells his/her friends and family about bad experiences at the company, a reputation emerges within the community that causes workers to avoid the organization. This negative reputation makes it more difficult to attract workers, which means that the company must increase wages to attract enough people to meet production demands. This produces a negative spiral of discontented employees, high turnover, a negative social reputation in the community, and upward pressure on wages and benefits.

The good news is that the spiral need not be negative, as Figure 9-9 shows. In this scenario, increased applications for employment and a positive work culture lead to low turnover and a rewarding atmosphere in which to work. As each person stays and recruits more employees, all relay their positive experiences with the company to friends and family, creating a positive reputation in the community. With a positive reputation it is easier to attract employees, which means that the company can pay a lower wage yet people will travel farther to come to work. A bonus is the fact that the company will not have to pay to advertise vacancies because it will have a waiting list of people who want to work for it. Because turnover is low, new recruits and associated training costs will decline, maintaining a self-reproducing upward spiral.

Lessons Learned

An organization's success (or failure) can be attributed to many factors, but one that can be created and reinforced is an organization's corporate culture. A company's executives usually establish the culture at the top level, but once in place it is reinforced continually by both the executives and the other employees. Because whatever corporate culture is put into place tends to reinforce itself, it is critical to the long-term success of the company that it creates a positive work environment. The lessons illustrated by this case study follow:

1. If there is a positive atmosphere in an organization, people are willing to travel to obtain this unique experience.
2. Employees are willing to work for a lower wage because the positive work environment is an added benefit.
3. High turnover is not "natural" for any industry. The companies in these industries have not produced the right mix of work environment, management approach, benefits, and culture to retain their employees.
4. Benefits such as medical and retirement plans are important in recruiting employees, but to retain employees you must have a strong employee-centered culture and an added bonus benefit related directly to the company's business, such as the free flight benefits at Happy Airways.

ARE YOUR CSRS THERE FOR THE MONEY?

Most people, when asked why they work somewhere, have an immediate answer, such as "it pays the bills" or something similar. However, besides earning a paycheck, employees are also engaged many hours per day in an environment interacting with other people, some in close proximity and others on the phone. The ideal response to the question "Why do you work here?" should be, "Because it pays the bills and I really enjoy the work, the environment, and my co-workers. I would do this job for $2 less an hour, but don't tell my manager that." As the case study

Table 9-2. Why Did You Choose to Work at This Call Center?

Answer	Number	Percentage	Total Respondents
Good benefits	267	76.3	350
Good pay	217	62.0	350
Job hours	172	49.3	349
Possibilities for advancement	160	45.7	350
The type of work	138	39.5	349
Close to home	102	29.3	348
Fit with partner's schedule	36	10.3	350
Close to children's school or daycare	9	2.6	350
Access to public transportation	3	0.9	350

Source: David L. Butler

on Happy Airways demonstrates, employees are willing to give up substantial money to work in a corporate culture that creates a great work environment. How much is it worth to actually ENJOY going to work, interacting with colleagues, and being part of a collective team to help the company move forward with great customer service?

This researcher asked call center reps in numerous call centers why they chose to work at the particular center they were in at the time. Table 9-2 indicates the responses.

Interestingly, the number one item mentioned for employees choosing to work at the call center is benefits, not pay. Benefits include not only medical, dental, and retirement benefits, but also access to company products at a discounted rate and similar incentives. Pay is number two, and job hours (flexibility) are number three. Because many call center employees live in a household with another adult worker, flexibility in working hours is often sought out, especially if there are young children in a household. Number four, possibilities for advancement, suggests that many of these employees believe that there is room for advancement through a company from a call center. Research to date indicates that the likelihood of call center employment being a springboard into management over time is small.

WHAT DO YOU PRODUCE?

As demonstrated in Table 9-2, customer service reps take their benefits seriously. Quite often, people will take a job with lower pay just to receive the monetary benefits associated with the job that may not be possible to acquire in another similar job that pays more.

Call centers, because of their back-office status, often are disconnected to a tangible product of the company the call center supports. For example, a reservation center is usually not inside the hotel or airport terminal. If a center takes orders for a product, most centers are not in the delivery warehouse or manufacturing plant of the product. Because of the freedom of location of call centers as back offices and the differential requirements of each division of a large company, all parts of the company will not be housed in one location. However, a call center is a major component of the corporation, especially its voice and customer service functions. Given this reality, how can call center employees be fully attached to the product the company produces and the reps service and sell? One way is to have the company's product(s) found throughout the center. Another way is to have the company's sales teams visit the center and introduce the new products to the call center staff, allowing them to see, hear, touch, smell, and interact with the products/information/processes they support. If reps are expected to be the ears and the voice of the company with the customers, then the employees should experience the products themselves so that they can relate to the customers on the phone.

Besides the reps being briefed on the products, interacting with the company's products, and having these products throughout the center, a critical question is whether or not to offer these product(s) as a direct benefit to the employees. If the company is a prescription refill company, do the employees have full prescription benefits? If it is a cell phone call center, do the employees receive a free cell phone with unlimited call time? If it is a banking institution, do the employees have access to all banking services with no fees? If the answer to any of these question is no, then there is a potential problem, because the employees do not have first-hand experience with the products they sell and support, thus they cannot relate, sympathize, or empathize with the customers, making it very difficult to provide a excellent level of service.

Many readers will have heard of the phrase "a dollar-a-day man." This phrase comes from Henry Ford, who helped introduce the fully integrated assembly line process for automobile manufacturing in the United States. Ford made a decision early on that his employees on the assembly line should make enough money to afford one of the vehicles they were producing. A similar logic should exist in call centers. Whatever products or services the call center sells or services, the employees should receive that product or service as part of their benefit package or, if not for free, at a very substantial discount. Once again, the point is not to spend money frivolously; instead, the goal is to increase the ROI of the center. By having reps actively participating in receiving product/services, they will become active proponents of the product, which will show when they are interacting on the phone. The stories they will hear on the phone will enable them to share their own experiences, making a solid customer service connection with the customers. If this benefit is substantial, it will discourage turnover, because once the employee leaves the center the benefit ends. Therefore, the higher the value of the benefit, the increased incentive for a rep to stay employed at the center, thus reducing turnover. As turnover is reduced, training costs decline, also adding to a stronger ROI for the center.

Positive Culture and ROI

A positive organizational culture is beneficial not only to retention and recruitment, but also in terms of the bottom line. Using the ROI model outlined in Chapter 9, this section will examine the potential savings and strong ROI that be accomplished with steady improvement to the work environment within a call center.

Using Happy Airways and another local call center as examples, an ROI evaluation of the costs of not having a positive culture and/or savings from a positive culture can be evaluated.

First a benefits/cost ratio must be created. Before the benefits and costs are known, they need to be tabulated from the collected data. The formula for arriving at the total cost of employee training per year is

(# of existing employees × \$1000) + (# of new employees × \$5000)

If we assume 500 employees per call center and an average turnover rate of 30% for other call centers and a turnover rate of 3% for Happy Airways' call center, the total training costs for new employees look like this:

Year One Training Costs

Happy Airways = 3% turnover
     3% × 500 = 15 new employees per year
     15 employees × \$5000 new rep training = \$75,000 training costs for
                                                   new employees
     97% retention rate
     97% × 500 employees = 485 retained employees

485 employees × $1000 annual continued training = $485,000
  recurring training costs for retained employees
Total annual training costs at Happy Airways
$75,000 + $485,000 = $560,000 total annual training costs

Other call center = 30% turnover
  30% × 500 = 150 new employees
  150 employees × $5000 new rep training = $750,000 training costs
                                                      for new employees
  70% retention rate
  70% × 500 employees = 350 retained employees
  350 employees × $1000 annual training continued = $350,000
    recurring training costs for retained employees
  Total annual training costs at other call center
  $750,000 + $350,000 = $1,100,000 total annual training cost

To enable a manager to create a positive culture in his/her center, which leads to a decrease in turnover, the hypothetical multi-week ROI evaluation project would cost $100,000. The benefits from the new positive culture would be the difference between the other call center's annual training costs and that of Happy Airways. That would formulate to $1,100,000 − $560,000 = $540,000. Therefore, the benefits/cost ratio (BCR) would be

$$BCR = \text{Program Benefits/Program Costs}$$
$$BCR = \$540,000/\$100,000 = 5.4$$

This means that for every $1 invested in creating a positive culture in your call center, a net return on investment of $5.40 was created or saved. The ROI for this type of intervention would be

$$ROI\% = \text{Net Program Benefits/Program Costs} \times 100$$
$$= \$540,000 - \$100,000/\$100,000 \times 100$$
$$= \$440,000/\$100,000 \times 100 = 440\%$$

This means that every $1 invested in creating a positive call center culture returned $4.40 in net benefits for the call center. Once again these are conservative numbers. Some call centers have much higher training costs and higher turnover rates, and the tangible and intangibles associated with a lower turnover rate are too numerous to formulate in this section.

Furthermore, the ROI was calculated according to savings in 1 year. This savings can be multiplied for many years out, which would be into the millions of dollars.

Another example of how a positive call center culture can have a strong and positive ROI is by using the trading board as an employee-centered approach within a center. Let us say that a manager sets up an employee shift trading board. In a normal day the manager would have spent 1 hour reworking schedules of the employees for the following week.

1 hour of 8 hours per day for the manager = 0.125 or 12.5% of total time

If the manager is earning $100,000 a year base salary, then 12.5% is equivalent to $12,500 per year spent with changes on schedules. The total cost of the trading board including materials and labor costs would be approximately $500.

The difference in total cost of schedule changes and trading board implementation would be

$$BCR = \text{Program Benefits/Program Costs}$$
$$BCR = \$12,500/\$500 = \$25$$

This means that for every $1 invested in creating a positive culture (the trading board) in this center, a net return on investment of $25 was created or saved from the manager's/staff's time. The ROI for this type of intervention would be

$$ROI\% = \text{Net Program Benefits/Program Costs} \times 100$$
$$= \$12,500 - \$500/\$500 \times 100$$
$$= \$12,000/\$500 \times 100 = 2400\%$$

This means that every $1 invested in creating a positive call center culture returned $24 in net benefits for the call center. Once again these are conservative numbers. The added value of employee empowerment in being able to take charge of their own schedule has a strong multiplier. Likewise, not only the real time value saved for the manager/staff is created, but the opportunity costs alone are enormous. Other changes in a call center parallel the schedule trading board and can offer substantial costs savings and revenue generation. Can you imagine the ROI on having the manager work at a station for 1 hour a week in terms of decreases in complaints and increases in productivity? What about the ROI of employee-directed training?

It has already been demonstrated that a strong and more positive work environment within a call center can lower turnover rates, which in turn can yield substantial savings in terms of training costs. What is the ROI for a more positive culture and wage rates?

Happy Airways paid an average of $10.44 an hour for each rep. The other call center with the 30% turnover rate paid an average of $11.85 per hour per rep. To enable a manager to create a positive culture in his/her center, leading to a decrease in turnover, the manager attended a week-long call center culture-building workshop that cost $25,000. The manager then hired a consulting company to create an evaluation and action plan for positive culture building for the center at a cost of $100,000 over several weeks. The total costs would equal $125,000. The benefits from the new positive culture would be the difference between the other call center's per hour wage and that of Happy Airways. That would formulate to:

Happy Airways per hour wage rate = $10.44
Happy Airways reps work 6 hours a day for 6 days a week = 36 hours per week per rep
Happy Airways reps work 50 weeks a year: 36 hours per week × 50 weeks per year = 1800 hours a year per rep
Happy Airways has 500 reps × 1800 hours a year per rep = 900,000 work hours paid per year for the call center
At $10.44 an hour × 900,000 hours = $9,396,000 a year in base per hour wages for Happy Airways reservation center

The other call center per hour wage rate = $11.85
The other call center reps work 6 hours a day for 6 days a week = 36 hours per week per rep
Other call center reps work 50 weeks a year: 36 hours per week × 50 weeks per year = 1800 hours a year per rep
Other call center has 500 reps × 1800 hours a year per rep = 900,000 work hours paid per year for the call center
At $11.85 an hour × 900,000 hours = $10,665,000 a year in base per hour wages for the other call center

Therefore, the expected benefits would be the total annual labor costs from the other call center versus the total annual labor costs of Happy

Airways. This equates to:

$$\$10,665,000 - \$9,396,000 = \$1,269,000$$

Therefore, the BCR would be

BCR = Program Benefits/Program Costs
BCR = $1,269,000/$125,000 = $10.15 (rounded)

This means that for every $1 invested in creating a positive culture in a call center, a net return on investment of $10.15 was created or saved. The ROI for this type of intervention would be

ROI% = Net Program Benefits/Program Costs × 100
= $1,269,000 − $125,000/$125,000 × 100
= 1,144,000/125,000 × 100 = 915.2%

This means that every $1 invested in creating a positive call center culture returned $9.15 in net benefits for the call center. Once again these are conservative numbers. Some call centers have much higher per hour wage costs as well as larger total hours worked per year. Once again, as this book has articulated, the tangible and intangible benefits associated with a positive culture are great multipliers that strongly influence the call center's bottom line. Furthermore, the ROI for wages was calculated according to savings in 1 year, which can be multiplied for many years out, which would be the savings of tens of millions of dollars.

The final example related to a positive culture within a call center and a strong ROI revolves around benefits employees received for working at a call center. As the data indicate, benefits are a strong motivating force for many people who work at call centers. The question for a manager is how can this knowledge be turned into an action step that would help improve the bottom line of the call center? Let's walk through an example of how offering benefits of what the company produces can add value to the call center. Let's use a new example and call it Not So Happy Airways. The Not So Happy Airways has a call/reservation center. The employees are paid a standard wage of approximately $11.85 an hour and work for 36 hours a week for 50 weeks a year. The employees of this reservation center do not receive any benefits related to what the airline produces, i.e., tickets. This fact bothers some of the reps, while others really do not even think about it. Now, imagine if Not So Happy Airways chose to start offering free flight benefits to each employee in their reservation center in an attempt to become a Happy Airways with a strong culture, ROI, and bottom line. What value would this offer in terms of monetary performance from the reps? What ROI could be expected from offering such benefits?

The new benefit of the company would equate to one free round-trip airline ticket for the employee and/or their family member every other month within the lower 48 states within the United States. The actual ticket price value a regular customer would pay would be approximately $150. The actual cost to the airline, assuming a load factor of 80%, would be the extra fuel spent on the weight of the passenger and their bags as well as any food consumed en route. Since the policy is to calculate using conservative numbers, then for the purposes of this example we will use the $150 figure and assume that every other month the employee uses the new benefit.

First, it would be necessary to calculate the cost of the program. Assuming a 500-person call center and each rep receiving six $150 value tickets per year, the total cost would be

$$500 \text{ reps} \times 6 \text{ tickets each} \times \$150 = \$450,000$$

What would the expected benefits be? The first benefit that comes to mind is a lower turnover rate since this benefit has a much larger value than the monetary value associated with it. For example, these tickets may represent the ability of someone to take a vacation that they could not have done otherwise. These tickets may represent the ability of someone to carry on a long-distance relationship that would be impossible without them. It could also have a strong social value in that the rep does not use the tickets, but instead offers them to his/her family members for use, thus having a strong positive effect from other family members. Each of these factors, along with countless others, would strongly discourage an employee from leaving the company because they know that this perk would disappear when they left. However, since decreasing turnover has already been demonstrated above, another production value will be used instead.

Before the reps received the flight benefits, some had never even flown on the airline they worked for. Now that they receive the benefits, they are more connected to the company and have a much stronger empathy to the customers on the phone ordering tickets, receiving seat assignments, changing tickets, and a host of other customer service functions. Because of the strong culture in the center represented by the desire of the employees to be able to enjoy the product the company produces, employees have begun to work harder, creating a stronger loyalty in the customer base as well. This increase in productivity and revenue is represented by an average 10% increase in productivity value of each call center rep. This is the benefit to the company from the creation of a strong positive culture placing the employees first. The total monetary benefit to the company would be:

> The Soon to Be Happy Airways call center per hour wage rate = $11.85
> The reservation center reps work 6 hours a day for 6 days a week = 36 hours per week per rep
> Center reps work 50 weeks a year: 36 hours per week × 50 weeks per year = 1800 hours a year
> Soon to Be Happy Airways call center has 500 reps × 1800 hours a year per rep = 900,000 work hours paid per year for the call center
> At $11.85 an hour × 900,000 hours = $10,665,000 a year in base per hour wages for the call center

A 10% increase in productivity, without an increase in wages, would give $10,665,000 × 10% = $1,066,500 in increased benefit for the company.

Therefore, the BCR would be

$$BCR = \text{Program Benefits/Program Costs}$$

$$BCR = \$1,066,000/\$450,000 = \$2.37 \text{ (rounded)}$$

This means that for every $1 invested in creating a positive culture in this reservation center, a net return on investment of $2.37 dollars was created or saved. The ROI for this type of intervention would be

$$ROI\% = \text{Net Program Benefits/Program Costs} \times 100$$

$$= \$1,066,000 - \$450,000/\$450,000 \times 100$$

$$= 136.8\%$$

This means that every $1 invested in creating a positive culture in the reservation center returned an additional $1.37 in net benefits for the call center. Once again these are conservative numbers. Some call centers have much higher per hour wage costs as well as larger total hours worked per year. Furthermore, the actual total cost of the ticket to the airline is marginal (less than the $150). However, as stated several times, the ROI formula articulated here uses conservative numbers to ensure the strength and rigor of the analysis.

Final Thoughts

If a manager is to be effective, he/she must fully understand the full dynamics of his/her center and be able to communicate these to the executives in a meaningful manner. The ROI is one of the measures that can be utilized to the manager's benefit to ensure to the upper management that the call center is not a cost center, but, in fact, is a strong and powerful asset of the company. Though the employee-centered positive call center culture at a surface glance may appear to be less efficient in terms of the number of calls answered per minute, the reality is the reformulating of the center around the "employee first" principle will generate positive returns from every angle in the center including ROI. Good luck and get to work on building a culture of accountability and customer service in your center!

CHAPTER 10

From the Present to the Future

The purpose of this chapter is to lay the groundwork for where the globalizing call center industry is heading and articulate how a manager of a call center should best position his/her center with the highest return on investment (ROI) possible no matter the location of the center. Only by creating a call center with a great culture, creating a strong ROI, and effectively communicating these items to the leadership of a company or organization will the center manager begin to feel a bit more secure in his/her position given the dynamic call center environment.

STATE OF THE INDUSTRY

A manager reading the call center trade press the past few years knows that the industry is in a state of flux and undergoing realignment. All indications are that the industry will continue along this path for the next 5 years or so until a determination is made whether the offshore call centers will deliver the expected promises of increased revenue generation or not. Though most managers understand the macro trends of the realignment, no solid numbers have emerged that allow a call center manager to see overall trends for centers, including winners and losers. In an attempt to obtain some solid numbers and to begin to understand patterns, if they exist, the researcher collected hundreds of news articles on the call center industry over the past 13 months and combed these articles for relevant data. The news items came from *Call Center Ops*, a weekly call center news digest with articles from around the world. Each week the researcher read each article and determined if it included enough data to be placed into the database. After 13 months and hundreds of articles later, a non-scientific sample of the past year's industry growth, decline, expansion, and contraction is available in Table 10-1.

Table 10-1. Summary of Call Center Industry Movement from July 2002 to August 2003

	Opened	Closed	Expanded	Contracted	Jobs Gained	Jobs Lost
United States	27	40	12	9	8,534	11,938
United Kingdom	10	4	10	2	5,815	1,403
India	9	1	1	1	9,312	2,335
Philippines	5				3,450	
Canada	3		4		2,295	
Pakistan	2				226	
Australia	1	2			150	295
Ireland		1	2		585	108
South Africa	1				1,500	
Ghana	1				20	
Hungary	1				500	
Malaysia	1				60	
Oman	1				80	
Panama	1				176	
Poland	1				250	
Total	64	48	29	12	32,953	16,079

Source: Data-Call Center Ops, Table and Summaries – David L. Butler.

Table 10-1 begins, along the top row, with the heading Opened. This heading represents the total number of call centers from the database that were opened in a specific country (see left-hand column). The next heading along the top of the table is Closed. This represents the number of call centers that were closed from the database within the 13-month period. The next headings are Expanded and Contracted, each representing an existing call center that either grew in total number of employees or began to lay off employees but did not close its doors, respectively. The final two headings along the top are Jobs Gained and Jobs Lost. This column represents the total number of jobs within the database that companies hired people for or people who lost their jobs due to contraction or closing of a center. The furthermost left-hand column shows the countries that were listed in the database as either having gained or lost jobs due to call center activity.

From July 2002 to August 2003, the big winners were everyone but the United States and Australia. The United States lost almost 12,000 call center jobs, but only gained approximately 8500 during the same period. Australia lost almost 300 jobs, but only gained 150. The United Kingdom, which has recently had many protests against the movement of call centers to India, actually lost only 1403 jobs while gaining 5815. Newer call center growth countries that showed impressive gains included India, the Philippines, Canada, and South Africa, each of which appear to be opening much larger than average centers than commonly found within the United States or United Kingdom. Once again, each of these countries because of years of colonization by either the United Kingdom or the United States, has a large segment of English-speaking people who can earn good wages in their country working for a call center servicing customers in the United Kingdom or United States. It is noteworthy that the overall call center industry grew strongly during this 13-month research period when many of the developed nations were in an economic recession. Call center managers in every country listed in Table 10-1 should be aware of the growth of decline of centers within their country, as well as the underlying economic reasons for the shifting location of centers over time.

CALL CENTER LIFE CYCLE

The call center industry is an amalgam of different types of centers that cross-cut almost every other existing industry. Some centers have been around since the early 1960s, while others are in the early planning stages. Each call center goes through a series of cycles; however, each proceed at a different pace based on the parent industry, the level of technology utilized, the average labor costs, and a host of other variables.

Call centers first began as an idea for a self-contained unit that customers could contact (or sales made) for a market without this unit necessarily having to be located in or near the headquarters of the business or organization. Centers are launched, and, like all businesses, some succeed and some fail. If successful in the market, the center usually grows in both size and number of employees, often opening multiple centers for redundancy in the system and seeking out other cost savings and efficiencies. Eventually, as the market becomes saturated and labor costs increase, other locations where positive revenue generation can be created and/or cost saving achieved are sought. Sometimes, this is in the form of moving from a city to a suburb or rural location. If increasing costs are realized early, some businesses choose to consolidate their 6–10 existing centers in different locations into just a handful in an attempt to gain some economies of scale and/or scope from the new agglomeration. More recently, companies are seeking newer locations, often

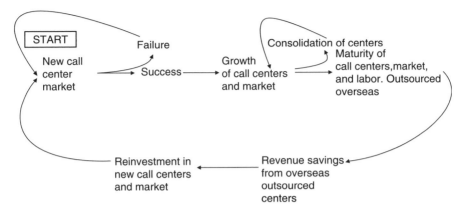

Figure 10-1. Call center life cycle.

relocating to developing nations with large English-speaking workforces
(see Table 10-1). If revenues are generated or cost savings are achieved,
then this capital can be reinvested in new pieces of the business or new
businesses that could create new call center opportunities in the future
(see Figure 10-1).

POSITIONING THE CENTER

A call center manager needs to be fully aware of where his/her center is on
the call center life cycle and how fast his/her industry is moving through
the cycle. The location of a call center in the cycle will help determine
a particular strategy a manager will use to effectively run and make a
strong case for his/her center.

New Market

The benefits of becoming a manager of a new call center in a new industry are to be able to get in on the ground floor of something new and
make him/her a name through effective call center management. Like
entrepreneurship, the opportunities abound. On the flip side, if the new
industry fails to have any market penetration, like entrepreneurship, eventual bankruptcy will occur, and the call center manager will lose his/her
employment.

In developing as well as developed nations, the challenges abound.
In developing countries, besides the potential for political and economic

instability comes the risk of a backlash in customer service for (1) movement of jobs overseas and (2) linguistic differences which can cause frustration on both sides of the communication line. Moving centers overseas comes with the expectation that a company will avoid high labor costs, poor customer service, decreasing revenues, and unacceptably high turnover rates. These requirements land squarely on the shoulders of the call center managers in these countries. There are some indications that these expectations may be harder to meet than originally conceived. "BT chairman Sir Christopher Bland came under fire from shareholders and staff who attacked management over the low share price, high executive pay and the outsourcing of services to India.... The meeting was picketed by union activist parading an inflatable pink elephant in protest at the decision to create 2200 jobs in Asia" (*The Guardian*, 2003). Reports indicating that up to 97,000 jobs will be lost in the United Kingdom call center industry to India increase the level of tension around this issue (*Contact Center World*, 2003).

Furthermore, there are early indications that India is beginning to have some of the same problems which seem to plague the call center industry in the United States and Britain, turnover and increased labor costs. Recent news reports indicate that the turnover rate in India, though it has not reached the same proportions in the United States, is growing. "Amid growing opposition to outsourcing technology jobs to Indian firms, the local back office services providers are also battling with a serious issue back home—high attrition levels. According to a study conducted last year, some of the larger and more established call centres in India are experiencing a 40% attrition rate, compared to the global industry average of 28%. Although lower than attrition rates of 70–120% in the US, the situation in India's money spinning sector is cause to worry" (SiliconIndia.com, 2003). It is true that India has a great reserve of labor that would be difficult to expend, but there are high costs associated with training a person to serve the customer service needs within the United States and Britain. Furthermore, Indian firms are beginning to cannibalize each other for labor, thus driving up labor costs. "India's call centres provide cheap English-speaking workers and high-speed telecoms to provide customer service helplines for companies around the world. They're a boon for India's army of job-hunting youth, but there is a murkier side to the industry. Retaining stressed and bored workers is one challenge for their managers. Poaching by mushrooming rivals is another" (Daga, 2003). Though the wage rate is still much lower than in the United States or Europe, all increases in labor costs decrease one of the main attraction criteria and potential advantage of an overseas center and increase the likelihood of repatriation of that center or services if the trend continues. Therefore, call center managers in the developing countries face the same challenges that a domestic center does: To create a culture in a center that encourages full participation by the employee, lowering turnover rates, keeping wages reasonable, and indicating the value-added nature of the center with a strong ROI.

Growth Market

Managing a call center in a growth market provides many challenges and opportunities. The challenges are in trying to keep pace with the advancing business needs and the continuous need to hire new people and open new centers. The opportunities lie in the fact that if a manager can effectively handle the scaling up of the required call center(s) and can do so while drawing down the precious capital, the center manager will be seen as golden by the leadership of the company. To achieve this golden status, it will be the responsibility of the call center manager to articulate the strong ROI for the center, demonstrate the great culture that exists within the center, and articulate why his/her center can have a 5% or less turnover rate while the industry average is above 30%. This means that as the parent organization continues to expand in a growing industry, the upper management will do everything it can to squeeze the last investment dollar out of all operations that will allow the company to continue to expand so that it does not lose market share to the emerging competition. Once again, a solid performing center with a strong ROI will look favorable to the leadership.

Consolidation Phase

If there are more than three call centers in an organization, rest assured that as strategies are debated at headquarters, consolidation plans will be put on the table. When a group of call centers are consolidated, savings accrue from not only lower equipment costs and expected economies of scale and scope, but also from the reduction of several call center manager's salaries. It is paramount that if the consolidation banner is acted upon by the leadership in the organization, that one center is considered to the most effective, efficient, and with the largest positive ROI of all the centers. With a positive label, a manager could be asked to absorb another center or two instead of the manager losing his/her job to another manager in the organization running another center.

If an industry is going through a phase of consolidation, then there is a chance that a company could be bought out or could buy out another company. When a business is purchased by another organization, the best position for a call center manager to have is the necessary updated documentation, including ROI, for the center ready to give to the executives of the purchasing organization. It is not uncommon when one business purchases another that most or all of the leadership of the purchased company are fired. If a call center manager is armed with valuable, realistic, and convincing data that articulate the value added the center offers, then the manager has the chance not only to escape the pink slip, but to also be the focal point of revisioning and restructuring the two sets of call centers from the merger.

If the parent company of the center is the purchaser, this is a much stronger position to be in than being purchased. To position a center in the best of all worlds, make sure that the leadership in the company is aware of the value-added nature of the center and that it stands shoulders above all the other centers in the organization. If this is the case, then this manager could be asked to create a plan bringing together the two sets of centers to ensure that they all perform as well as his/her center does.

Mature Market, Brace for Offshoring

Even a manager of a mature call center has some risk. Even if performance has been solid for the past 5–10 years, unless the manager of the center can demonstrate not only a great ROI for the center but also great customer service through a great call center culture, then there is a chance that someone in headquarters will offer the plan to follow the trend and talk about relocating the center offshore.

Managing a call center in a mature industry offers some strong challenges. If revenues are flat or not as strong as shareholders or the executive leadership desire, they will systematically go through each division and unit within the company seeking opportunities for efficiency, cost savings, and/or increased production to help boost revenues. An easy target at present is the call center. Since many managers have not done an effective job in communicating the importance and value-added nature of a center, many of these are now being either outsourced and/or moved to lower labor costs regions around the world. Since many managers have not articulated an ROI for their center and have not tried to, or failed at, developing a strong and positive culture within a center, turnover has continued to increase, costs are going up, and service has spiraled down. Outsourcing an unproductive center to Asia for many executives will not hurt customer service, since they believe that customer service is marginal to begin with. So the equation in the boardroom is based on cost only, mainly to the detriment of the manager, staff, and reps domestically. So to effectively protect a center from relocation, a manager must make a case for the success of his/her center loud and often. And remember, the decision makers in the upper management do not know how to read or even care to know the number of calls per minute and such frequency reports. Their interest level is in customer satisfaction measured by happy, paying, and repeat customers and the ROI of their investment in the call center.

Though there are certain advantages and disadvantages being in a different phase of the call center lift cycle and in a different location during the cycle, the reality is that if a center is performing up to and beyond expectations, few people in the upper management will be willing to risk changing a success model since there is the potential for failure. To ensure that a center is viewed as a success, the manager must be willing to build a center with a strong culture that facilitates employees first which produces a lower overall turnover rate and lower overall costs for the center. A great culture can also build upon the revenue side by directly selling to customers or by ensuring that the market share grows through multiple generations of customers. To demonstrate that the budget for a call center is being used wisely, a call center manager needs to utilize an ROI model that is rigorous and conservative and that can be communicated to the upper management to demonstrate that the manager of the center knows what he/she is doing and is doing it well.

FINAL THOUGHTS

The call center industry is growing as more industries realize the potential savings that can accrue from a more location-flexible customer support center versus their old way of doing business. Some centers will move from the domestic country to a developing nation, and some of these centers that are moved will be repatriated in the years to come. One market, city, or country will not be a winner and the rest losers. In reality, there will be winners and losers in each location. A major determining factor of success, no matter the location, will be the effectiveness of the manager of the center. If the manager is ineffective, then no matter the location, turnover will rise, labor costs will increase, and customer service will be poor. Similarly, if a well-managed center exists, no matter the location, it will have a low turnover rate and lower than average labor costs, and customer service will be excellent, driving operating costs lower, increasing revenues for the business, and creating a strong ROI for the center. The only question that remains for the manager would be: Is he/she up to the challenge to control his/her own future, and the future of his/her employees in the center, by implementing the strategies outlined throughout this book. GOOD LUCK!

REFERENCES

BBC News . "Call Centre Faults under Fire." http://newsvote.bbc.com.uk, July 2, 2003.

Daga, A. "Indian Firms See Darker Side of Call Centre Boom." *Yahoo! India News*, July 11, 2003.

SiliconIndia.com. "Call Centres Grapple with High Attrition Rates," June 30, 2003.

Call Center OPS. www.callcenterops.com. 2002–2003.

Contact Center World. "100,000 Jobs to Go in UK Call Centres." www.contactcenterworld.com. July 18, 2003.

MacAlister, T. "BT under Fire Over Indian Call Centres," in *Guardian Unlimited*, July 17, 2003.

Index

A

Accountability, managers
  definition, 17
  employee accountability, 17
  executive accountability, 17
  goals, *see* Goals
  return on investment, *see* Return on investment
  scenarios for success, 29–31
  SWOT analysis, *see* Strengths, weaknesses, opportunities, and threats analysis
Attitude, productivity relationship, 62–66, 69

B

Benefits
  importance to call center representatives, 73, 156
  return on investment analysis, 152–153
Building, call center selection factors, 40–42
Business culture
  boot camp model versus teamwork, 1–4
  employee name memorizing importance, 13
  human nature considerations, 8
  incentive program effect on performance versus cultural change, 15
  manager connection with employees, 9–12
  negative versus positive retention spirals, 153–155
  open door policy, 14–15
  positive culture company example, 7
  respect earning by managers, 5–8
  return on investment impact, 158–165
  salary effects, 96–97

C

Call center industry
  consolidations, 171–172
  developing markets, 169–171
  growth markets, 171
  offshoring, 172–173
  trends, 166–168
Challenged employees
  management, 72–73
  outcomes, 72
  prevalence at call centers, 71–72
  return on investment analysis, 151
Community college, workforce development, 44–46

Commuting
    impact on call center labor, 35–40,
        49–55
    return on investment analysis, 149
Competency modeling, hiring, evaluation,
    and training, 62
Consultants
    employee satisfaction measurement,
        84–86
    hiring, 87
    strengths, weaknesses, opportunities,
        and threats analysis, 25–26
Culture, *see* Business culture

D
Developing markets, call centers, 169–171

E
Employee evaluation, *see* Performance
    measures
Employee satisfaction
    consultants, 84–86
    importance, 83–84
    measurement, 84–86
    responses to feedback, 86
Employee turnover
    call center rates, 57–58, 91
    negative versus positive retention
        spirals, 153–155
    return on investment analysis, 148–151
Employee turnover, call centers,
    57–58, 91

F
Financial transparency, rationale, 83
Flexible hours
    facilitation of schedule swapping, 81–82
    importance to call center
        representatives, 73–74, 156

G
Geographical Information System (GIS),
    labor shed construction, 51–55
GIS, *see* Geographical Information System
Goals
    achievement measures, 23–24
    alignment, 20–23
    assets for achievement, 25

communication with employees, 22
current status assessment, 25
definition, 18
examples in call center, 19–20
flexibility, 23
functions, 18
scenarios for success, 29–31
setting guidelines, 18–19
simplicity importance, 23

H
Hiring
    abundance in call centers, 57–58, 91
    agent skill requirements, 60–61
    attitude and productivity, 62–66, 69
    competency modeling, 62
    consultants, 87
    employee first attitude, 68–69
    filtering layers in interview, 66–68
    steps in recruitment process, 58–59
    success factors in potential
        employees, 58
    supervisor skill requirements, 59–60
    training considerations, 61–62
    whole person concept of hiring, 82, 94
Human capital, physical capital
    comparison, 4–5

I
Incentive programs
    effect on performance versus cultural
        change, 15
    employee retention effects, 91–92
    perfect attendance award, 92
India, call center industry, 168, 170–171

J
JetBlue, business culture, 7

L
Labor costs, *see also* Salary
    comparison with all other call center
        costs, 47
    importance of management, 47–48, 93
    overtime, 48–49
    spatial fix for rising labor costs, 97–98

Labor shed
  call center site selection, 35–36, 49–51
  data collection, 49
  Geographical Information System,
    51–55
Labor unions
  avoidance importance, 99, 101
  contract negotiation, 103–108
  demographic trends, 99–101
  European model adaptation, 108
Life cycle, call centers, 168–169
Location of call centers, *see* Site selection,
  call centers

M

Managers
  accountantability, *see* Accountability,
    managers
  connection with employees, 9–12
  employee name memorizing
    importance, 13
  empowering of employees, 80–82
  executive level promotion, 78–79
  knowledge requirements in upper
    support management, 77–78
  open door policy, 14–15
  promotion from representatives
    advantages of internal recruiting,
      76–77
    needs assessment, 75
    phases, 75–76
  respect earning, 5–8

O

Open door policy, importance in positive
  business culture, 14–15

P

Parking facilities, call center needs, 42
Performance measures
  common elements in employee
    evaluation, 89
  consistency, 88
  establishment for employees, 87–88
Product briefings, call center
  representatives, 156–158
Promotion potential, importance to call
  center representatives, 74–75, 77

R

Reputation of company, importance to
  call center representatives, 79–80
Respect, earning by managers, 5–8
Return on investment (ROI)
  accountability, 128–129
  call center evaluation checklist,
    141–142
  candidate call center identification,
    141–144
  case study of hypothetical airline call
    center
    benefit effects, 152–153
    challenged employees, 151
    commuting effects, 149
    employee turnover, 148–151
    key values of call center, 146–147
    lessons learned, 155
    organizational profile, 147–148
    salary effects, 150–152
    survey process, 148
  historical perspective, 129
  implementation
    barriers, 138–139
    benefits, 139–141
    criteria, 132–133
  Phillips' model
    calculation from benefits and
      costs, 136–137, 159
    cost tabulation, 136
    data collection, 133–134
    data conversion to monetary
      values, 135–136
    evaluation planning, 133
    impact study reporting, 137–138
    intangible benefit identification, 137
    isolating effects of call center
      program, 134–135
    overview, 128–129
  positive business culture impact,
    158–165
  rationale for measurement, 129–131
  technological change, 120–123
  training costs, 159
ROI, *see* Return on investment

S

Salary, *see also* Labor costs
  business culture value, 96–97
  call center location effects, 95–98
  competing business compensation
    considerations, 96
  employee retention effects, 91
  importance to call center
    representatives, 73, 91, 155–156
  principles of agent compensation, 93
  return on investment analysis,
    150–152
  setting of wages, 93–96
  supply and demand of wages
    generalization, 94–95
Site selection, call centers
  building selection factors, 40–42
  clustering of needed services, 42–43
  community college as labor asset, 44–46
  community factors, 34
  commuting impact on labor, 35–40,
    49–55
  government incentives, 43–44
  labor factors, 33–35, 95–96
  legislation factors, 34
  offshoring, 172–173
  parking facilities, 42
  redundancy, 41
  spatial fix for rising labor costs,
    97–98
  technological infrastructure, 44
Southwest Airlines
  employee attitude and productivity,
    64–65, 69
  interviewing policy, 67
Strengths, weaknesses, opportunities, and
    threats (SWOT) analysis
  Facilitators, 25–26
  Functions, 28–29
  matrix creation, 26–28
SWOT analysis, *see* Strengths,
    weaknesses, opportunities, and
    threats analysis

T

Technology
  adoption steps
    annual assessment, 116–117
    assessment, 114
    evaluation, 114
    implementation, 115–116
    reevaluation, 116
    testing, 114–115
  change success measurement, 120
  control options, 123–124
  cost reduction and revenue generation,
    113
  enabling of customer contact versus
    gate-keeping function, 124–125
  importance of personal interaction
    above technology, 111–113
  resistance to change scenarios, 117–120
  return on investment, 120–123
  technological infrastructure, call center
    needs, 44
Training
  competency modeling, 62
  costs and return on investment, 159
  hiring considerations, 61–62

U

Unions, *see* Labor unions

W

Wages, *see* Labor costs; Salary

About the Author

David L. Butler, Ph.D.

 David Butler is president of Butler and Associates, Inc., a research consulting firm in Hattiesburg, Mississippi. Dr. Butler is also a professor and director of the International Development Doctoral Program (IDV) in the Department of Economic Development at The University of Southern Mississippi. Butler earned a Ph.D from University of Cincinnati and a masters of science and bachelor of arts from Texas A&M University. In the past five years, Dr. Butler has published fifteen articles, presented at more than eighteen conferences, and worked on a variety of grants and consulting projects.

In 2002, Dr. Butler was asked to testify before the National Commission to Ensure Consumer Information and Choice in the Airline Industry in 2002 in Washington, D.C. as an expert witness. At the hearing Butler provided expert testimony from his research involving information technologies and the U.S. airline industry. David Butler has been researching the call center industry for almost a decade and specifically created his consulting company, Butler and Associates, Inc., to put into practice the findings from his extensive research.

Dr. Butler can be reached at Butler and Associates, Inc., 100 South 22nd Avenue, Hattiesburg, Mississippi 39401, 601-310-9372 (phone), ButlerandAssociates@yahoo.com.

The Value of Belonging

ASTD membership keeps you up to date on the latest developments in your field, and provides top-quality, *practical* information to help you stay ahead of trends, polish your skills, measure your progress, demonstrate your effectiveness, and advance your career.

We give you what you need most from the entire scope of workplace learning and performance:

Information
We're your best resource for research, best practices, and background support materials – the data you need for your projects to excel.

Networking
We're the facilitator who puts you in touch with colleagues,experts, field specialists, and industry leaders – the people you need to know to succeed.

Technology
We're the clearinghouse for new technologies in training, learning, and knowledge management in the workplace – the background you need to stay ahead.

Analysis
We look at cutting-edge practices and programs and give you a balanced view of the latest tools and techniques – the understanding you need on what works and what doesn't.

Competitive Edge
ASTD is your leading resource on the issues and topics that are important to you. That's the value of belonging!

For more information, or to become a member, please call 1.800.628.2783 (U.S.) or +1.703.683.8100; visit our Website at www.astd.org; or send an email to customercare@astd.org.

ASTD

Linking People, Learning & Performance

900-31410

"Going to college and getting the most out of it has never been more important. Henry J. Eyring's advice for doing just that is utterly engaging and extraordinarily rich with spiritual insight and practical wisdom, born of powerful personal experience and keen observation. Whether you are just starting college, preparing to go to college, or thinking you can get by without some higher education, you need to read this book!"

—Matthew S. Holland, President, Utah Valley University

"*Major Decisions* is about acting and not being acted upon. This is not a book of theory. It is a practical, realistic, 'how to' book that addresses both the challenge of getting into a university that will bring out the best in your abilities, and once you are accepted, making the most of the educational opportunities so that you will graduate with momentum, confidence, and a career."

—Steven C. Wheelwright, Edsel Bryant Ford Professor Emeritus at Harvard Business School; President, BYU–Hawaii

"There is much clutter on bookstore shelves about 'How to Go to College.' It is refreshing to find a book that asks fundamental questions about not only how one selects a college, but what type of education is best for an individual. This book also provides the reader with a real sense of self-worth and self-analysis. I would recommend it highly."

—Gordon Gee, President, Ohio State University

"Henry J. Eyring has written a tremendous book that can profoundly alter the trajectory of the lives of students (and prospective students) everywhere. This is one of those rare books that is immensely practical and realistic while simultaneously being filled with wisdom and insight. I highly recommend it."

—Stephen M. R. Covey, author of the *New York Times* bestseller *The Speed of Trust*

"This book is a wonderful mix of information, insight, advice, and exploration. It helps smart students create a path that maximizes their educational experience and puts them in charge of their future. Only someone with Dr. Eyring's educational experience and teaching abilities could craft a book this concise and yet this full of information. I am delighted to recommend it with genuine enthusiasm to friends and colleagues around the world as a valuable guidebook for anyone seeking an extraordinary and transformative education."

—Michael Young, President, University of Utah

"While so many people speak of the importance of going to college, far fewer focus on what you need once you get there. Henry Eyring's thoughtful book helps students look ahead to see the implications of early choices. It also provides the helps and guides students will need to be prepared when they are done. As a longtime mentor to college students, I'd want all of them to have this resource. As an employer, I'd demand it. This book is a gem!"

—Clark G. Gilbert, former Associate Academic Vice-President, BYU–Idaho; President and CEO, Deseret Digital Media

Acknowledgments

I'm grateful to many friends who made contributions to this book. They include Merv Brown, Steve Cannon, Tony Carpenter, Jordan Clements, Kent Davis, Rob Eaton, Glenn Embree, Clark Gilbert, Greg Hazard, Brian Memmott, Justin Miller, Sheldon Lawrence, Thomas Lee, Ben Packer, Rhonda Seamons, Richard Siddoway, Troy Spratling, and Gary Wallace.

Three groups reviewed the manuscript and made important suggestions: the students of professor Josh Allen's professional editing class; the members of BYU–Idaho's iComm Student Media Lab; and the members of the Idaho Falls Young Professionals Network.

Also, the team at Deseret Book went above and beyond the call of duty in editing, illustrating, formatting, and promoting the book. They include Chris Schoebinger, Richard Erickson, Scott Eggers, Barry Hansen, Kayla Hackett, Emily Watts, Gail Halladay, and Patrick Muir.

I also acknowledge gratefully the many teachers and mentors not mentioned in these pages; their names are written in my heart.

Taking Charge of Your College Education

HENRY J. EYRING

DESERET
BOOK

To Kathleen Johnson Eyring,
my first and dearest teacher

Library of Congress Cataloging-in-Publication Data

Eyring, Henry J.
    Major decisions : taking charge of your college education / Henry J. Eyring.
        p. cm.
    Includes bibliographical references and index.
    ISBN 978-1-60641-636-5 (paperbound)
    1. College student orientation. 2. College students—Conduct of life. 3. Vocational guidance.
4. Success—Religious aspects—Church of Jesus Christ of Latter-day Saints. I. Title.
    LB2343.3.E97 2010
    378.1'98—dc22   2010004010

Printed in the United States of America
Malloy Lithographing Incorporated, Ann Arbor, MI
10 9 8 7 6 5 4 3 2 1

CONTENTS

Introduction . . . . **vii**

Part One: Understanding the Higher-Education Path **1**

1. Education and the Gospel **5**

2. The Growing Need for Education **17**

3. High-Stakes Judgments . . *HSJ page 43* **37**

4. Is College for Me?. **71**

5. Getting Ready **93**

6. Choosing a School **115**

Part Two: Being Your Own General Contractor **151**

7. *General Contractor's Rule #1:* Always Have a Career Dream. **155**

8. *General Contractor's Rule #2:* Always Have a Major **165**

9. *General Contractor's Rule #3:* Customize Your Degree **175**

10. *General Contractor's Rule #4:* Find the Best Teachers. **189**

11. *General Contractor's Rule #5:* Do Your Best Work **205**

12. *General Contractor's Rule #6:* Connect Your Degree to What Comes Next . . . **217**

13. *General Contractor's Rule #7:* Get All the HSJ Skills You Can. **227**

Conclusion: Lifelong Learning **237**

Index. **241**

INTRODUCTION

his book is about education, especially the "higher education" that comes after high school. It's the kind of book I wish I had read before going to college and graduate school. It might have helped me get more from my education. It might also have helped me avoid some mistakes along the way.

I began to lay my plans for higher education at a young age. By the time I was eight, I was determined to attend the Harvard Business School. My father, then a professor at Stanford, had earned both an MBA and a doctorate in business administration from Harvard. I admired both Harvard and Stanford, but knew that Harvard was number one. So of course I wanted to go there.

My father's father also had a PhD, one in chemistry from the University of California, Berkeley. Grandpa was always nice to me, but for some reason he seemed to think that a boy my age should know advanced algebra; he patiently tried to teach me math that was way over my head. He counseled me to major in physics, which he considered the ideal combination of science and math. Dad told me that the Harvard Business School would like a science major. So, based on their counsel, I was all set with both an undergraduate and a graduate education plan:

I would get a bachelor's degree in physics and a Harvard MBA. (It didn't bother me that I really didn't know what physics was.)

My early awareness of higher education and focus on a major field of study proved a great blessing. Even during my junior year of high school, when I finally got a driver's license, cut classes, and finished with a two-point-something GPA, I knew that college loomed in my future. That long-held vision kept me from going entirely over the edge. Thanks to good grades during my freshman and sophomore years, when I had been a responsible young pedestrian, I entered the twelfth grade with a college-worthy high school transcript.

One of the classes I cut most that junior year was physics. Whatever beauty Grandpa found in "the ideal combination of math and science," I literally didn't get it. Nonetheless, I stuck to the science major/Harvard MBA game plan: I majored in geology, the academic version of the rock collecting that I had loved as a kid.

Brigham Young University accepted me, and I thrived in its student-friendly geology department. My grades were solid, and I got a good score on the GMAT, the standardized exam required by the top graduate business schools; in fact, on both of these dimensions, I looked better than the average student admitted by Harvard the year before. Everything seemed to be going according to plan.

But Harvard denied me. (Warning: If you bought this book expecting to learn the secrets for getting into an Ivy League graduate school, now would be a good time to list it on eBay.) In a panic, I applied to Stanford but was again denied. In both cases the denial letter said something to the effect of, "You're a good candidate, and we recommend that you reapply after gaining two years of full-time work experience."

My grandfather, father, and brother Matthew, who did get into Harvard

That presented a huge problem. I wasn't qualified to work as anything but a geologist. And, unfortunately, oil was selling for $8 a barrel, one-third of the price it had been at the time I started my geology degree program. No one was exploring for oil or gas, and even experienced geologists were being laid off. In that down market, a brand-new bachelor's graduate in geology had little chance of getting the kind of job necessary to win admission to either Harvard or Stanford. My lifetime's dream was dead. Worse, I felt unemployable.

More than twenty years later, I am happy to report that things worked out well. In fact, looking back, I see evidence of a kind Providence leading me down an even better path than the one I had dreamed of from boyhood. Outstanding professors in both college and graduate school helped me gain valuable education and insight into the things that matter most. I've enjoyed a rewarding career that has included not only the intellectual challenges and financial rewards I had hoped for but also deeper professional friendships and more time for family than I had imagined.

But you have to wonder: How could such carefully laid educational plans fail? I started young and got expert advice. I worked very hard, and my university professors paid unusual attention to me and my fellow students. And yet, with a college degree finally in hand, I felt unprepared to get a good job.

At the time, I found myself wondering whether my investment in higher education had been worth it. I've learned since that I'm not the only person who has felt this way. In fact, you may be having doubts about higher education yourself. Maybe you're thinking about attending college but wonder whether it's worth the cost. Maybe you're now a college student and are worried about whether you'll be able to get a good job in your field, or whether graduate school makes sense.

In the nearly thirty years since I enrolled in college, I've discovered some things that the typical newly admitted student would never guess. They include the following:

- Many undergraduate majors and even some graduate programs aren't designed to ensure job readiness.
- Professors with both the talent and the time to nurture students are rare.
- Good grades alone don't guarantee real learning or preparation for life after graduation.
- Graduating with a four-year college degree in just four years is difficult.

You're right to be thinking about these issues. At the same time, though, I've learned that higher education is essential to a successful, secure career. There are good reasons why Dad and Grandpa encouraged me to get all the education I could. In today's competitive world, even an intelligent, hardworking person faces a difficult life without a college degree.

Education also makes life richer in non-monetary ways. It can open your eyes and heart to the world and to the people in it. The point of making money, after all, is to provide for the physical necessities of life so that its true pleasures can be fully experienced. Higher education makes both of those things easier.

I've also learned that the people you meet in college and graduate school can shape your life for the better. I particularly treasure the influence of professors who not only taught well but also took the time to mentor me and my fellow students. I owe many of my most valued skills and perspectives to teachers who went beyond the call of duty.

Here's something else I've learned about higher education, probably the most important thing: You can get everything you hope for—and more—if you take personal responsibility for the design and construction of your education. The key is to be your own "general contractor," the one who puts all of the pieces of a higher education together according to a careful personal plan.

You *can* get an outstanding higher education, one that will prepare you to make decisions of great economic and social value and to enjoy the best things in life. You can succeed at college and in graduate school even if you're the first person in your family to try. The key is to take charge of the process yourself. If you don't have that eBay buyer yet, read on and find out how.

PART ONE

UNDERSTANDING THE HIGHER-EDUCATION PATH

This section will guide you along the first part of the higher-education path, with stops along the way designed to help you make decisions about why and where to go to college.

First, we'll put your education in its broader perspective. Education is important for everyone, but it means most to those who appreciate the real purposes of life. Learning is a fundamental reason for our being on earth. Understanding that truth not only increases our desire to learn, it also gives us the right motives for learning—providing for our loved ones, serving our fellow men and women, and preparing for our divine destiny. That's why we'll start our journey with a study of what life is really about and the divine assistance we can receive as we learn.

Next, in a chapter called "The Growing Need for Education," we'll explore why a college degree is becoming ever more essential to making a good living. Over your lifetime, the difference between having only a high school diploma and a college degree could be worth well over $500,000, and perhaps more than $1 million. To understand why the relative value of higher education is growing, we'll look at the forces in the world that are making working with your hands alone, rather than with your head, less profitable. We'll see why you need higher education even more than your parents did.

Then, in "High-Stakes Judgments," we'll explore just what it is that makes higher education so valuable. We'll do that by looking at the puzzling differences in the earning power of different jobs. It's not hard to see, for instance, why an airline pilot makes at least twice as much as a flight attendant and three or four times as much as a baggage handler; the pilot has spent thousands of hours training for the job, compared with just a few days or weeks for the others. Also, the pilot has the lives of passengers literally in his or her hands. But how do you explain the fact that the executives who run the airline, whose decisions don't have life-and-death consequences, outearn the pilots—sometimes by a lot? We'll study these surprising salary differentials, as well as the super-valuable decision-making skills that can be developed through higher education. We'll also talk about why that education is valuable in this life and in the eternities for reasons that go far beyond money and job security.

Even after hearing about the benefits of higher education, you may not be convinced that it's right for you. Maybe you don't have the best high school grades; maybe you don't even have a high school diploma. Or perhaps you just don't want to give up your current job and go into debt to get a college degree. We'll discuss those doubts in a chapter called "Is College for Me?"

Having explored the cost and benefits of college, we'll talk about "Getting Ready." We'll see why the things that most college-bound high school students worry about—perfect grades, AP courses, and application-enhancing extracurricular activities—may not be as important as some other things, such as getting excited about learning and exploring different careers.

Finally, we'll create a strategy for "Choosing a School." We'll find out just how much it matters to attend a school with ivy-covered buildings or a tradition of football greatness. We'll also learn how to build an individualized college "ranking" system, one focused on your personal learning and future success and happiness.

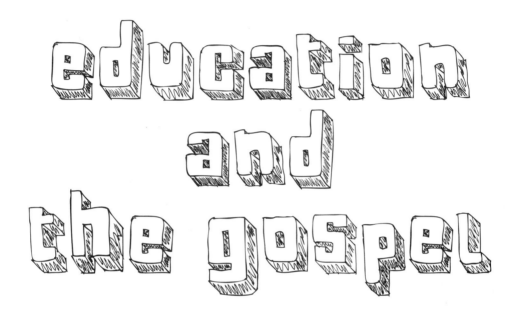

education and the gospel

Whatever principle of intelligence we attain unto
in this life, it will rise with us in the resurrection.
DOCTRINE AND COVENANTS 130:18

ducation matters to everyone, but it has special value for those who sense the deeper meaning and purpose of life. My grandfather had that kind of big-picture view of education. Once, when he was president of the American Academy for the Advancement of Science, an association of 100,000 scientists, he wrote these words to his colleagues: "I believe that every brilliant conquest made by man is but a manifestation of the divine spark which sets him apart from the rest of creation. Man is in the image of God, destined to go on learning and perfecting himself throughout eternity."[1]

Grandpa learned that principle from his grandfather, who learned

"Joseph Smith, as a very young man, translated the Book of Mormon from plates inscribed with a language no one on earth understood. He did it by a divine gift of revelation from God. But he later hired a tutor to teach him and other leaders of the Church ancient languages. Joseph Smith had essentially no formal schooling, yet the effect of the gospel of Jesus Christ on him was to make him want to learn more so that he could be more useful to God and to God's children."[2]

PRESIDENT HENRY B. EYRING

it through Joseph Smith, the founding president of The Church of Jesus Christ of Latter-day Saints. Joseph Smith recorded the divine direction to study and learn all we can "of things both in heaven and in the earth, and under the earth; things which have been, things which are, things which must shortly come to pass; things which are at home, things which are abroad; the wars and the perplexities of the nations, and the judgments which are on the land; and a knowledge also of countries and of kingdoms" (Doctrine and Covenants 88:79).

Joseph Smith applied this principle in his own life. His family's poverty prevented him from attending school past the second grade. However, he spent his life studying many of the subjects mentioned above—astronomy, history, languages, law, and others.

Joseph Smith was not only a dedicated student, he was also a great teacher and a builder of schools. In the frontier settlements of Kirtland, Ohio, and Nauvoo, Illinois, he directed the early Mormon pioneers to create schools at the same time they were constructing temples. School building became a pattern for these pioneers when they went west. As soon as they had established a new settlement, they built a school for their children. My grandfather, for example, attended a frontier "academy" in Colonia Juarez, Mexico; his parents and their fellow settlers paid 8 percent of their income to operate the school. Many schools like that one, initially built for grade-schoolers, grew larger: BYU, BYU–Idaho, and the University of Utah all started as Mormon academies.

EDUCATION FOR ALL

The pioneer schools were filled equally by boys and girls. My great-grandmother Caroline Romney Eyring taught at the Juarez Academy,

and she made sure that all of her children attended. The educational head start they got propelled them to later success. Of Caroline's eight children, six earned bachelor's degrees, four went on for master's degrees, and three earned PhDs. That was in a day when only one in twenty-five people in the United States had a college degree.

That kind of emphasis on education is exemplified by the family of Elder William Grant Bangerter, a pioneering missionary to Brazil. He and his wife were the first people in their families to earn college degrees. When they married, they set a goal to ensure the blessing of higher education for each of their children. As it turned out, they had ten children, making the goal unusually difficult to achieve. But all ten earned college degrees. It took a long time; the Bangerters had one or more children in college for a period of twenty-five years.

One of their daughters, Julie Bangerter Beck, was called in 2007 as general president of the Relief Society, the world's largest women's organization. Of her parents' ten children, President Beck took the longest to graduate. She started college but married young and left school for a time. Several years later, one of her older sisters offered to babysit President Beck's children so that she could return and finish her degree. It took a total of eight years, and she ended up attending college with five of her siblings at one time or another. When President Beck finished, she and her siblings passed their love of learning and education on to their children. Today her parents, the Bangerters, have sixty-five grandchildren, and all those who are old enough have had the opportunity to earn college degrees.

My grandfather Henry Eyring believed that education was invaluable for parents, who play the central role in their children's education and development of character. He argued that all parents, mothers and fathers alike, have to know enough science to answer their children's questions, especially questions about how the things taught in school relate to the principles of religion. He said:

"The influence that you have on your children and grandchildren depends very much on how well you understand the world. It is surprising how much they will listen to you if they think you are talking sense, and how little attention they will pay to you on the things that you talk nonsense on, that you do not even pretend to know very much about. **It is important to everybody to be as widely acquainted with the things going on in the world and to understand what people are thinking and saying as clearly as they can if they want to influence other people.** I think that each of you has a definite obligation to understand something about science in this world.

"You could not live in a more exciting time. We have the true gospel, the gospel that the Lord revealed here, to learn, to guide us, to understand where we came from, and where we are going. We live in a time when science is the most exciting it has ever been. You have heard the figure that **ninety-five out of every hundred scientists that ever lived are living right now,** and science is moving faster than it has ever moved before. Every day you can read something exciting in the paper. If you do not keep up, you will be an old fuddy-duddy; you will not have any influence with your kids. We owe it to ourselves to understand the world we live in—science, music, and art."[3]

PREPARING FOR OPPORTUNITIES

My father has often described his own education, noting both learning opportunities he missed and times when Heaven helped him to learn beyond his natural capacity. His stories and counsel helped me in developing my own learning plan; they may be helpful to you, too. He once said this:

"Part of the tragedy you must avoid is to discover too late that you missed an opportunity to prepare for a future only God could see for you. The chance to learn another language is for me a painful example. My father was born in Mexico. He grew up speaking Spanish as his first language. I lived in his home for more than 20 years. Sadly, I never asked him to teach me a word of Spanish. Several years ago I was the first contact . . . for the Church in Mexico, in Central America, and in Colombia, Venezuela, and Ecuador. It was no accident that I was born into a home with a Spanish-speaking father.

"But there was another opportunity. My father was a great teacher. He was a chemist. He even kept a blackboard in our basement for his children. He was eager to teach me mathematics. He spent hours trying to help me solve problems for my physics classes. He pled with me to think more often about those things that then seemed so uninteresting and so unimportant. Years later I was called by the Lord to the Presiding Bishopric of the Church and given responsibilities for computing and communications systems. What a blessing I might have had by taking the counsel I give you now. …

"The real life we're preparing for is eternal life. Secular knowledge has for us eternal significance. Our conviction is that God, our Heavenly Father, wants us to live the life that He does. . . . **All we can learn that is true while we are in this life will rise with us in the Resurrection. And all that we can learn will enhance our capacity to serve.** That is a destiny reserved not alone for the brilliant, those who learn the most quickly, or those who enter the most respected professions. It will be given to those who are humbly good, who love God, and who serve Him with all their capacities, however limited those capacities are—as are all our capacities, compared with the capacities of God."4

DIVINE GUIDANCE

Perhaps the greatest benefit of having a truly long-range perspective on education is knowing that our decisions matter not just now but in the life to come, and that we can expect divine guidance in making them. I certainly see that as I look back on my formal education and career choices. In spite of denial letters, economic downturns, and my own sometimes wrongheaded choices, Heaven has guided my path.

My experiences remind me of Autopia, the Disneyland attraction where you drive small cars along a track. When that ride was created in the 1950s, impulsive drivers nearly destroyed the cars by crashing them. So the Disney people had to install bumpers and steel guide rails. The steering wheel still turns now, but you can steer the car only to the point that the wheels hit the guide rail, and then you go where the rail takes you, whether you like it or not. Also, you can only go so fast.

My life as a student and family provider has sometimes been like that. For instance, I steered for the Harvard Business School, but the divine guide rail didn't lead that way. I had a similar experience as an MBA student at BYU (which, it turned out, was precisely the right place for me, even though I'd dreamed of Harvard all my life).

I had a similar experience looking for my first job after graduate school. During the summer of 1987 in the BYU MBA program, I worked to arrange job interviews with investment banks in New York. I really didn't know anything about being an investment banker, except that it was very prestigious and high paying. In spite of my ignorance, half a dozen people on Wall Street were kind enough to set appointments with me. I bought my plane ticket, reserved a room at the cheapest hotel in Manhattan, and counted down the time.

Just three days before my departure, the stock market fell further in one day (25 percent) than it ever has before or since, including during the worst days of the Great Depression.[5] Almost everyone with whom I had an appointment was still willing to see me, but none of their companies were even thinking about hiring new MBAs; that left us with little to talk about. I flew home dejected, wondering how my dreams could have been foiled yet again.

Within just a few months, though, my Autopia rail took me in another direction, one I hadn't considered. During a job-hunting trip to Boston I met a group of people at a consulting firm called Monitor Company who not only offered me employment but have since become lifelong friends. In hindsight, I'm grateful that Heaven spoiled my dreams so as to give me something better.

My father has described how and why such things happen in our lives:

"Your life is carefully watched over, as was mine. The Lord knows both what He will need you to do and what you will need to know. He is kind and He is all-knowing. So you can with confidence expect that He has prepared opportunities for you to learn in preparation for the

service you will give. You will not recognize those opportunities perfectly, as I did not. But when you put the spiritual things first in your life, you will be blessed to feel directed toward certain learning, and you will be motivated to work harder. You will recognize later that your power to serve was increased, and you will be grateful. . . .

"The Lord loves you and watches over you. He is all-powerful, and He promised you this: 'But seek ye first the kingdom of God, and his righteousness; and all these things shall be added unto you' (Matt. 6:33).

"That is a true promise. When we put God's purposes first, He will give us miracles. If we pray to know what He would have us do next, He will multiply the effects of what we do in such a way that time seems to be expanded. He may do it in different ways for each individual, but I know from long experience that He is faithful to His word."[6]

Keep that in mind as you read the chapters to follow. **God cares about you and your education. He will not only help you get the education you need, He will take you to the people He wants you to encounter.** Those people are in only one place, and so you can be sure not just that there is a right school for you to attend and particular subjects for you to study, but that your choice should be based more on people than on prestige. You will always be grateful for what you learn in school. But even more, you will be grateful for service you give and are given as you learn.

[1]Henry Eyring, *The Faith of a Scientist* (Deseret Book, 1967), 184.
[2]Henry B. Eyring, "Education for Real Life," *Ensign,* October 2002, 14.
[3]Henry J. Eyring, *Mormon Scientist: The Life and Faith of Henry Eyring* (Deseret Book, 2008), 241–43.
[4]Eyring, "Education for Real Life," 18, 21.
[5]http://en.wikipedia.org/wiki/Black_Monday_(1987).
[6]Eyring, "Education for Real Life," 18–20.

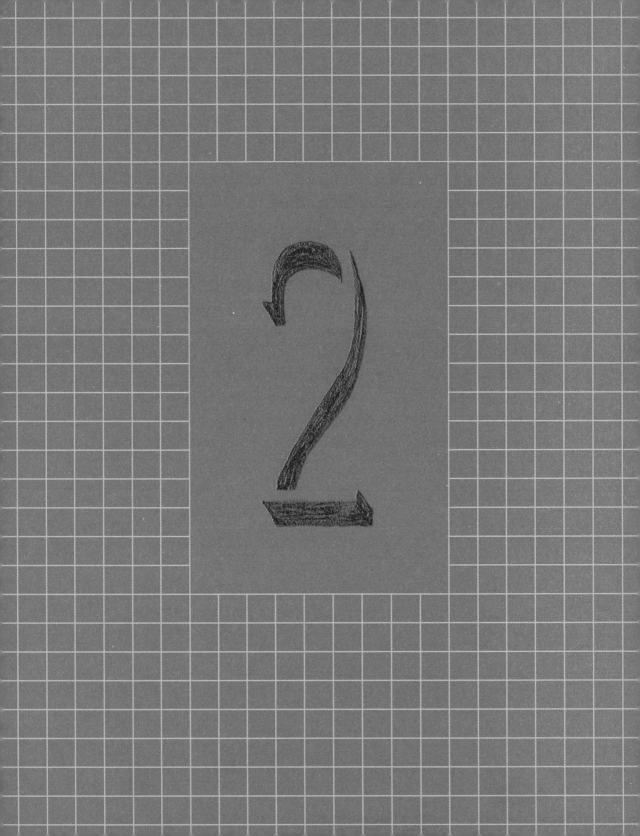

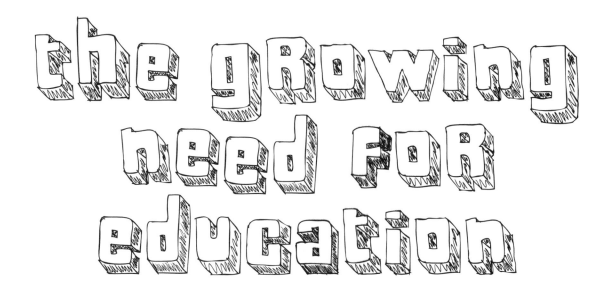

the gRowing need FoR education

Be willing to work diligently and make sacrifices to obtain learning.
Education is an investment that brings great rewards.
You live in a competitive world where a good education opens the
doors of opportunity that may otherwise be closed to you.

FOR THE STRENGTH OF YOUTH

here are many reasons for seeking all the formal education you can get. Education increases your awareness of the world and your ability to get around in it. It gives you the chance to learn from the experiences and insights of others. That learning can help you avoid painful mistakes. For example, a class in biology might convince you to avoid smoking, or to stop if you've already started. And a good math teacher could show you why your credit card can be as dangerous to your bank account as smoking is to your body. Education can help you learn from the mistakes of others and avoid making those mistakes yourself.

Education can also help you live a happier life. For example, a little psychology can teach you a lot about getting along with your friends and family members. And, through the study of history, you can learn to understand cultures different from your own and to appreciate the value of peace among countries and races.

Of course, as Latter-day Saints, we know that **learning is one of our major purposes for being on this earth**, and that the knowledge we gain here will go with us into the next world. That is the great eternal reason for seeking education.

But, if you're like me when I was in high school, you may be looking for more tangible benefits, such as a better wage than you can make as a lifeguard. That's a worthy desire and a great reason for getting education. In fact, if you hope to graduate from the lifeguard's chair to something more interesting and better paying, you had better think seriously about higher education. If you don't, you could be in real trouble, because the world is changing in ways that are hard to see but will have a powerful effect on you.

Looking around, you may have noticed that life is getting better for most people. For example, the biggest houses built when your parents were teenagers are small compared to some of the mansions going up today. Your parents probably like to remind you that they never had their own cell phones or laptops or iPods when they were your age. They may say, "You don't know how much better you have it now than we did."

In fact, there *is* much greater wealth in the world today, and more people are sharing in it. However, the way wealth is created is also changing. **In the past, human muscle was the source of the products that made life better. Today, those products are increasingly created by the power of the human mind.** That change is important for you. It can be good news if you're well educated, but bad news if you're not.

My grandpa recognized that inevitability when he was young. Grandpa was born in a Mormon settlement in Mexico in 1901. In 1910,

Grandpa Eyring on horseback

revolutionaries—"bandits," he called them—took his family's ranch and drove them from Mexico. As refugees in remote Pima, Arizona, they borrowed money to buy land and broke baked ground to start a farm.

Grandpa didn't like this kind of desert farm work. That increased his natural enthusiasm for school. He studied hard and won a scholarship to the University of Arizona. He applied his farmer's work ethic in the classroom and ultimately became a well-known research chemist at Princeton, where he knew Albert Einstein, another American immigrant.

Grandpa was a story-teller with a quirky sense of humor. Grandpa liked to tell, for instance, of walking one day with Dr. Einstein through a garden planted with soybeans. He asked Einstein what kind of plants they were, and Einstein said, "I don't know." Grandpa, the old farm boy said, "They're soybeans." For the rest of his life, he enjoyed telling this story and joking, "Einstein didn't know beans."

a penny a week

In a 1964 speech my grandfather Henry Eyring gave to a group at Brigham Young University, he addressed the need for education to make a living in the modern world. After describing recent developments in science, he said this:

"What does it mean? I will tell you what it means. It means that we are going to do everything more and more using our heads and less and less using our arms. Any young man or woman who is so ill-advised at the present time, if their mind is good enough to let them, to not go to the Brigham Young University, or one of the other universities, and get training is a very brave person. I mean, it is almost guaranteed that unless they are much smarter than the people who go to college and get the training that way, they will have a subservient position in the community. Society needs us to go ahead and get training if we possibly can, if we are able to.

"I would like to use an analogy. Let's suppose you have twenty tons of coal and a ten-foot fence. When I was down in Pima I could have thrown that over the fence—and I can still do it—twenty tons in a day. Now, twenty tons of coal weighs 2,000 pounds per ton, and twenty times 2,000 is 40,000, and if you lift it ten feet over the fence, that is 40,000 times ten; that is 400,000. And you don't belong to a union, you remember, so you can work for six days a week. That is 2,400,000 foot-pounds. Do you know how much that is worth? It is worth about a penny in power. It is a kilowatt hour. A kilowatt hour is 2,650,000 foot-pounds, and this is only 2,400,000.

"If you do not have anything but muscles you are not worth anything. We can only afford to pay you about a penny a week."[1]

Of course, when Grandpa spoke of "worth," he was referring only to financial earning power, not to character or other personal qualities of eternal significance. He meant no disrespect for those who labor without the benefit of education. In fact, he believed he could learn something from everyone, regardless of their level of formal education. But he wanted you and me to appreciate how machines have changed things.

In this modern world, we can't begin to make a living on muscle alone. Even minimum-wage jobs, which usually require at least *some* thinking, don't provide a decent living for a family. At the current minimum wage, a family of just three people with just one minimum wage earner would fall below what the U.S. government calls the poverty level.[2]

You might ask, "Well, why don't we just raise the minimum wage?" That's a good question, and the minimum wage *is* raised periodically. However, there is a limit on what employers are willing to pay. That limit is set by something called "the market."

THE COMPETITION FOR JOBS

An easy way to envision the market is to think about buying a video game. Let's say you want the latest version of your favorite game. You could buy it at any number of places—at a store in your neighborhood, online, or even from a friend who bought the game and didn't like it that much. You might be willing to pay more at the store, where you can play a demo and get the game right now, with a warranty. But if the price is too high there, you'll look at the other options, where the price is lower. In other words, the market—the other places you could buy the game— sets a cap on the price that can be charged by the most expensive seller.

When you go looking for a job, you are like a video game seller, but instead of selling a game you are selling your labor. Just like the case of the video game, employers won't pay you much more than what the next-best applicant is willing to work for. In other words, **you are in competition with other sellers of labor, and you will get a higher price for your work only if it is more valuable.**

For example, let's say that you have your own lawn-mowing business. Your father lets you use the family lawn mower and electric trimmer, so all you have to buy is gas. You have a dozen neighbors who pay you between $20 and $40 per job, depending on the size of the lawn. Each lawn takes between two and four hours to do, so you're making about $10 per hour, minus what you pay for gas. It's a great summer job for someone your age.

But then a professional lawn service comes to your neighborhood. They work as a two-man team, one mowing while the other trims and cleans up. They have a giant riding mower, the kind you stand on; it can do even a large lawn in under twenty minutes. They've also got a powerful blower for cleaning the sidewalk and driveway, instead of the push

broom you use; the blower is not only faster, it also leaves fewer grass clippings than you and your broom do.

The bad news is that the lawn service charges the same rate you do. At first, you can't understand how these professionals can afford such low prices when they use expensive equipment and send two people for each job. But then you figure out that they're getting maybe nine or ten lawns done in the time it takes you to do one. So they can afford to have two guys and lots of machines.

With this new competition, you face a difficult choice. To keep your customers from switching, you're either going to have to do a better job—for example, by spending more time sweeping up the grass clippings—or reduce your price. The quality of your service hasn't changed, but market competition has made it worth less.

This kind of market competition is increasing everywhere around us. If you're a frequent video game buyer, you know there are more places to buy games today than there were even a few years ago. And the competitors for the lawns in your neighborhood are no longer limited to just the other kids who live there.

You'll face market competition all your life; in fact, it will increase every year. To stay ahead, you'll need lots of education, as we'll see in the next chapter. For now, though, let's focus on where the competition will come from. One clue is in that big blower the professional lawn guys are using. The blower is both much faster and also more effective at getting the grass off the sidewalk than you and your broom. You'll never win in a competition with that kind of machine.

MAN VERSUS MACHINE

That takes us back to Grandpa's story of shoveling coal. When he did those fancy calculations to put a one-penny price on a week's worth of

shoveling, he was comparing the efficiency of people versus machines. Machines, because they are built for a specific purpose and employ mechanical principles such as leverage, can perform repetitive tasks much faster than humans can.

That's true not only for physical labor such as shoveling coal or sweeping sidewalks, but also for some basic mental tasks, such as mathematical computations. Computers are machines that increasingly perform tasks that people used to do. Computers aren't "smart"—they can't make decisions the way a human or even an animal does. But they can execute simple instructions, such as adding one number to another, literally at lightning speed.

saw a classic example of the slow but steady takeover of jobs by machines during the summer after my first year of college. I worked for an oil company in an office with a friendly fellow named Doyle, a draftsman.

Back in the days before digital printers, the only way to create a high-quality architectural drawing of a building or an oil refinery was with a pen, by hand. The people who did this kind of technical drawing were called draftsmen. They sat perched on stools at large, high tables to do their work. Doyle was a master draftsman, with a steady hand and a great eye for detail.

Doyle loved his work, but he hated the constant noise coming from a new machine in the office. It was a "plotter," a six-foot-long monster that spat out rough architectural drawings. The plotter received its image from a high-powered computer and drew images by moving mounted pens back and forth across the paper with wires, like a giant Etch A Sketch. The plotter's work wasn't very pretty; the pens sometimes didn't stop at the right place, leaving a gap or an overshoot where two lines were supposed to meet. But it was very, very fast. The plotter could create in a few minutes a drawing that would take Doyle a whole day to complete.

Doyle took comfort in the thought that his drawings were worth the price of a day's labor, at least when the image had to be perfect. But I was glad for his sake that he was close to retirement. I had a feeling that the company making the plotter would soon find a way to keep the pens from stopping in the wrong place. In fact, the plotters didn't just get better—they were ultimately replaced with high-tech digital printers, which make more precise images than even the steadiest human hand.

Computer technology hasn't eliminated the need for draftsmen. But today these workers are more likely to be called CAD (computer-aided design) specialists. Their tools are not pens but computers. They are much more productive than traditional draftsmen, and they are better paid. They are also very likely to have college degrees (something few draftsmen did). The old job of draftsman no longer exists. Without formal training in the new technologies, Doyle wouldn't be able to sell his services today at any price.

Because of their high power and low cost, machines—especially computer-controlled machines—have taken over many jobs that once employed not only the human body but also the brain. Even a "high-tech" job may be less safe than it sounds. For example, just a few years ago, PC networking was one of the newest and hottest professional opportunities. However, improved software, such as the kind in an Apple Mac, makes networking easy even for untrained computer users. Even highly trained workers like PC network engineers are in competition with ever-smarter machines.

COMPETITORS FROM AROUND THE GLOBE

In addition to smart machines, uneducated workers increasingly find themselves competing with two other forces. One is immigration. During the middle of the twentieth century, when Grandpa was talking about the power of machines, immigration to the United States slowed to a trickle. If he were giving advice about education today, though, he'd warn you that you're in competition not only with technology but also with a flood of immigrants. These newcomers are relatively uneducated, but they are hardworking and enterprising. They are also willing to work for low wages. **Many of the jobs that can't be performed entirely by machines, such as building construction and landscaping, are now being done by industrious immigrants.** In fact, the lawn-care team you were working against may have been from someplace outside the United States. This new source of labor pushes hourly wages down. That's a good thing for consumers, like the homeowners who get better services at lower prices. But it's hard on the workers providing the services.

A related downward force on wages is something called globalization. Globalization means that billions of people around the world can now compete for jobs that used to be performed only in the United States. Even without being here, these people can get many of our jobs done at a much lower price. This changes the way all kinds of products are made.

Several things make this kind of globalization possible. One is the low cost of transportation. New super-cargo ships, for instance, allow not just computers but even very heavy products such as steel and automobiles to be sent halfway around the world quite inexpensively. Another relatively new technology, the Internet, makes communication essentially free. This means that people producing computers or steel or cars or anything else can talk to buyers anywhere in the world as though they were making the products right next door.

The early computers were made in U.S. factories by relatively well-paid assembly-line workers. They were sold in retail stores by salespeople trained to help you. These computers were very expensive, so you tried to make yours last for a long time. If it broke, you took it to a computer repair shop.

Today, nearly all computers are made overseas by foreign manufacturers. Most of us order our computers online rather than going to a traditional store. If you need customer service, you call someone in India. If your computer breaks, it makes little sense to fix it, because the repair will be more expensive than a new machine, which is cheaper and faster than the old one anyway.

Another contributor to globalization is free trade, the reduction or complete elimination of charges on foreign-made products. Until just a few decades ago, U.S. companies and workers were protected from foreign competition by high import fees ("tariffs") put into place during the Great Depression. Today, though, those tariffs are much lower or, in some cases, gone altogether. Thus, the foreign goods that can be ordered via the Internet and shipped by supercargo ships are now imported without any tariff disadvantage. To see how common this has become, check the labels on things you find at your local Walmart and see how many of them were made in other countries.

Finally, globalization is driven by the rapid development of formerly backward nations. Just a few years ago, for example, "Made in China" was something you expected to see only on the back of a cheap plastic toy. However, China and India and dozens of other countries have

changed. These countries are still very poor, and their average citizens are undereducated by our standards. But they are modernizing at a breathtaking rate. They already have high-tech factories capable of manufacturing the world's most sophisticated products. Because their workers are willing to work for a few dollars a day, their factories can make high-quality products at very low cost. And, as we've seen, getting those products to the United States doesn't add much to that cost.

THREATS AND OPPORTUNITIES

Think of what this means for the U.S. workers and companies involved. To go back to our computer example, the jobs on the computer assembly line are gone. So are many of the jobs selling computers or providing customer support by phone. You may know some people still doing computer repairs and upgrades, but their business isn't what it used to be; if they're smart, they don't see a career in it. Much of the work of making and servicing computers that was once done by people in the United States is now done by machines or people overseas. You may be getting a Dell, dude, but you're not getting it from where you used to.

I'm making all the money I need!

BRAIN OUT!

There's a negative side to these changes. Some people will lose their jobs. Also, the minimum wage will stay low. That's a bigger problem than you might realize if you're still living with your parents. It may be all right to make seven or eight dollars an hour when your housing, food, health care, and maybe even access to a car are provided at no cost. But that kind of minimum-wage job wouldn't pay for those things if you had a family of your own; that's why the government would classify you as below the poverty level.

Fortunately, in addition to the negative effects of global competition, there are very positive sides to the change occurring in the world. For one thing, the products and services we buy are much less expensive. Our computers are cheaper and more powerful, our cars are safer and more comfortable, and our wardrobes are larger and more fashionable.

On top of all that, our best jobs are better. **It's true that many once-giant companies now employ fewer people. But the employees who remain have greater influence and productive capacity.** Though Dell and HP and Apple may have outsourced their factory operations to others, they have retained the important decisions about what products to make, how to make them, and where to sell them. A relatively small group of people are now making these decisions for workers and customers around the world. Because these decisions affect the whole world, the people who make them are well paid. Fifty years ago, Grandpa said it this way:

"A man using his mind can direct a machine which can do an amount of work a thousand slaves could never accomplish. For a few dollars we can telephone to the ends of the earth, or if need be can fly non-stop to any spot on earth. The untrained mind with only physical strength to offer has become economically valueless in competition with a machine. By the same token, anyone who can see a little more clearly how to use the tremendous forces at our bidding can multiply his strength beyond limit. Calculating machines are now being built which can make calculations faster than a small army of brilliant humans. If one must compete with the machine, one is lost. **If one can really master machines, one's value is beyond price.**"[3]

That's the silver lining in the change occurring everywhere around us: The old jobs that we've lost have been replaced by new ones that pay better and are more intellectually engaging. However, they require more education. If you want to make a good living and enjoy the full benefits of this exciting, changing world we live in, you'll need to be a learner all your life. You'll especially want to consider attending college. We'll see why in the next chapter.

---

[1] Henry J. Eyring, *Mormon Scientist: The Life and Faith of Henry Eyring* (Deseret Book, 2008), 274–75.

[2] In 2009 the federal government defined the poverty level for a family of three in the mainland U.S. as $18,310 (*Federal Register* Vol. 74, No. 14, January 23, 2009, p. 4199). The minimum wage in 2009 was $7.25 (see http://www.dol.gov/esa/whd/flsa/). At 2,080 hours per year, this wage would produce a gross income of only $15,080.

[3] Eyring, *Mormon Scientist*, 273–74.

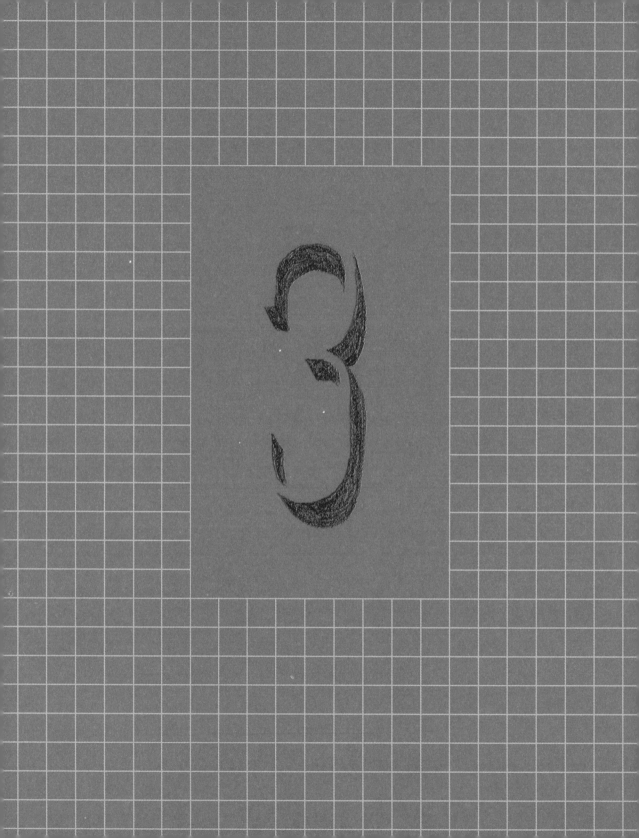

high-stakes judgments

Know ye not that we shall judge angels?
How much more things that pertain to this life?
1 CORINTHIANS 6:3

s the world becomes more mechanized and more global, the potential power of each person grows. A single individual can have worldwide impact. That can be very beneficial. But sometimes it's not such a good thing.

For example, early in 2008 it was discovered that one "rogue trader" at a French bank had lost 7.2 billion dollars. This fellow, named Jerome, was making huge financial bets that the stock market would continue to rise. Hoping to outsmart fellow traders who were betting that stock prices would go down, Jerome used the bank's money to borrow much more money and essentially gamble with it. For a while, Jerome was wildly successful, as stock prices went up. He kept what he was doing a secret, though, because his high-stakes gambles violated company policy.

Unfortunately, the stock market finally began to fall, and Jerome's huge gains turned to even larger losses. His bosses eventually discovered his unauthorized gambles, and they quickly cut the bank's losses by selling the things that Jerome had bought, at far less than he had paid. But the cost of doing so was staggering. The bank, one of the world's biggest, will survive. However, all of its 130,000 employees felt the impact of the loss. So did the millions of people who owned stock in the bank.

Seven point two billion dollars sounds like a lot, and it is. Amazingly, though, the total pool of funds that thirty-year-old Jerome was investing, including what he had borrowed, amounted to ten times that figure. He controlled a mountain of money that exceeded the value of the whole bank. It was an incredibly high-stakes game, played by just one person.

Jerome's case is unusual. He acted alone, and he took outsized risks. However, teams of "investment bankers" like Jerome routinely invest gigantic sums of money as large as his. With so much at stake, it's no wonder that a senior manager at an investment bank typically makes millions of dollars a year; even a new college graduate can earn $100,000 or more.[1] The decisions of these investment bankers, when made well, are worth a lot. That is true in today's highly mechanized, global world to a degree that was unimaginable a few decades ago.

the wii-markable value of good decisions

To help you visualize the vast value of good decisions, let's consider an example that may be close to home. In the late 1990s, the Japanese computer game company Nintendo had lost its lead in video games to Sony, whose PlayStation had become the world's most popular game console. The PlayStation's awesome power and amazing graphics made it seemingly unbeatable.

In 2001, though, a team of Nintendo designers began cooking up something entirely new. They took a fresh look at what video game players really wanted. They guessed that amazing graphics and even the ability to play movies didn't matter to game players as much as the competitors, Sony and Microsoft, seemed to think.[2] They envisioned a console that had only "good-enough" graphics and didn't play movies; this would make it much less expensive to manufacture and thus more affordable to game players.

The Nintendo team's real breakthrough, though, was in putting a new kind of fun into video game playing. They created a magic wand controller called the Wii Remote (or "Wiimote"). The Wiimote wand converts the movement of a game player's hand into movement on the video screen. The result is a game controller unlike any before, one that appeals to children and adults beyond just the tra- ditional video game players. Nintendo's breakthrough was made pos- sible by an ingenious application of technology: The Wii development team found a way to take an "accelerometer," the device that triggers an automobile airbag, and put it into a game controller.[3] It was a brilliant invention. But it also represented a great risk: If game players disliked the unusual Wiimote and its relatively low-powered console, Nintendo might be finished as a company. As any game aficionado (or parent) knows, when it was introduced in 2006 the Wii became an instant smash. In spite of its affordability, it was almost impossible to actually get one, because shipments from the factory sold out as fast as they arrived in stores. What most game players don't know is that the Wii helped increase the market value of Nintendo by eight times. The company's shareholders made tens of billions of dollars; in fact, Nintendo's biggest shareholder became the richest man in Japan. All of this happened largely because of the ingenuity of a few creative thinkers.

Even though developing a new video game console is very different from swapping piles of money, as investment bankers do, it is the same in one way: Success depends upon good decisions. And when good decisions are made by people in large organizations, such as a global investment bank or a large company like Nintendo, the value of those decisions can be astronomically high. People who can make such high-stakes decisions are accordingly well paid.

MONEY REALLY ISN'T EVERYTHING

Now, you may be thinking, "Wait a minute. Why are you so focused on money? I want to make a good living, but I also want my job—and my education—to be about more than a fat paycheck." Good for you. **If you're wise, you'll see money not as your reason for getting a good education and working hard, but rather as a by-product of it.** And you won't choose a college major or a job solely on the basis of your expected salary.

Even in this increasingly competitive world we live in, well-educated, hardworking people can make a good living pursuing the things they love and still have time outside of work to spend with the people they love.

But you're more likely to succeed in any job if you understand why some types of decisions are worth so much money. When you understand that, you'll be able to pick a career that allows you to strike the right balance among the things you want, such as serving people, pursuing your unique talents, and providing for yourself and those dependent on you. You'll also begin to understand what it will take to avoid being replaced in your chosen career by the machines and the people from around the world who will compete with you whether you like it or not. So, with those goals in mind, let's take a look at the kinds of decisions most valued by the marketplace.

HIGH-STAKES JUDGMENTS

The most economically valuable decisions have two qualities. One is that they have far-reaching impact. If the decisions are good, the benefit to the world is great; if the decisions are bad, the cost to the world is equally great.

The other quality of these important decisions is that they require good judgment. In other words, there's no simple formula for making them. **Experience may help, but the most valuable decisions ultimately require good educated guesses, or judgment calls. We can put these two qualities under a single name: high-stakes judgments** (HSJs for short).

One way of recognizing an HSJ is to contrast it with what it is not. To see this contrast in a real-world setting, let's return to the airline employees we met at the beginning of Part 1. As you'll recall, we talked about a baggage handler, a flight attendant, a pilot, and an airline executive. We noted that the average pilot's pay exceeds the flight attendant's pay by at least two times and the baggage handler's by three to four times. We also saw that the executive makes more than the pilot, potentially much more. That seems strange, because the pilot is the one performing the life-or-death job. But all of these differences in pay make sense if we understand the high value of high-stakes judgments.

Imagine a small grid, or matrix, with four boxes. On one side of the matrix, let's distinguish between decisions that are "high stakes" versus "lower stakes." The pilot, for instance, has a job that is obviously high stakes. If the pilot fails to follow proper procedure or doesn't react well in an emergency, everyone aboard the plane can die. The baggage handler,

by contrast, performs a relatively lower-stakes job. It's true that passengers don't like it when their bags get broken or sent to the wrong destination. But the price of this kind of mistake isn't very high compared to the life-or-death situations the pilot has to engage in. That difference in risk, along with the related difference in time required to train for the two jobs, explains why the pilot makes more money than the baggage handler. The pilot is rewarded for making high-stakes decisions.

Now let's contrast the baggage handler with the flight attendant. Neither of them has a high-stakes job compared to the pilot; both the baggage handler and the flight attendant will occasionally make a mistake, but those mistakes are unlikely to put passengers in grave danger. They receive training, but not nearly to the degree that the pilot does. Both, not surprisingly, are paid less.

The difference between these two jobs, though, is that the flight attendant's work requires more judgment than the baggage handler's does. That's because the flight attendant has to work with people rather than inanimate objects. Every passenger is different. Some are afraid of flying. Others complain about the small seats and frequent delays. Occasionally, an unruly drunk will cause a scene and potentially put other passengers in danger. Baggage, by contrast, never acts up. Aircraft delays often make it hard to get the bags where they're supposed to go on time, but the baggage handler's job is simply to send the bag to its specified destination as quickly as possible.

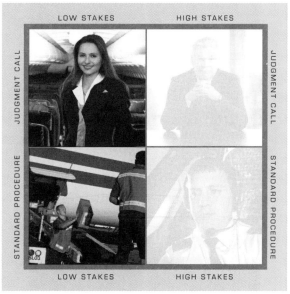

In addition to serving passengers, the flight attendant is also responsible for their well-being. Flight attendants are trained to organize the evacuation of passengers in the event of an emergency landing. They also have to attend to those who become ill while in flight or who are injured by heavy air turbulence.

Keeping passengers happy and safe thus requires more judgment than handling bags. The flight attendant has to be capable of making good decisions in the moment, with sensitivity to all of the unique variables, many of which—a passenger's mood or state of health, for instance—may be hard to read. In other words, the flight attendant literally has to think on his or her feet.

The baggage handler, meanwhile, relies mainly on muscle. From a thinking standpoint, handling bags primarily requires following standard procedures. The flight attendant's greater need for judgment is the reason that he or she is paid more than the baggage handler, even though the latter is likely to go home more physically exhausted. The baggage handler may be a great person, but the market price for his or her labor is capped by the growing number of people who can do the job equally well with a little training and experience. In fact, the baggage handler is also in competition with new machines

that handle bags faster and less expensively with each passing year. Those machines will keep the baggage handler's wage low, and in time they may eliminate that job altogether.

All of this is relatively intuitive; it naturally makes sense, given the differences in judgment required. It's also what you'd expect given the training required for each job. The baggage handler trains for a matter of days, the flight attendant for a few weeks, and the pilot for years; it makes sense that their pay would reflect those differences.

How can you explain, though, the airline executive's earning more than the pilot? What makes the executive's decisions more financially valuable than the pilot's, particularly when the latter is entrusted with the lives of passengers? Let's give that question some thought.

First, it's important to realize that high-stakes decisions aren't limited to matters of life or death. The executive's decisions can affect the economic and psychological well-being of thousands or even millions of people, just like the decisions of Jerome, the rogue trader, or the developers of the Wii did. The executive's ability to affect *many* people a *little* is thus on par, in terms of being high stakes, with the pilot's ability to affect a *few* people a *lot*.

The executive's job is not only equivalent to the pilot's in terms of being high stakes, it actually exceeds the difficulty of the pilot's job in an important way—the need for judgment calls. To appreciate that, let's look first at the task of flying a plane.

The rules of flying are well established. It's true that weather is unpredictable and that engines sometimes fail. When that happens, we're very grateful for pilots with good judgment. However, a pilot is surrounded by impressive decision-making support and safety systems. Air traffic controllers warn of approaching aircraft and storms. Airplane manufacturers and airline maintenance personnel work hard to ensure that airplanes rarely malfunction. Electronic warning systems, as well as a

human copilot, watch for signs of danger and provide correction in cases of pilot error. (You can see that pilots are increasingly competing, in a way, with machines, much like the baggage handlers are.) With all of this mechanical and human support, the pilot who follows the rules and is open to counsel rarely makes a major mistake. That is why so few planes crash.

Airline executives, on the other hand, "crash" their companies with alarming frequency. Any big company is hard to run. Compared to today's high-tech, ultra-safe aircraft, a large company sometimes behaves more like the early flying machines you see in old newsreel footage, plummeting to the ground or collapsing in a heap on the runway.

That's especially true of airline companies. They are unusually difficult to manage. In recent years, the airlines have faced unprecedented disasters, such as 2001's September 11 terrorist attacks, which stopped all U.S. flights for days and cost the airlines

billions of dollars. In addition, the airline industry has suffered for most of its history from poor labor relations. Battles between executives and unions have sometimes led to workers' calling in sick or going on strike. The unique problems that plague airlines have made bankruptcy common, even for the largest and apparently strongest companies. Looking back at the troubles of the airline industry, superstar investor Warren Buffett made this joke: "Sizing all of this up, I like to think that if I'd been at Kitty Hawk in 1903 when Orville Wright took off, I would have been farsighted enough, and public-spirited enough—I owed this to future capitalists—to shoot him down. I mean, Karl Marx couldn't have done as much damage to capitalists as Orville did."[4]

You might ask, "Why, then, if their companies do so badly, do airline executives get paid so much?" The reason is that an executive who can keep an airline out of bankruptcy—or better yet, lead it to profitability—is very valuable. Airlines are critical to the economy and to our individual happiness; our world couldn't function as it does without them. We're willing to pay a lot for the convenience and safety of air travel, which means there is a lot of money to be made in the airline business.

But airlines are also hard to run. There's no manual of rules and standard procedures. What do you do when the union threatens to strike? Or when the price of jet fuel doubles and passengers won't pay higher ticket prices? Making these decisions well requires outstanding judgment. That's why an airline executive is paid so much, or fails and gets fired. He or she is held responsible and rewarded for making high-stakes judgments.

Now, the purpose of this analysis isn't to argue that you should be an airline executive instead of a pilot or a flight attendant or a baggage handler. The HSJ framework we've created doesn't prescribe a way of life for anyone. It merely explains why some people make more money than others. There can be great nonfinancial rewards in jobs that don't involve HSJs. Those rewards may include the satisfaction of forming close relationships with coworkers and customers, or of applying unique talents such as working with your hands.

But **understanding the concept of high-stakes judgments will help you make an informed choice about your career and how much money you are likely to make. It will also help to develop skills** we'll talk about in a moment **that will increase your market value—and protect you from being put out of work** by machines or people willing to work for lower wages—regardless of the kind of job you take.

Remember, the forces of mechanization and globalization can't be stopped. Jobs that don't require a high degree of *judgment* will increasingly be performed by machines. And jobs that aren't *high stakes* can be performed by other people, including immigrants and overseas workers. Keeping one of these jobs will require you to understand HSJs and find ways to make

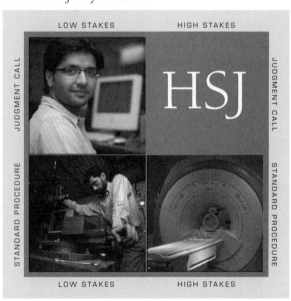

as many of them as you can, moving yourself toward the upper-right box of our matrix, where you have a better chance of staying ahead of smart machines and the flood of global workers. You don't have to be a corporate executive to make a good living. And you don't have to be a natural-born genius. But, in whatever job you take, you need to always be increasing your ability to make high-stakes judgments.

hsj matrix exercise

Though every job is a little different, the link between HSJs and compensation holds true in most fields of work. Try your hand at putting each of the jobs below into the HSJ matrix. (For suggested answers, see page 69.)

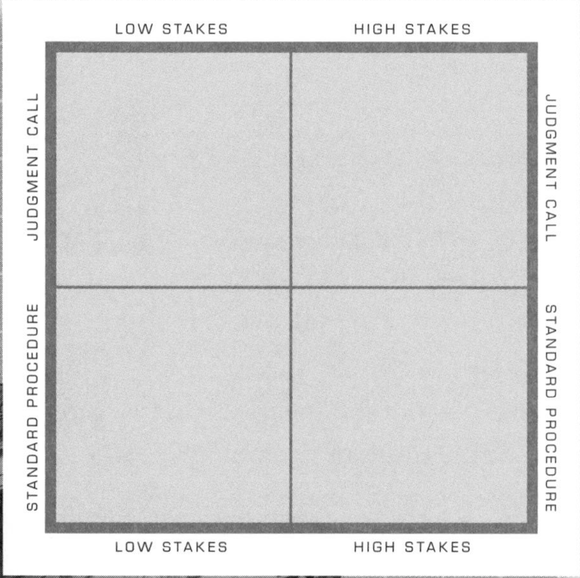

Banking

Loan Officer

Teller

Investment Banker

Local Branch Manager

	LOW STAKES	HIGH STAKES	
JUDGMENT CALL			JUDGMENT CALL
STANDARD PROCEDURE			STANDARD PROCEDURE
	LOW STAKES	HIGH STAKES	

Restaurants

Fast Food Franchise Manager

Corporate Marketing Vice
  President

Pastry Chef

Cashier

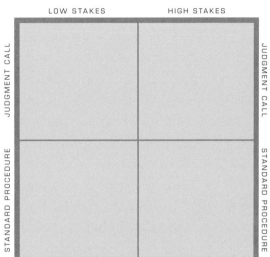

LOW STAKES   HIGH STAKES

JUDGMENT CALL

JUDGMENT CALL

STANDARD PROCEDURE

STANDARD PROCEDURE

LOW STAKES   HIGH STAKES

LOW STAKES   HIGH STAKES

JUDGMENT CALL

JUDGMENT CALL

STANDARD PROCEDURE

STANDARD PROCEDURE

LOW STAKES   HIGH STAKES

Automotive

New Car Design Team Leader

Dealership Manager

Oil Change Specialist

Custom Auto Builder

NOT JUST A BIG COMPANY THING

High-stakes judgments are needed in almost all large organizations, from airlines to video game companies to banks. "But," you might say, "I'm not sure I want to work for a big company. I like serving people. How does your theory of HSJs apply to me?" It's a good question, one perhaps best answered with another example.

Consider these four providers of services who perform their work for one person at a time: a barber, a hairstylist, a registered nurse, and a doctor. The barber's job pays the least because the stakes are low and the procedure is relatively simple. A stylist, however, must master not only scissors and clippers but also complex cuts and dyes. His or her customers are demanding; pleasing them requires good judgment, which comes only with training and experience. A trusted stylist's customers will pay more than they would to an ordinary barber. But of course in both cases what is at stake is just the way one looks until the next haircut; bad hair may be embarrassing, but isn't forever.

The nurse's job, by contrast, is high stakes, because nurses hold their patients' health in their hands. Still many of the tasks a nurse performs, such as taking blood pressure or administering

medicine, are relatively routine, and they often are performed at the direction of a doctor. Thus, the nurse's job requires some judgment, but not as much as the job of the doctor giving the instructions.

The doctor, of course, is the one who must constantly make HSJs. The doctor's judgment calls are high stakes not because they affect multitudes of people, like those of a corporate executive, but because many of his or her decisions are a matter of life or death; that's particularly true, for example, of decisions made in the operating room. For that reason, the doctor's compensation is many times higher than the nurse's.[5]

MOVING UP AND OVER

When I think of stylists and nurses, I remember my friend Martha Bray. She has had both of these jobs. I'm bald as a billiard ball now, but Martha used to cut my hair before it all fell out. Martha is an outstanding stylist; she has great judgment when it comes to un-

derstanding her clients' preferences and making them look good. And she always took extra time for me. She was even willing to come in at seven o'clock on the snowy morning I was married to give me a last-minute trim. Because of Martha's personal commitment and good judgment, I was happy to pay her more than the big, low-priced haircutting chains were charging. So were a lot of other people. She built

Henry Eyring with his fiancée, Kelly, when there was still hair for Martha to cut

up a great clientele, eventually bought the salon where she worked, and began to employ other stylists.

In the beginning, styling hair had been Martha's way to pay for college (she got one bachelor's degree in music and started another one in nursing while doing hair). But Martha turned out to be a natural entrepreneur. She had a knack for making high-stakes decisions such as renting space and hiring people; in fact, she enjoyed the challenge. Soon, with her own salon, she was making more money than many college graduates, and she put the nursing degree on hold to work full-time.

However, after several years Martha realized that her real passion was not just for making people look good but for helping them become healthier. That led her back to school to complete her nursing education. She earned not only an RN (registered nurse) degree but continued on to become a nurse practitioner (someone who has a master's degree and can perform some of the functions a doctor does). She worked several years as a hospital nurse while still running her hair salon.

With this nursing education and experience, Martha was ready for her next entrepreneurial move. She sold the studio and created a new

business, a wellness clinic. In this new venture, Martha combines the client service skills she honed as a hairstylist and the medical knowledge she gained in nursing school. She now employs dozens of people dedicated to the health and happiness of hundreds of patients. Her high-stakes judgments are equivalent— both in terms of the good they do for others and the income they generate for her—to those of corporate executives and doctors. By the way, she still cuts the hair of a few favored clients, including my father, who is mostly bald but needs an occasional trim.

Martha's career path illustrates the principle of always increasing your HSJ capabilities. As a hairstylist, she exceeded her competitors in good judgment, serving her clients unusually well. That moved her up relative to other barbers and stylists in the HSJ matrix. Then, as she took the risk of opening her own studio and hiring employees, allowing her to effectively serve many more clients, her decisions became more high stakes; that moved her to the right in the matrix. Now, by earning two nursing degrees and creating a wellness clinic, she has moved into the realm of high-stakes judgements. That's a great example of how you and I can increase our HSJ capabilities throughout our lives.

hsj work that doesn't pay well

Now, if you think about it for very long, you'll realize that some jobs requiring high-stakes judgments don't pay very much. Good teachers, for example, make judgment calls that can turn out to have very high stakes for their students. Parents do the same for their children.

The same thing is true for many important volunteer positions. Consider the case of a school board chairman. In most communities, there is never enough money or political support for the public schools. Some people will never vote to build a new school—not if it means an increase in their taxes. Other people want funds earmarked for their

own school or for their favorite program, such as music or competitive athletics. A good school board chairman builds common ground and sets policies that will affect the welfare of generations of students and teachers, as well as the economic health of the community. But he or she won't be paid for those HSJs. Nor will a host of other volunteers, from soccer coaches to Scoutmasters to Sunday School teachers.

My father has talked about the great spiritual rewards that await people who skillfully serve others in their work without high pay or public recognition: "Your service may not be in what the world would recognize as a lofty calling. **When the real value of service becomes clear in the judgment of God, some people who worked in quiet anonymity will be the real heroes.** Many of them, perhaps most of them, will be the underpaid and under-recognized people who nurtured others. I never visit an elementary school and watch the teachers without thinking about that future day when the rewards will be eternal. I never visit a hospital and watch those who nurse and those who clean without thinking of that. I never visit a workplace where someone serves me and others well, earning wages barely enough to provide the necessities for a family, without thinking of the future. And I never see a mother juggling three little children who are crying while she is smiling, as she shepherds them gently, without seeing in my mind's eye that day of honor in the presence of the only Judge whose praise will matter."[6]

MY MOTHER THE POLITICAL SCIENTIST

Though the market doesn't reward some people who make high-stakes judgments, those people often receive other forms of compensation in this life. **My mother,** for example, **has never reported her HSJ activities to the Internal Revenue Service; none of her six children has ever paid her for the decisions she made that shaped our lives. But her HSJs on our behalf are duly noted and deeply appreciated.** We're grateful not only for her efforts but for her education. She got her degree in political science from the University of California, Berkeley, one year before I was born. She's been practicing an invaluable form of political science—and making HSJs—in our home ever since.

I particularly remember one of Mother's biggest HSJs. My brother and I were in front of the TV one Saturday night around midnight. We were watching a comedy show that had been banned in our home. Over the years, Mother had been more than patient with our excessive TV watching. She drew repeatedly on her training as a political scientist. We had one family council after another. Deals were struck; approved viewing schedules were written up and posted on the refrigerator. But my brothers and I never honored our agreements.

The political battle all came to a head that night. The basement room was dark except for the light from the television. Without warning, Mother walked in. She was wearing a white, flowing nightgown and carrying a pair of shears. Silently, she reached behind the set, grabbed the cord, and gathered it into a loop. Then she inserted the shears and cut the cord with a single stroke. Sparks flew. The set went dead, but not

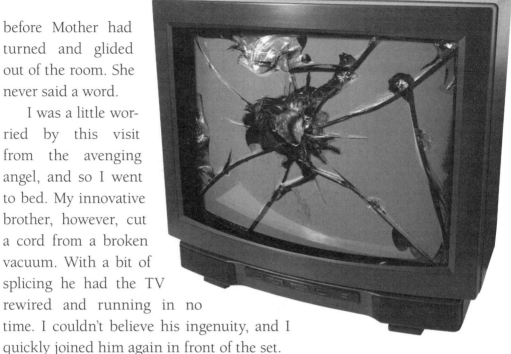

before Mother had turned and glided out of the room. She never said a word.

I was a little worried by this visit from the avenging angel, and so I went to bed. My innovative brother, however, cut a cord from a broken vacuum. With a bit of splicing he had the TV rewired and running in no time. I couldn't believe his ingenuity, and I quickly joined him again in front of the set.

Mother, however, got the last laugh. When we came home from school the next Monday, we found the TV set in the middle of the floor with a crack running the length of the screen. We immediately suspected Mother. When confronted, she responded with a perfectly straight, diplomatic face: "I was dusting under the TV, and it slipped."

To put Mother's claim into perspective, you need to know that TVs were much heavier in those days; this one probably weighed fifty pounds. I've spent a lot of years trying to imagine Mother holding the TV in one hand and dusting under it with the other. Obviously, it was an act of intentional vandalism.

But it was also a carefully calculated HSJ. We only owned that one set. And back then there were no home computers or DVD players. With that TV gone, there was no television watching in our house. For the next twenty years (until the last child left home), the house was a TV-free zone. As a result, my younger siblings grew up reading more books and having more meaningful conversations with Mother and Dad than I did. They were much better prepared for college and all that comes after it, thanks to one whopping HSJ.

My paternal grandmother, Mildred Bennion Eyring, brought similar blessings of education and insight into my father's home. When Grandma met my grandfather, she was a PhD student at the University of Wisconsin. For Grandma, marrying Grandpa meant giving up not only her doctoral studies but also her position as head of women's physical education at the University of Utah. However, my father often speaks of how the dinner table conversation in his home was perfectly balanced, with his mother complementing (and sometimes correcting) his father's ideas about the world. They were well matched both spiritually and intellectually, to the great benefit of their three sons.

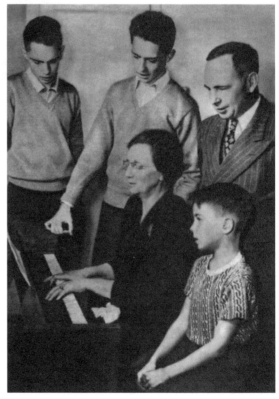

The Eyring family (Ted, Hal, and Henry standing; Mildred and Harden sitting) newly moved to Utah, in 1949

These cases of well-educated mothers illustrate an important principle: Not everyone capable of making high-stakes judgments gets paid a lot.[7] But *all* high-paying jobs require HSJs. And the better you can make high-stakes judgments, the more you'll be worth in *any* job. For example, you may have correctly guessed that the pastry chef we saw a few pages back makes less than the marketing vice president of a restaurant chain; the latter job has higher stakes than the former does. But the pastry chef is also in competition with other pastry chefs. If he wants to protect his job, he'll continually have to find ways to make better pastries that cost less, because that's what his competitors will be trying to do. (Think, for instance, of the inexpensive, high-quality pies and cakes you can now get from large grocery chains.) For the pastry chef, that will mean making high-stakes judgments, trying new recipes, and taking risks just like the marketing VP does. **No matter what kind of job you want**—whether it's in a restaurant executive's office, a pastry kitchen, or a kitchen at home—**you're more likely to perform it well if you know how to make HSJs**. Let's take a look at how to do that.

MAKING HSJs

Making high-stakes judgments requires three things: (1) analysis skills, (2) people skills, and (3) moral sense. To get an idea of what these things mean, suppose that it's 2001 and you are Shigeru Miyamoto, the creator of Mario, Donkey Kong, and dozens of other Nintendo video games. You've just released your Nintendo GameCube, but it's not selling well; PlayStation 2 and Xbox have taken the first and second spots in the game market, and they look unbeatable. If you don't find a Super Mushroom power-up fast, you and Mario are in big trouble.

Analysis Skills

The first thing you have to do is figure out what is happening in the game industry. That will mean carefully studying what Sony and Microsoft are doing better than you are. In addition, you'll need to gather lots of information about what game players want. You must be humble enough to admit your weaknesses, but at the same time not fall prey to faulty arguments and assumptions. If your analysis is very good, you'll recognize something the opposite of what you'd expect—that the answer isn't to imitate Sony and Microsoft's strategies of adding power and features, but to go in an entirely new direction by creating a less expensive console with a revolutionary user interface. You'll see the possibility of making video games interesting not just to testosterone-driven young men, but to girls and older people. You won't be entirely sure about your answer, but **the high quality of your analysis, combined with your good judgment developed over many years of experience, will give you the confidence to proceed.**

People Skills

Even with a good idea of the new product you want to create, you're still a long way from success. As my mentor Mark Fuller, founding chairman of the business consulting firm Monitor Company, says, "The right *analytical answer* is never more than 50 percent of the *solution to the problem*." What Mark means is that figuring out what needs to be done (the analysis part) is only half the battle; the other half is getting other people to join you in the task. High-stakes jobs can rarely be accomplished alone. And **no matter how clearly you think you see the answer, you'll never succeed in leading other people without understanding their abilities and feelings as well as you understand what you want to get done.** You'll need to recognize their strengths and weaknesses, their doubts and fears, their aspirations and ambitions. You'll have to build bridges among people of vastly different skill sets and personalities—for instance, the mechanical engineer who knows accelerometer technology 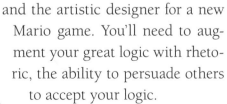 and the artistic designer for a new Mario game. You'll need to augment your great logic with rhetoric, the ability to persuade others to accept your logic.

Moral Sense

In all of your analytical thinking and working with people, there must be an essential, intangible factor: moral sense. This **moral sense is more than just knowing the difference between right and wrong; it is knowing how to get the right thing done in a given situation.** For example, Nintendo has historically been known for having less "mature" content in its video games than its competitors do.[8] But the relative lack of violent and sexually suggestive titles may have contributed to the Nintendo GameCube's failure. For the sake of competing against the better-selling consoles, will you relax this self-imposed policy, at least a little? Can you really afford to be a moral leader in the game industry when investors' money and employees' jobs are at stake?

Consider a similar high-stakes judgment that will require great moral sense. Nintendo, a Japanese family company more than 100 years old, has a tradition of treating its employees well. But now the survival of the company is in question. You can't be sure that the Wii will suc-

ceed, and your investors want to see increased profitability right now. With these future uncertainties and immediate financial pressures, should you temporarily cut salaries and even lay some people off? Isn't it better to play it safe, when you can always bring those workers back if the Wii succeeds?

These questions can't be answered by pure analysis; there's no law or financial calculation that will determine the right answer. Nor, with morally ambivalent characters like Jerome around, can you simply take a poll and follow the opinions of the crowd. HSJs require moral sense, the quality that separates truly great leaders from those who are merely intelligent and persuasive.

high-stakes judgment

ANALYSIS SKILLS   PEOPLE SKILLS   MORAL SENSE

THE NEED FOR A COLLEGE DEGREE

Now you see why the people who can make high-stakes judgments are in such demand: It's not easy to make the triple play of analysis skills, people skills, and moral sense. You might even see that in yourself. "I don't like math," you may say, "I'm a people person." Well, you are to be congratulated, perhaps, on your people skills. But if you're uncomfortable with numbers, your analysis skills will be inherently limited, and you're less likely to succeed in making HSJs. You're also at risk of losing the job you want to someone who has both people *and* analysis skills.

That is why you need to think seriously about attending college and, if possible, getting a graduate degree. High school is designed to provide basic analysis skills—reasoning with words and numbers, learning from history's most important decisions, understanding how science is changing the world. It also enhances (mostly through out-of-class experiences) your people skills and moral sense. You learn, for instance, that talking behind someone's back almost never pays off; gossiping may momentarily increase your popularity, but in the end what goes around comes around, and you end up sorry.

High school, though, doesn't offer much practice in making HSJs. You may study the basics of statistics and psychology, but you're unlikely to be presented with the challenge of interpreting statistical survey data on what video game users want from their console. To be honest, you'll have to look hard for applied problem-solving opportunities in college, too (something we'll discuss in detail later). But college allows you to build on the skills you gained in high school. By focusing on a major area of study, you can develop more of what is required to make HSJs. A psych major, for example, can begin to make sense of that game-user survey data.

College also provides you a potential ticket to graduate school, where HSJs are the focus of study. In an MBA program, for example, you'll spend all day every day making high-stakes decisions based on cases drawn from the business world; the Wii case might be one of them. In medical school you'll get to test your judgment while making rounds with instructors who are treating real patients. Even if you got nothing else from college, the ticket to graduate school would be worth the price of tuition.

But you can get much more than that from college; you can begin to develop the skills for making high-stakes judgments. We'll see how later. In the next chapter, though, we're going to discuss some doubts you may have about whether college is for you.

Answers to HSJ Matrix Exercise

Banking

	LOW STAKES	HIGH STAKES	
JUDGMENT CALL	Loan Officer	Investment Banker	JUDGMENT CALL
STANDARD PROCEDURE	Teller	Local Branch Manager	STANDARD PROCEDURE
	LOW STAKES	HIGH STAKES	

Restaurants

	LOW STAKES	HIGH STAKES	
JUDGMENT CALL	Pastry Chef	Corporate Marketing Vice President	JUDGMENT CALL
STANDARD PROCEDURE	Cashier	Fast Food Franchise Manager	STANDARD PROCEDURE
	LOW STAKES	HIGH STAKES	

Automotive

	LOW STAKES	HIGH STAKES	
JUDGMENT CALL	Custom Auto Builder	New Car Design Team Leader	JUDGMENT CALL
STANDARD PROCEDURE	Oil Change Specialist	Dealership Manager	STANDARD PROCEDURE
	LOW STAKES	HIGH STAKES	

[1] Careers-in-business.com, *Investment Banking: Salaries,* http://www.careers-in-finance.com/ibsal.htm.

[2] The genius behind the Wii has been insightfully analyzed by Michael Olenick in "Nintendo Wii Blue Ocean Strategy—Strategy Canvas," *Blue Ocean Strategy and Technology Businesses,* April 1, 2008, http://www.valueinnovation.net/2008/04/nintendo-wii-blue-ocean-strategy.html.

[3] Michael Olenick, "Create: ≠ Tech Innovation," *Blue Ocean Strategy and Technology Businesses,* February 2, 2008, http://www.valueinnovation.net/2008/02/create-tech-innovation.html.

[4] Warren Buffett and Carol Loomis, "Warren Buffett on the Stock Market," *Fortune,* November 22, 1999, http://money.cnn.com/magazines/fortune/fortune_archive/1999/11/22/269071/index.htm.

[5] The Bureau of Labor Statistics puts average registered nurse compensation at $65,130 (see http://www.bls.gov/oes/current/oes291111.htm); the comparable figure for doctors is $165,000 (see http://www.bls.gov/oes/current/oes291069.htm).

[6] Henry B. Eyring, "Education for Real Life," *Ensign,* October 2002, 19.

[7] There are many reasons why certain jobs that require high-stakes judgments don't pay as much as others. In some cases, it's a matter of supply and demand, or more people wanting a job than there are available positions. That's the case, for instance, for the president of the United States, who makes less than nearly all chief executive officers in the business world; the pay can be low because so many people would like to be president. In other cases, jobs that require high-stakes judgment pay less than others because the quality of the work is hard to measure and reward. That's true of teaching: "Education" is very valuable, but it's hard to demonstrate that one teacher imparts more of it than another.

[8] J. J. McCullough, "Nintendo's Era of Censorship," *Filibuster,* http://www.filibustercartoons.com/Nintendo.php.

CHAPTER FOUR

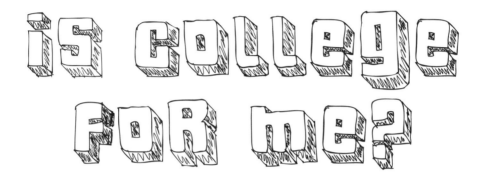

Seek ye out of the best books words of wisdom;
seek learning, even by study and also by faith.
DOCTRINE AND COVENANTS 88:118

 ou may have been dead set on going to college even before reading the preceding chapters about the importance of education. You may already have good grades and test scores and a plan for financing college. If that's you, feel free to skip this chapter and go on to the next one, "Getting Ready."

But even if you're pretty sure that college is a good thing for some people, you may not be convinced that it's the right thing for you. For example, you may be more interested in certifying to become an electrician or a hairstylist. As we've discussed, people in skilled trades like those can find great satisfaction in their work, and they can make pretty good incomes. It may be hard to imagine how a college degree would be worth the cost if that's your preferred career.

In fact, the cost of college is a concern for almost everybody. College is awfully expensive. You and your parents may not have that kind of money. "Even if I can borrow enough," you may think, "do I really want to go that far into debt?"

And what if your high school grades aren't that good? Maybe you didn't finish high school at all. What would it take for you to get into college? Would the kind of college you could get into be worth the investment?

Then there's the question of whether you'd finish. You may have heard that only about half of the people who start college actually get their bachelor's degrees.[1] What are the odds that you'll be one of the successful finishers? If you're not, will your time and money have been wasted?

Those are all good questions. Let's talk through them and try to find some good answers, the kind you'll need to feel confident that college is for you.

IS COLLEGE THE BEST PLACE FOR ME TO LEARN?

Depending on who you are and what you want from life, college may in fact not be for you. The classroom-based approach to learning doesn't appeal to everyone, and many people choose a different route. Some very bright college students drop out to start businesses; Bill Gates, the founder of Microsoft, and Michael Dell of Dell, Inc., the computer company, did that. Other people skip college entirely in favor of skilled trades such as plumbing or dental technology. If you're a high school student interested in pursuing an applied trade or starting your own business, you should explore opportunities in vocational education (also called applied technology training). Those opportunities include technical schools as well as apprenticeships.[2]

But **even if you've got a strong practical bent, don't skip college just because you can't stand the thought of spending more time in the classroom** studying theories with no apparent real-world application. Some people do start businesses straight out of high school, and others do make a good living practicing a skilled trade. However, the average person fares much better financially with a college degree than without one.[3] Higher education almost always increases your earning potential, whatever job you end up taking.

My mother's father, Grandpa Sid Johnson, taught me that. He was a poor Utah farmboy who went to California to seek his fortune after high school. He found a job working on the Golden Gate Bridge during the Great Depression. He saved his money and began to buy land and build apartments in what had once been cherry orchards near San Jose. Those cherry orchards soon became Silicon Valley, and Grandpa Johnson made a fortune. But he knew that without good luck (and heaven's blessing), his hard work wouldn't have been enough. Even though he hadn't followed the higher-education path himself, he recognized and emphasized the value of it to his posterity. Not wanting his children and grandchildren to face the risk and hardships he did, Grandpa helped all of them go to college.

Grandpa knew that a college degree does more than just prepare you for your first job. It also prepares you for the unexpected. Remember that the world will continue to change, the way it did for Doyle the draftsman. Let's suppose, for example, that you dream of being an automotive technician. In fact, you may already be working as one. The pay can be good, especially if you are "factory certified" by a car manufacturer. With that kind of certification you might be able to make as much as or more than a college graduate.

But think about the changes that are likely to affect you in that job. Car engines are becoming more sophisticated. All are now computer controlled. Some car engines are complex hybrids that run on both gasoline and electricity. The engines of the future will have even more computer controls, and before  long they may run on hydrogen instead of gasoline. With this kind of change coming, you'll need to retrain continually. Otherwise, you'll lose your job to someone who may have less experience but is trained and certified in the new technology.

The effects of change could be even worse than that, though. For instance, the car company that certified you could go out of business; that could mean being unemployed until you can certify with another manufacturer. Likewise, new technologies could lead to engines that need less maintenance; that would mean fewer work opportunities for you, just as it has for TV and computer repair technicians. Trained only to work in today's world of automotive technology, you could find yourself fighting the same kind of losing battle with change that Doyle did.

Suppose, on the other hand, that you pursue your dream of automotive technology at a college. **Your experience in college could better prepare you to handle the inevitable changes that the future will bring.** At the right school you could take classes in engine maintenance and repair and even earn credits toward a factory certification. But you could do more than just that. For example, you could study mechanical engineering (ME, for short). In those ME classes you could learn not just how engines work but also the scientific principles behind building engines that work *better*. With that knowledge, you'd see a new engine design from the factory and quickly understand it. Your college education, in other words, would enhance your analysis skills.

You could also take classes in computer technology. That would help you understand the complex computerized cars of today and imagine the more complex ones of the future. You might even take a class in chemistry and another one in physics. If you did that, you'd have a basic understanding of the difference between engines that burn gasoline and those that run on hydrogen. When hydrogen-fueled cars become common, as they are likely to do during your career, you can more easily master the new technology.

In fact, at the community college you could become more than just an automotive technician ready to handle change. You could also prepare to be the technician who runs the shop or maybe even owns it. You might pick up business courses, including one in accounting, that would give you the analytical skills to manage the shop's income and expenses. Courses in writing and communication would enhance your people skills, preparing you to manage employees and negotiate with customers.

Even after doing all of this, you may decide to stay under the hood of the car and pursue your love of automotive technology one engine at a time. But your college degree is still likely to be worth the investment. By increasing your HSJ capabilities, your college experience will make you more valuable under the hood and more secure in the changes that will inevitably take place there.

You may still wonder, though . . .

CAN I AFFORD IT?

College is definitely expensive, and it's getting more so every year. There are costs of all kinds. First, there is the cost of tuition and books. Then, unless you live with your parents (something we'll talk about later), you'll also have to pay for rent and food. You might even need to buy a car.

remember how poor I felt as a college student. I'll never forget an embarrassing incident buying textbooks. The bookstore took only cash, so I stopped at the cash machine just outside and withdrew most of what I had in my account. Inside, I began searching for my textbooks. They were unbelievably expensive, way more than I had expected. By the time I'd put the last book into my basket, I knew I wouldn't be able to afford them all.

I left the books inside and went out to the cash machine for more money. But it still wasn't going to be enough. So I decided that I would put a few of the most expensive books back; I thought maybe I could check them out of the library. (This, in case you're wondering, never works; the library has only one copy, if any, and someone else has already checked it out way before you get the idea.)

I went back and forth across the bookstore, putting some books back on the shelves. It was embarrassing to look so indecisive and so destitute. I hoped that no one would notice.

Unfortunately, someone did. Having watched me shuffling books from my basket to the shelves and going in and out of the store, two undercover floorwalkers identified me as a probable shoplifter. They started to tail me, making sure that one or the other had me under surveillance at all times. When I figured this out, my face went red and I started to sweat. That must have convinced them of my guilt; they began to converge. Luckily, I gave them the slip. I beat them to the checkout stand, turned over my last dime to the cashier, and made my getaway. The irony was that *I* felt like the robbery victim.

It's not just the college-related expenses that set you back. In addition to those out-of-pocket costs for tuition and books and room and board, college also creates something called opportunity costs. An opportunity cost doesn't involve taking money *out* of your pocket, but it can mean not putting it *in*. For example, going to college may require that you quit your job. If that job pays, say, $25,000 a year, you'll be that much poorer than you would be if you didn't quit. If it takes just four years to get your bachelor's degree (which would be fast), your opportunity cost of giving up that job would be $100,000 (less whatever you might make during summer internships as a result of your college experience). The total of your out-of-pocket and opportunity costs could run into hundreds of thousands of dollars.

"Ouch!" you say. "Why would anybody do that?" But wait a minute. Before you decide college is a bad deal, let's think about what college is worth. Suppose that, after graduating, you were able to get a job paying $50,000 (a reasonable hope, depending on your major).[4] That is $25,000 more than you were making before. And you'll enjoy that salary differential and maybe even more, thanks to the power of your degree, for your whole career; let's say it's forty years. In that case, the total benefit of your college degree would be at least a million dollars. You have to account for your tuition

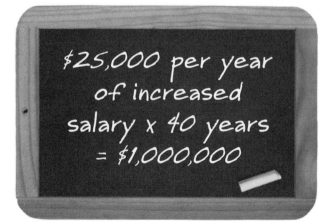

$25,000 per year
of increased
salary x 40 years
= $1,000,000

and other school-related costs and something called the "time value of money," which means that the million dollars is worth less because it comes later than the money you lost when you gave up your $25,000 job to attend college. But even when you factor those things in, you still come out way ahead financially. You also will likely enjoy a career that is more secure and more intellectually rewarding, because your education will qualify you to make more high-stakes judgments.

There's still the challenge, though, of coming up with the money. Unless your parents are wealthy, you'll probably have to borrow.[5] The good news is that government and private bank loans are more available than ever before. And you may also qualify for government "grants" (money you don't have to give back); the Pell grant is the most common.[6]

Take care in your borrowing. You'll be tempted to borrow too much and spend it on the wrong things. Some of your friends, for instance, will use their education loans to buy cell phones and even cars. In addition to avoiding this kind of irresponsible spending, you'll want to look hard at the cost of the college you're attending. In Chapter 6, "Choosing a School," we'll talk about getting your money's worth for your tuition. You'll find that some colleges are much less expensive than others and still provide good HSJ fundamentals.

CAN I GET IN?

Even if you can afford it, you may not consider yourself college material. You might have barely graduated from high school. Perhaps you got a low score on the SAT or ACT (the standardized tests required for admission by many colleges). Maybe you don't even have a high school diploma.

But don't give up just yet. If you're still reading this book, you must be smarter and more diligent than the average bear. And remember that almost nobody is at their best in high school. The social distractions alone are enough to explain a lot of your high school troubles. On top of that, your HSJ skills were underdeveloped back then. In fact, researchers have discovered that your brain was literally still getting its act together in high school. Certain parts of it, especially the ones needed to make complex decisions, weren't all there yet. When your parents asked you, "What were you thinking?" and you said, "Nothing," you were actually telling the truth.

That happened to me in my junior year of high school. As I mentioned earlier, I got my driver's license and drove off a cliff, academically speaking. I also got thrown on my head (literally). One day before a swimming workout, my friend Matt and I decided to gang up on our coach. In our two-on-one wrestling match, I got dumped on my head. I lost twenty-four hours' worth of memory. My dad joked (at least I hope it was a joke) that I also lost ten IQ points. In any case, it was a bad year for my brain. It took me all of senior year to put things back together. But I've overcome high school, and you can too. It is our nature as children of Heavenly Father to learn not just when we're young, but throughout our lives and into eternity. **Your best learning is still ahead of you.**

Poor Grades and Test Scores

Let's suppose that your high school transcript isn't exactly suitable for framing. That's not as disastrous as you might think. Many colleges have "open enrollment" policies, meaning that they'll take anyone with a high school diploma. At the beginning you may want to invest in remedial courses in essential subjects such as math and English; in other words, before taking the introductory college course, you could take one that covers the basics that you didn't get in high school. This could cost you a bit in time-to-graduation. However, the price may be well worth paying, as you'll lay a strong foundation that will continue to serve you well throughout your time in college.

You also shouldn't write yourself off on the basis of that low SAT or ACT score. As a university administrator, I've looked at the link between low test scores and college grades. From what I've seen, **hardworking students, especially those who are a little**

The good news is that once you're in college your high school transcript is irrelevant. With a college diploma in hand, you won't likely be asked by an employer what your high school GPA was. College allows you to turn over a new leaf.

older and more mature, can perform well in college in spite of low test scores. You could be one of those students.

After taking the entrance test once you might decide to take it again. That may be a good idea, especially if you didn't study for it the first time. A higher score could increase your self-confidence; it could even qualify you for scholarship money. And raising your score is a real possibility. In spite of the SAT and ACT often being called aptitude tests (meaning measures of your inherent capabilities), careful preparation can produce a higher score.[7] There's great benefit, for instance, in simply being familiar with the format of the test. If you're more comfortable with what the test is asking you to do, you'll think more clearly. Taking practice tests can increase your comfort level. You may be surprised at how much that advance preparation can improve your score.

No High School Diploma

If you didn't finish high school, you've probably heard of the GED (short for General Equivalency Diploma). The GED is a test that substitutes for a high school diploma. It was created during World War II for war veterans who hadn't completed high school but wanted to go to college. Today, the GED also helps students who were home schooled, as well as immigrants and students who started high school but didn't finish.

If you're in the last category, don't consider yourself a high school dropout. Instead, think of yourself as a veteran. **The things you have learned in the battles of life are going to make you a better college student.** And getting a GED isn't too difficult. More than 15 million people have received a GED. One of every seven high school graduates got their degree that way; so did one in every twenty college students.[8]

The GED is a test with five parts that, in most places, is administered over two days. You can find a free or very low-cost preparation program in whatever state you live in. There are practice tests, and the test itself can be retaken if you fail. The time you put into preparing for the GED will pay off not only when you take the test but later in college as well, because it will enhance your basic analysis skills.

CAN I FINISH?

You may be thinking, "If I have to work that hard just to get in, what are the odds that I'll actually finish? Half the people I know who started college didn't get their degree. Will I be able to make it to graduation?"

The good news is that you don't have to answer that question now. Just start. Ease in if you need to. You can take a light load the first semester, focusing on refresher courses in math and English and basic science. You might also take a class or two just for fun. Have faith in your ability to become a better student than you were in high school.

If you run into academic trouble, as many new college students do, you can seek special help. Most schools provide some kind of tutoring, and many schools offer courses on study skills and time management.

If you make the most of these resources, your study skills will improve. As that happens, you're likely to discover fields that you like. You don't have to graduate at the top of your college class; just do your very best. The things you learn and the power of the degree itself will open doors to good jobs and HSJ opportunities.

Even if you don't finish all four years, you'll still benefit from the effort. You might be able to get a two-year associate's degree. But even if you decide to leave college after just a semester or two, the things you learn will increase your potential to make high-stakes judgments in whatever career you pursue.

a Success Story From harlem

One of my friends, Sandra, has shown how a dedicated student can overcome almost any obstacle and get a college degree. Sandra's mother, who brought her family to the United States from the Dominican Republic, had no formal education. Very few young people from Sandra's Harlem neighborhood were going to college. As a junior in high school, Sandra didn't think she was the "college type."

Fortunately, Sandra found a student mentoring program at church. Her mentor, a Manhattan attorney, not only helped her with her school assignments and study habits but also encouraged her to prepare for college. Knowing of Sandra's concerns, the mentor arranged for her to meet other Dominican students who were home from college. Sandra decided to go for it. She applied to two schools, one of which admitted her. She chose public relations (PR) as her major.

The first semester was tough. The college had few Dominican students, and Sandra didn't make many friends. She also struggled in class; after midterm exams she knew she was in trouble. Then, in a phone conversation, her mentor from home encouraged her: "Take responsibility for yourself, and get help." Sandra did both. She set regular study hours, as if going to school were a real job. And she went often to the college tutoring center. With personal discipline and tutoring help, her natural analytical abilities showed through; she began to realize that her "street smarts," developed when she was learning English in the New York City public schools and working part-time jobs, were in fact valuable analysis skills. Her grades began to rise.

With her academic life under control, Sandra started to reach out socially. She joined a student organization that planned cultural events on campus. Almost immediately, she had a new group of friends and many opportunities to apply and enhance her people skills. In fact, Sandra discovered that working with people was one of her great gifts.

I saw that the first time she came to my home for a potluck dinner with a dozen fellow students. Having lived in so many different cultures, Sandra appreciates others' unique interests and can find common ground with almost anyone; that makes her a great conversationalist. She is also thoughtful of people's needs. When the party was over she asked my wife, Kelly, what she could do in the kitchen. Kelly said, "I'm fine; just take home whatever you brought." Sandra replied cheerfully, "I brought hands to help. My mother taught me that."

Later in her college career Sandra joined another volunteer group, one that mentored students who were struggling. That provided opportunities to apply sympathy and charity—essential aspects of moral sense that she had learned from being mentored by others. Before graduating, she went back to New York for a public relations internship. During that time, she helped young high school students—the kind she had been just five years earlier—get excited about higher education. Sandra not only made it through college herself, she set others on the same path. Along the way, she discovered that growing up in Harlem had given her many of the HSJ skills needed for success in life at college and beyond.

HSJs ON THE FARM

I saw another great example of determination and success in a man named Craig Moor, a friend and mentor who was also my first boss. Craig started college in 1933, at the bottom of the Great Depression. His family couldn't afford to keep him in school, so he dropped out without getting his degree. He spent the next four and a half decades on the family dry farm in rural Idaho.

It was a hard way to make a living. A dry farm has no irrigation system; you try to plant the right crop at the right time, and then you pray that it rains. Any number of uncontrollable forces, from drought to hail to low market prices, can ruin your year. In a very good summer, when the weather is just right and the price of grain is high, you can make money, hopefully enough to cover the lean years. Through it all, you have to manage your expenses and save what you make as though your life depended on it. Craig's modest college education, along with common sense learned through years of hard experience, gave him a much needed advantage in this high-risk business.

When I was ten years old, my dad asked Craig if I could help him on his farm. I was very lucky that he said yes. I loved the work. Every summer morning, Monday through Saturday, Craig pulled his old pickup to the curb of our house and honked the horn. I would run out and hop inside the truck. As he pulled away he would ask, "What's the good word?" At this cue, I was supposed to respond, "Save your money."

Training me to recite that slogan was just one of the ways that Craig taught me the risky economics of farming. We always listened to the daily crop report on the radio. Craig helped me to compare grain prices with our costs for seed and diesel fuel, to forecast whether we would make or lose money. At that time, I thought it was just common sense; in the years since, I've learned that Craig was developing my analysis skills.

Craig also taught me people skills. He rarely lost his cool, and he never scolded anyone for an honest mistake. If a green farmhand mistook a water can for a gas can, there was no lecture, just a lesson in siphoning water back out of the gas tank.

In the beginning I did simple tasks like tightening bolts on machinery. Craig taught me to give even these small chores everything I had. When I thought a bolt was tight enough, he would say, "Give it one more turn, for good measure." He was sharing with me his moral sense; I noticed that he gave good measure in all of his business dealings, always making good—and then some—on his promises.

During my second summer, Craig trained me to drive his big eight-wheel tractor by myself. He showed me how to start a turn early, so that the plow swinging wide behind the tractor wouldn't tear into rocks and trees on the edge of the field. "Always leave enough room for the turns," he would say. I learned this lesson the hard way, occasionally taking down an aspen. It was an early exposure to HSJs.

FIFTY YEARS TO GRADUATION

In the early 1980s, when farmers all across the country were losing their farms to mortgage foreclosures, Craig lost most of his acreage too. By then I had moved away. Craig had been struggling to operate the farm alone, and the foreclosure was the last straw. He had to retire from farming.

But he didn't stop working. At age sixty-six, he went back to college. The nearly fifty-year educational layoff was hard to come back from. He needed lots of special help from the tutoring center, just like Sandra, and even with that his grades weren't great. It took him several years to

Craig Moor, college graduate

finish. He certainly wasn't class valedictorian. But he graduated, and the local newspaper carried the story.

Whether you are young or old, from the inner city or a rural farm, your life's experiences have prepared you more than you may realize. Life has given you important HSJ skills. Even if you're not a classroom standout, you've learned the street smarts and common sense that are the foundation of analysis skills. You have learned respect for others and how to have "helping hands," the key to great people skills. You also have acquired the moral sense to give "good measure" and the judgment to leave room for life's "turns." Just like the experienced veterans for whom the GED was invented, you may be ready to get on the path leading to college and high-stakes judgments.

---

[1]Actually, the national graduation rate is much lower than 50 percent for students seeking associate's degrees, according to data published by The National Center for Higher Education Management Systems in 2009. (see http://www.higheredinfo .org/dbrowser/index.php?level=nation&mode=graph&state=0&submeasure=24). The graduation rate is higher than 50 percent for bachelor's candidates (see http://www.higheredinfo.org/dbrowser/?level=nation&mode=graph&state=0&sub measure=27), but varies substantially according to the selectivity of the institution, as demonstrated by Frederick H. Hess, et al., *Which Colleges Actually Graduate Their Students (and Which Don't),* American Enterprise Institute, June 2009, http://www .aei.org/docLib/Diplomas%20and%20Dropouts%20final.pdf.

[2]You can find many technical schools on the Internet. For an overview of apprenticeships, go to http://www.doleta.gov/OA/.

[3]The Census Bureau reports that an associate's degree increases annual earnings over a high school diploma by nearly $8,000 and a bachelor's degree by more than $25,000. See U.S. Census Bureau, *Current Population Survey, 2008 Annual Social and Economic Supplement,* PINC-03 (Education Attainment—People 25 Years Old and Over, by Total Money Earnings in 2007, Work Experience in 2007, Age, Race, Hispanic Origin, and Sex), http://www.census.gov/hhes/www/macro/032008/perinc/ new03_001.htm.

[4]The National Associate of Colleges and Employers puts the average starting salary for bachelor's graduates at $48, 515 (see http://www.naceweb.org/press/display.asp?year=2009&prid=300).

[5]About 60 percent of college students borrow money for school (College Board, *Trends in Student Aid 2008,* 11, http:// professionals.collegeboard.com/data-reports-research/trends/student-aid-2006).

[6]For information on Pell grants, follow this link to the U.S. Department of Education's Web site: http://www.ed.gov/programs/ fpg/index.html.

[7]Derek C. Briggs, "Evaluating SAT Coaching: Gains, Effects and Self-Selection," in *Rethinking the SAT: The Future of Standardized Testing in University Admissions,* ed. Rebecca Zwick (Routledge, 2004), 222.

[8]For more on the GED, see http://en.wikipedia.org/wiki/GED.

CHAPTER FIVE

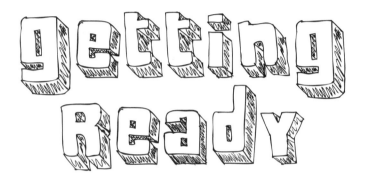

Be ready to every good work.

TITUS 3:1

reparing early for college can give you great advantages when you get there. Ironically, though, some of the high school students who have spent the most time "getting ready" may have been emphasizing the wrong things.

Take Advanced Placement (AP),[1] for example. AP courses can provide tremendous learning experiences. They attract some of the most intelligent and hardworking students. They also tend to be taught by outstanding teachers. That was true of my AP European history and English classes. Andy Odoardi and Donna Parker brought those subjects to life for me and my friends. Fortunately, they were also patient with my juvenile distractedness.

Mr. Odoardi had the misfortune to encounter me during my junior year. I was genuinely interested in European history. But I was also a junior class officer on a teenage power trip. Citing the duties of my elected office, I obtained my own book

EXCUSED ABSENCE

TEACHER _____

DATE _____

NAME _____

CLASS _____
_____
_____

MESSAGE _____
_____
_____

of pink "excused absence" slips. I began to make a habit of excusing myself from AP European history.

On the Friday afternoon before Memorial Day weekend, Mr. Odoardi stopped me in the hallway with the news that I would fail his class due to excessive absences. It made for a pretty bad holiday weekend; I spent three days feeling like a condemned man looking for any possible escape.

The following Tuesday I begged Mr. Odoardi to let me retake the course the next year. Not surprisingly, he wasn't keen on letting me back into class. But he offered a deal: I would spend the year studying on my own, writing a set of essays and preparing for the AP exam. My grade on the exam would be my grade for the course. I gratefully took the deal. **Thanks to my teacher's generosity, I got the chance not just to learn what I'd missed about European history but also to learn how to "make things right."** It was a powerful lesson in people skills and moral sense.

Donna Parker helped me learn a similar lesson in the spring of senior year. I loved her AP English class, and by then my brain was gelling a bit. But there were still "What-were-you-thinking?" moments. One of those occurred on a morning a few weeks before the AP exam. Mrs. Parker gave us a poem to analyze, as practice for the exam. The poem was about flowers blooming in the spring, a pretty obvious metaphor for birth and rebirth.

I can't explain what happened next. In a moment of apparent mental breakdown, I decided to write a rant about the poem, its author, and poetry in general. Of course, it was only a matter of hours before I began to feel not only foolish but also guilty for having indirectly attacked Mrs.

Parker. It didn't surprise me to come to class the next day and find that I'd gotten a bad grade on my paper. I was surprised, though, to find that the grade was a C, rather than a D or an F. And I was dumbfounded by what Mrs. Parker said when I went up and apologized to her after class. "That's all right," she replied. "Everyone's entitled to a tantrum once in a while." On that day and many others, she taught with a degree of understanding and kindness that I didn't deserve. That's one of the highest of people skills.

With teachers like Andy Odoardi and Donna Parker, I couldn't be a bigger fan of AP courses. There are few high school classes in which you can learn so much, especially about yourself. That, though, is the way to view AP: as a great learning experience. The temptation is to focus on two other perceived benefits. One is the potential to impress a college admissions committee. The other is shaving time off the four years required to graduate with a bachelor's degree.

A STRONG FOUNDATION

There's something to be said for both of these objectives. However, it will help you to view them from the perspective of your future college professors. They have built your major (the subject in which you'll specialize as you get a bachelor's degree) with the assumption that you'll take the college's foundational courses in subjects such as English and math and science. These courses are designed to a known level of quality, which is high enough to ensure that you'll start your major well prepared. Your professors won't have to stop and teach you things that should have been covered already.

Consider an AP course in this light. The AP course is the creation of a gifted high school teacher. But it hasn't been designed with an understanding of the specific college courses for which it will serve as a foundation. And it hasn't been taught to a known level of quality. Thus, to a college curriculum committee, it represents a threat to the integrity of the major. Quite possibly, having the AP course accepted as a substitute for its college equivalent will mean that the AP student will perform poorly in subsequent courses and have to be helped along. **Many curriculum committees will** therefore **discourage students from substituting AP credit for required courses. They may even prohibit it.** All of this is likely to come as a surprise to the enterprising student who loaded up on AP courses in high school, thinking that it would be a time-saver and even a badge of distinction in college. More likely, those AP courses will be viewed by your professors with some concern, particularly if you scored less than a five on the test.

I wonder what I could have learned if I hadn't used good AP scores

I'm glad, in hindsight, that I got a two on the AP Calculus test. (Now you're really thinking about selling this book, aren't you?) That failing score meant I had no choice but to retake calculus as a college freshman. I was scared to death; the class was full of people who looked old enough to be my aunts and uncles. But I studied like a maniac, and I got an A. In fact, I really mastered basic calculus. Math became a strong subject for me, not only as I pursued a bachelor's degree in geology but also later in my MBA program.

in English and European history to skip those courses in college. I was probably okay because my scores on those tests were high; I really knew those subjects. But if you get just a three on an AP test, be careful about using it to skip the equivalent college course.

Now, after all of that explanation of why college faculty members might not like AP, you should know that a college admissions committee may favor students with lots of AP experience. Their first responsibility, after all, is to recruit the brightest and most capable students, and a high school transcript heavy on AP can be a good indicator of both intelligence and capability. However, you have to be careful here, too—a low grade in an AP course could do more harm than good in the admissions process. And, in any case, you shouldn't select courses based on whether they'll get you into an elite college. **You should take the courses in which you, given your unique interests and skill level, can learn the most.**

The bottom line, then, with AP is this: Take an AP course if it offers the best learning experience. Don't do it to impress anybody or to get a jump on graduation. And don't do it unless you think you can perform well in the class.

The same thing is true of concurrent enrollment courses, classes you take in high school that are sponsored by a particular college. These courses have the advantage over AP of the *guarantee* of being accepted by the sponsoring college. However, the same AP concern applies; you should ask yourself whether the concurrent enrollment course is as good as the one offered at college. Remember, you won't be saving time by taking a course that doesn't provide the right foundation for the courses to come. There are better ways to graduate quickly from college than trying to get a head start in high school.

VOCATIONAL EDUCATION: SMARTER THAN YOU THINK

If AP is for the college-bound kids, then vocational education (we called it "Vo-Ed" at my high school) is just for the ones who want to go work straight out of school, right? That's what I thought. I would have been totally embarrassed to take a class in something like business or accounting.

bit of Vo-Ed exposure could have saved me some *real* embarrassment in my first professional job. When business schools at Harvard and Stanford denied me, I was fortunate to win admission to a combined MBA and JD (law) program at Brigham Young University. After the first year, spent in law school, I got a summer job with a private law firm. One day the partner I worked for sent me to the federal court building on a reconnaissance mission: I was supposed to review the monthly financial statements filed with the court by a fellow in bankruptcy. Our client was trying to collect a big sum of money from him, and we suspected that he had declared bankruptcy not because he was really broke but to avoid paying up. My task was to see what he might be hiding.

At the courthouse I paged through the fellow's monthly statements of assets (the stuff he owned, such as his house and furnishings and cash) and liabilities (the debts he owed). Almost immediately, my keen eye spotted something fishy. Every month, the assets and liabilities (plus something called "net worth") changed. But the assets

I HAVE SOLV-ED THE CASE: THE ASSETS ALWAYS EQUAL LIABILITIES PLUS NET WORTH!

and the combination of liabilities and net worth *always changed by the same amount! Right down to the penny!* I had found the smoking gun, the evidence of a massive fraudulent conspiracy. I immediately returned to the law office and reported my brilliant discovery.

Now, if you know anything at all about accounting, you're already laughing. The most fundamental accounting rule is this: "Assets must equal liabilities plus net worth." It's true *by definition*. In terms of being obvious, it's right up there with two plus two equals four. There was no fraud in the bankruptcy filings, just the basic law of accounting at work. I hadn't revealed anything except my own ignorance. It's a tribute to my boss that he didn't hear my report and laugh out loud. He just said, "That's very interesting." I had no idea how foolish I'd been until that fall, when I started the MBA program and took my first accounting class.

The amazing thing about my "it's-not-worthy" attitude toward high school Vo-Ed classes is that I already knew I wanted to go to business school; I knew that I'd have to take accounting someday. But for some reason I was embarrassed to study the subject in high school. It's true that, given the other courses required to get into college, I couldn't have taken more than a few Vo-Ed classes. But those classes might have been invaluable in at least two ways.

First, I could have begun thinking about the principles of business  and accounting at a much younger age. Warren Buffett, one of the world's most successful investors and generous philanthropists, started doing business deals when he was in elementary school.[2] I had a similar interest in business at that age, but focused it all on the formal education process, on the academic subjects I would need to study to get into an Ivy League MBA program. That's not the main reason that Warren Buffett is immeasurably wealthier than I am. But **I could have been a much better business student in graduate school if I'd taken time to understand the basics of business in high school.** As I studied English and history—or bought hamburgers and concert tickets after school—I could have been aware of the influence of the market and business that I now recognize in all of those things.

A second benefit of exposure to vocations in high school is that you can learn what you *don't* like. It would be a shame, for instance, to decide as a teenager that you want to practice medicine based only on what you've seen on TV or because you like the cars that the doctors in your neighborhood drive. If you can't stand the sight of blood, or if you can't tolerate people complaining about pain, it's good to find that out before your second year of medical school. A high school medical technology course, one that would let you dissect a frog or observe a real ER, could tell you in a hurry that you're not cut out to be a doctor. Or it could confirm your attraction to medicine and put you on the fast track to becoming a physician. So remember: Vo-Ed may or may not be cool, but a little Vo-Ed can go a long way in preparing you for college—and for life.

FOCUS ON THE FUNDAMENTAL SKILLS

Just as you can think in high school about the kind of job you might like doing, you can also be thinking about HSJs. You recall that the three things needed to make HSJs are analysis skills, people skills, and moral sense. You can work on all of those in high school. Let's see how.

Analysis Skills

Your high school courses provide good opportunities to build analysis skills. **Make the most of English and math especially. These two subjects are essential to understanding all other fields of knowledge**, and mastering them will be a blessing both in your professional work and in teaching your children.

Try to see the deeper power of the words and numbers. Math, for example, is an essential tool for sizing things up. In making HSJs you'll always be asking questions such as, "How much is this thing really worth?" or "What is the risk of that happening?" Numbers will help you to answer those questions with precision. You don't have to know advanced calculus or Einstein's theory of relativity. But, to consistently make good HSJs, you must feel comfortable talking and thinking in the language of numbers. You'll know you're there when you naturally start running simple calculations in your head, like Grandpa did when he was explaining why you can't make a living shoveling coal.

Here's a practical tip for learning to feel comfortable with math: Don't move to the next level until you've mastered the one you're on. That was part of my problem with AP calculus, which I took in my senior year of high school. Among the many courses in which I earned bad grades the year before was college algebra. Without a solid foundation in algebra, I was a sitting duck when it came to calculus; even if I'd studied calculus as intensely as a high school senior as I did the following year in college, I'd have performed below my ultimate ability level. Rather than taking AP calculus without the necessary foundation in algebra, I'd have been better off enrolling in a less difficult math class or even retaking college algebra. Math builds on itself, and so you have to make the foundation solid as you go, even if that means going slower. Remember, the fast track isn't fast if you arrive at

the end of the line unprepared.

Skill with words is equally important in making HSJs. Warren Buffett, for example, is of course good at reading an income statement, the numerical summary of a company's profitability. But he is also a brilliant writer. People who don't even own stock in his company, Berkshire Hathaway, look forward to reading the annual letter he writes to his stockholders. (You can find these by searching the Internet for "Berkshire Hathaway shareholder letters.") Part of the reason that people like to read these letters is that he's very funny. His annual letter often includes jokes and sometimes even favorite chili recipes. But Warren Buffett's writing is also just plain fun to read. His sentences are simple and clear; it's easy to see his logic. Writing with that kind of clarity requires clear thinking. **If you can write effectively, you will also think effectively.**

I noticed that as I observed my classmates from business school and law school. At law school, of course, all of the top students were good writers, because law school requires reading and writing from dawn to dusk. However, some of the sharpest mathematicians—the "quant jocks"—in business school couldn't express themselves nearly as well in writing as they could in numbers. That limited their performance, both in school and later in the workplace. The most effective business executives are, like Warren Buffett, good writers.

One way to become a good writer is to read good writing. Hemingway was a high school favorite of mine; his short, declarative sentences get right to the point. Another way to improve your writing is to do it a lot. I enjoy writing in my personal journal; it forces me to think clearly about what really went on during the day.

That's something else you can do in high school—try to see the deeper meaning behind the facts and figures you learn in history or the stories you read in literature. For instance, you're very likely to study Harry Truman's decision to drop two atomic bombs on Japan. Your teacher and even your textbook may describe this decision in simple, one-sided terms. But you can go deeper. With a few mouse clicks, you can find a multitude of additional perspectives and facts. And, with a bit of imagination, you can put yourself in Truman's shoes, trying to see the world the way he did, based on the information he had. You can join Truman in thinking about his HSJ, one of the most complex and difficult in history.

People Skills

Especially if you're itching to get to college, high school can be so … well, *high school*. The superficiality and social competition is completely over the top. With all of the game playing, it's natural to want to just find a group of like-minded friends and spend all your time with them. You may feel inclined to take the same classes together and participate in the same extracurricular activities. Being around them will help you feel comfortable during these uncomfortable high school years. Beware, though: You could be setting a lifelong trend. Particularly as you get more education, the temptation will always be to hang out with people who think like you do.

There are several big problems with that, from an HSJ standpoint. One is that the constant reinforcement of your worldview, the way you look at things, can seriously limit your analytical ability. **One of the most important analysis skills is spotting your own biases when sizing up a situation. You have to be able to look at things from many perspectives, especially the ones that run counter to your natural viewpoint.** Otherwise, you

risk being blindsided, as Sony and Microsoft seem to have been by the Wii. Always hanging with a crowd that shares your views can set you up for nasty surprises.

The other problem with limiting your circle of friends is that it will limit your ability to lead. Most of us are, by definition, average. The average person is thoughtful, but not a genius; eager to do well, but often not ready to do whatever it takes to succeed. Nearly all organizations are full of such people. Therefore, if you want to lead, you have to be able to work with ordinary folk. That means not only appreciating viewpoints different from your own but also leading some people who may not match your level of intelligence or enthusiasm.

I learned that lesson from Mark Fuller, of the business consulting firm Monitor Company. Mark taught me to be careful of falling into a trap that often catches well-educated business consultants. Much of the advice that consultants give isn't taken by their clients, even though the clients pay lots of money for it. When that happens, the consultants are tempted to say, "We gave the clients the right advice, but *they didn't get it.*"

Even if it's true that the consultants gave the clients the right advice, the excuse, "They didn't get it," misses the point. It's like a trapeze artist saying, "I delivered the bar at the right time, but my partner wasn't there to catch it." The fact is that a consultant is paid not only to give the right advice but to give the advice in such a way that the clients "get it." Especially as you pursue more education than the average person has, you have to be careful to stay in touch with people to whom you may not naturally be attracted. You can set that pattern in high school by taking a genuine interest in students who aren't part of your clique. In the process, you'll lay the foundation for great people skills—and you'll be appreciated as a true friend.

Grandpa Eyring had that gift: Almost everybody liked him. That was true in part because he respected every person he met for what that person knew. My dad often tells how, when he was a kid, Grandpa would embarrass him at the gas station. Back in those days, you didn't pump your own gas; there was an attendant who did it for you. (This is another one of those jobs that hardly exists anymore, thanks to smart machines.) Pumping gas, of course, didn't require any formal

My daughter Sarah, a high school student, has a wide circle of friends. When she throws a party at our house, all the kids at her school consider themselves invited. Sarah has learned to see the world through the eyes of very different people. They appreciate her for that, and she has great influence with her many friends. Even without the benefit of college education she has honed her people skills, just as you can.

education. But Grandpa would always get out of the car and start asking the attendant questions while he pumped. Dad, then a teenager, couldn't believe that his PhD father would value the insights of a fellow who might not have had even a high school degree. When the gas tank was full and they were on their way again, Grandpa explained, "I never met anyone I couldn't learn something from."

Moral Sense

Along with analytical and people skills, high school is also the time to start developing moral sense. That's true in part because it's in your high school courses that you'll first start to look hard at moral dilemmas. You might ask, for instance, "Was it right to use atomic weapons against Japan?" But high school is also fertile ground for developing moral sense because it is so full of contradictions. The kids with wealthy parents may drive expensive cars they won't be able to afford when they grow up. The popular kids may be admired by everyone while being kind to almost no one. The smart kids may be able to get good grades without studying hard. The star athletes may be able to smoke and drink and still win.

The apparent contradictions of high school don't end there; they continue on through college and graduate school and into the professional world and the home you'll create for your family. But, over time, certain truths become apparent. You learn, for example, that there's no substitute for hard work and that it's wise to keep the golden rule, treating others the way you want to be treated. You learn that things aren't always as they appear, especially when it comes to the houses people buy and the cars they drive. You learn to distinguish right from wrong by firsthand, and usually painful, experience.

You can get a jump on that learning process, and thus begin to prepare for making HSJs, by becoming aware of your moral decisions in high school. Step back and take a hard look at the way you and your classmates are behaving. Will it pay in the long run? If not, what needs to change?

eorge Washington worked on developing his moral sense when he was high school aged. As a writing assignment, he copied down 110 "Rules of Civility and Decent Behaviour in Company and Conversation."[3] He faithfully observed those rules throughout his life. Most of the rules are about treating others well, even when they don't deserve it. Think of how much more pleasant high school—and life in general—would be if everyone honored these principles:

"Show not yourself glad at the misfortunes of another though he were your enemy."

"In reproving show no sign of cholar [anger] but do it with sweetness and mildness."

"Speak not evil of the absent for it is unjust."

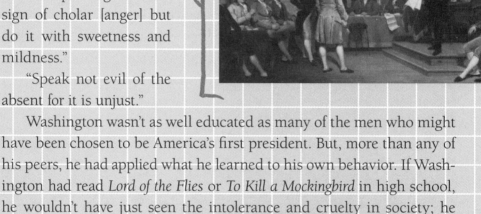

Washington wasn't as well educated as many of the men who might have been chosen to be America's first president. But, more than any of his peers, he had applied what he learned to his own behavior. If Washington had read *Lord of the Flies* or *To Kill a Mockingbird* in high school, he wouldn't have just seen the intolerance and cruelty in society; he would have seen it and systematically eliminated it *in himself*. That's why his countrymen, even those who were better educated, wanted him as president. Like Washington, you'll be ahead of the game if you start developing moral sense in high school.

So, there's your plan for preparing for college. Take classes that you can learn a lot in, whether they're AP or Vo-Ed or anything else that is well taught and stimulates your thinking; don't worry about appearances. And, in all of your high school activities, keep in mind analysis skills, people skills, and moral sense; you can acquire plenty of HSJ skills even before you earn your high school diploma.

With that preparation plan in place, you're ready to take the next step toward college—choosing the school you're going to attend.

[1] At your school the name for these courses may be IB, or International Baccalaureate.
[2] Alice Schroeder, *The Snowball: Warren Buffett and the Business of Life* (Bantam, 2008), 59.
[3] The Papers of George Washington, *Washington's Copy of Rules of Civility & Decent Behaviour in Company and Conversation*, http://gwpapers.virginia.edu/documents/civility/transcript.html.

choosing a school

I will lead them in paths that they have not known:
I will make darkness light before them, and crooked things straight.

ISAIAH 42:16

hoosing which college or university to attend is one of the most difficult decisions you'll make at this stage of your life. The good news is that you can get divine guidance in the process, because where you go to college really matters. You'll meet people and learn things unique to that particular place. So Heaven really cares about the decision and will help you make it.

That said, this is definitely one of those decisions that requires study before seeking a spiritual confirmation. You need to gather as much information as you can, and you need to think clearly. In particular, you must distinguish the good reasons for choosing a school from the not-so-good ones. Because some of those not-so-good reasons are often given too much weight, let's start with a look at one of them.

THE BIG GAME

On New Year's Day 2007 the Boise State University Broncos pulled off one of the biggest upsets in college football history. Using wacky trick plays and an overtime period, Boise State beat the heavily favored Oklahoma University Sooners by one point in the Fiesta Bowl. The game ended with a dramatic "Statue of Liberty" play, a risky gamble that, had it failed, would have meant an Oklahoma victory.

It was definitely an exciting football game and a tribute to the Boise State players and coaches. But some people apparently saw more than luck or even football skill in the victory. In the weeks immediately after the game, requests for applications to Boise State's graduate programs increased by 1000 percent (ten times).[1]

Of course, the outcome of one football game is a poor reason for choosing a college to attend. In fact, unless you're a football player, you shouldn't be thinking much about football at all as you make decisions about college. Yet many college students choose their schools for reasons not directly tied to education. Some just want to go where their friends are going. Others are interested in staying close to home (or getting far away from it). And yes, even last year's football record is a determining factor for some.

Prospective college students often fall back on such reasons because it's hard to judge the quality of one school versus another. There is no higher-education equivalent of *Consumer Reports,* in which

products are tested side by side. In fact, it's hard to measure the thing you *really* want to get from college, which is the ability to make high-stakes judgments. The difficulty of measuring HSJ skills means that it's hard to assess which college provides the best education. So, many students rely on the things they *can* measure, such as where most of their friends are going or whether the football team had a winning season.

It's frightening that such an important decision might be made this way. The choice of where to get your higher education is, until you buy a home, the most expensive decision you'll ever make. And the decision matters a great deal, because the differences in educational value and spiritual environment from one school to the next can be enormous.

TRANSFER COSTS

Your choice of a school also matters because changing schools, or transferring, is often expensive. In that respect, colleges are very different from high schools. When you move from one high school to another, almost all of your course credits will be accepted by the new school. You can see why that has to be the case. It would be a bad thing for everyone if moving meant that getting a high school degree took more than four years. Students would be unfairly penalized, and the high schools would have to spend extra time reteaching the courses they didn't accept.

Colleges, though, are different. For one thing, they are picky about accepting other schools' courses. (Remember the problem of getting AP credits accepted in place of required courses?) And colleges aren't financially motivated to accept transfer credit, the way public high schools are. If a college decides not to accept transfer credit, it's the student who pays, not the school.

For that reason, you need to think of courses as being like video games. You're best off assuming that the game you buy for one console won't work with any other console. That won't be true for all transfer credits, but it is very likely to be true for at least some. That means that **once you've started at one school, it will probably cost you something to transfer to another one. You'll likely**

have to take some classes over, and that will cost you not only extra money but also extra time. You're unlikely to be able to get your bachelor's degree in just four years.

The exception to that general rule is an associate's degree. All community colleges, as well as some four-year colleges, offer two-year degrees with the label "associate," in contrast to the four-year "bachelor" designation. In some cases an associate's degree may be accepted by a four-year college in place of all General Education (GE) requirements. Technically, that means that all of the two years' worth of associate's degree credit transfers and counts toward a bachelor's degree.

The catch, though, is that it may take more than two additional years to finish the remaining requirements for the bachelor's degree; that's especially true if your specialty, or major, requires lots of credits. If community college is the right place for you to start, this transfer-credit risk may be worth taking. It's better to do well in your first few years and take a little extra time to graduate than to start off at a school you're not ready for. But always assume that transferring will cost you something.

Because your higher education involves such a large investment, and because transferring is expensive, you'll want to commit right now to making a good, informed decision about where to go to school. Your goal should be to get it right that first time. This will be one of your first high-stakes judgments. You'll need to hone your analysis skills, your people skills, and your moral sense to make this decision. To help you do that, we'll first explore the questionable—or downright bad—reasons for choosing a college. It's a good exercise in analytical thinking.

WHAT WAS I THINKING?

You'll be pleasantly surprised to find how much you grow during college. By the time you finish, your perspective on life will be very different. You'll be more self-confident and patient. You'll also have a much better idea of what matters most to you. It would be sad if, with your new perspective, you looked back at your choice of a college and asked, "What was I thinking?" To help spare you that, here are some common reasons for choosing a college that tend to get more weight than they deserve. Let's look for the flaws of logic in each of them.

"All my friends are going there."

The value of true friendship can't be overstated. But, if you think about it, you'll see why it isn't a good idea to choose a college on the basis of where your friends are going. **What are the chances that one college will be right for everyone in your group of friends?** Do you all have the same interests? Are you all equally prepared for college? The school you choose needs to be right *for you*. Colleges can be as different from one another as one person is from another. Depending on your capabilities and what you want to accomplish in life, a school that might be good for your best friend could be wrong for you.

Let's suppose, for example, that your best friend is very outgoing, but you're naturally a bit shy. In that case, a small school might be better

than a big one for helping you develop people skills. If your best friend is set on going to a really big school, you might tell him or her that instead of attending college together you'll stay in touch by computer and phone, and plan to spend time with one another at home during breaks.

If that calculating approach sounds a bit heartless and even selfish, think a bit about this reality: High school friendships are all but impossible to preserve in college. As a new freshman, you'll find it difficult to get the classes you want at times during the day that don't conflict (freshmen get last priority in registering, and so often end up taking whatever they can get that contributes to their graduation plan). You'd be unlikely to schedule even one class per semester with a friend. You might be able to room together and thus spend time in the evenings and on weekends. But that's not everything it's cracked up to be. It's one thing to like playing video games with your friends; it's another to share a bathroom with them. Ask your parents or older siblings. Almost anyone who has roomed at college with a high school

friend will tell you that the much better way to preserve the friendship is to find ways to stay in touch as your lives take different paths. That's a people skill you'll want to have, and you can begin to develop it now.

"It's close to home."

With more than four thousand colleges and universities in the United States,[2] there is likely to be at least one within several hours of your home. You might naturally be attracted to the best of these nearby schools. You might even be glad to find that the one right in your hometown is pretty good. But you need to be careful about giving special preference to the schools close to where you live. Can you guess why?

Remember: you'll make new friends at college. You'll find study partners, for instance, among other students in your major. It's also possible that you'll become close friends with one or more of your roommates. The most probable candidates, though, aren't the ones who like your favorite video games; the roommates you'll most enjoy will be the ones who don't steal food from the refrigerator or leave dirty dishes in the sink. So be careful about making high school friendships the main driver of your college choice.

There can be good reasons for attending a local college. "In-state" tuition is a great bargain, especially at the best state schools. Let's assume, though, that your goal is not just to stay in-state but to save money by living with your parents and driving every day to the college in your hometown. Look hard at the logic behind that choice. Are you really going to spend all four years of college with your parents? Or are you planning to move out and transfer to another school as soon as you can afford it? In that case, you might end up losing credits, as we've discussed. The cost of repeating courses could be greater than what you saved in room and board at home. Staying in-state can make great financial sense. But, particularly as you consider attending a local college where you don't intend to finish your degree, be careful not to put too much weight on short-term financial savings.

The same goes for staying close to home for emotional reasons. Especially if you're prone to homesickness, being within a day's drive of Mom and Dad and high school friends sounds great. But doing well in class and getting the most from college is a 24/7 proposition. Coming home regularly will make it hard to succeed academically and to enjoy the social life of college. In time, you'll realize that and will come home less often. Your college years can be a great time to learn the important skill of being a faithful family member and staying close to your parents and siblings even when you're not under the same roof.

"It has the lowest tuition."

You're right to want to get the most from your financial investment in college. And there's good reason to think that a private college charging $30,000 isn't necessarily five times better than a state school where tuition is $6,000. But don't let high price alone scare you. The value of a good college education can be worth hundreds of thousands of dollars, maybe more, over your lifetime. For that reason, even an expensive school can be worth the price, if it prepares you to make HSJs.

As you compare the cost of schools, though, beware: You can't tell what you're getting just by looking at the price of tuition. On the one hand, high tuition doesn't ensure high quality. Prestigious schools can charge a lot because of their popularity, regardless of whether they actually spend your tuition on you. Sadly, they can just as easily divert the

money to their graduate programs and athletic teams. For example, you could pay $30,000 a year and find yourself being taught by graduate students in classrooms with hundreds of people. In other words, a high price tag doesn't necessarily mean a good education.

Similarly, low tuition isn't necessarily a sign of low quality. For instance, a state-sponsored school may be cheaper not because its quality is lower but because the state is willing to subsidize your education through tax dollars. Thus, if there's a rule of thumb for judging tuition, it is to avoid putting too much stock in either spending a lot or spending only a little. Find a high-quality school (using techniques that we'll explore), and view the cost of tuition as you would a good investment, one that will pay off in the long run.

"The team rocks."

Everybody loves to be associated with a winning team. A successful college athletic program builds spirit among students and alumni. It also enhances public perception. That is why many schools spend so much on intercollegiate sports. But can you see the limits on what athletic success really contributes to a college's educational reputation?

Think, for instance, about your favorite college basketball team. How

are they doing this year? When I was in college, the great basketball powerhouses were Georgetown and UNLV; they had tremendous success in the NCAA tournament year in and year out. Today, both teams are still very respectable, but they're not the perennial powerhouses they were in the 1980s. A student who chose one of those schools primarily for its basketball reputation back in my college days would probably be a bit disappointed now. Athletic success comes and goes; even the so-called "dynasties" don't last forever. One way to see the here-today-gone-tomorrow quality of athletic success is to ask yourself who won the national championship in your favorite college sport five years ago. Even if you can remember (without Googling), how is that team doing now?

Here's another question to ask yourself: "How likely are employers and graduate school admissions committees to equate a school's athletic record with its ability to nurture HSJ skills?" When your team is winning, it can be easy to overestimate the halo effect. I did that, for instance, when I applied to business school. As mentioned earlier, I applied without the full-time work experience that the Harvard Business School required of 97 percent of its students. Hoping beyond hope to be among the lucky 3 percent without work experience, I took comfort, even confidence, in the fact that my undergraduate school, BYU, had won the national championship in football the very month that I submitted my Harvard application. Looking back, it's laughable that I thought that would have made any difference. Just try to imagine the conversation among the members of the admissions committee: "Hey, this guy doesn't have work experience, but how 'bout them Cougars! Let's admit him." As if.

RANKINGS: BE SURE TO DOUBLE CLICK

There's another basis for choosing a college, one that seems more logical and reliable than the ones we've explored. "I'm not basing my decision on friends or football," you may say, "I'm looking at national rankings." The rankings certainly have some value. They're published by respected news magazines and other organizations with no tie to a particular school. And they have lots of hard numbers behind them.

In fact, the best rankings contain some potentially useful information that you ought to be aware of. But before you factor ranking information into your choice of a school, you need to do two things. One is to **decide what you're looking for, so that you can tell whether a particular ranking is measuring the things you care most about.** The other is to "double click" on the numbers and assumptions behind a given ranking. Otherwise, you might find that your school's high ranking is no better an indication of its worth to you than last year's football record would have been. Here are some ideas to guide you as you do that analytical double click on rankings.

One Size Doesn't Fit All

Many rankings order schools sequentially, starting with the "number one" school. Other rankings create categories or tiers of schools. **It's natural to conclude that the best schools are the ones with the higher rankings. But, if you're wise, you'll look at the "best" schools and ask, "Best for what?"**

To understand the importance of asking this question, let's imagine that you're shopping for a car. Suppose that you have been given a list of the world's car companies, ranked from one to twenty-five. You can guess the names likely to appear near the top of the list—Mercedes, BMW, Porsche, Ferrari. You might find some value in this list; other things being equal, you'd prefer to buy a car from a well-respected company. Pretty quickly, though, you'd realize something. "It's helpful to know which of these car *companies* is prestigious," you'd tell yourself, "but I'm looking for a particular *kind of car*. I want information that will tell me which car meets my needs."

Your needs will vary depending on the way you plan to use the car. Are you driving it, for instance, to work on Wall Street? Or will you use it for slick-rock fun in Moab? Will you be driving long distances or short? With few passengers or many? The best car for you depends on what you want from it. A $300,000 Ferrari might be just the thing for the Wall Street commute. But it would get high-centered on a rock pretty fast in Moab.

The same is true of your college degree. The private schools that top many of the national rankings turn out more than their share of HSJ decision makers. But they are expensive and difficult to get into. And they may not be the best place for you, given your capabilities and career interests. For these reasons, a simple ranking of colleges, like a list of car companies, doesn't tell all you want to know.

et's suppose that you dream of being on the team that designs the next great video game console, the one that will make the Wii obsolete. Let's also suppose that you've always dreamed of attending a particular prestigious school (we'll call it Top-Ranked University, or TRU for short). If you're wise, you'll say, "It's nice that TRU is highly ranked. But **prestige isn't enough**. I have to know whether TRU's electrical engineering degree will pre-pare me to be a great console designer."

In fact, TRU is probably quite expensive and likely to require lots of student loans. That heavy debt load could make it hard to live after gradu-ation on the salary of an entry-level game designer. And TRU's electri-cal engineering program could be strong on theory but weak on real-world application; it might be pres-tigious as far as national rankings go but not have a strong reputation with game console designers. If that were so, taking a TRU educa-tion where you're trying to go could be like taking a $300,000 Ferrari to Moab. You might be better off at a less expensive school with an elec-trical engineering department that has strong ties to Nintendo or Sony or Microsoft.

The lesson is to break any given ranking down to find the things it measures that you care about. Some rankings measure things that matter to everyone. For example, everyone should care about graduating in a reasonable time. Many college students drop out before getting a degree, and many of those who do graduate take much longer than they had planned. A ranking that emphasizes these easily measured and commonly reported statistics is valuable to you, regardless of your unique needs and aspirations.

Even after you've identified the components of a ranking that matter most to you, though, be careful not to accept all of the data at face value. That's because . . .

The Numbers Often Don't Tell the Whole Story

Many rankings are based on precise numbers. The fifth-ranked school, for instance, may have an overall score of 92, while the school ranked sixth scores an 89. Those overall scores are based on other numbers, such as the percentage of applicants who get in, the applicants' standardized test scores, and current-student satisfaction surveys. But you need to do an analytical double click on these and other numbers before you accept them as evidence of a school's value.

Let's start with the percentage of applicants who win admission, a credible-looking statistic that is often used as evidence of a school's quality. Some rankings reward a school for admitting only a small percentage of those who apply; the lower the admission rate, or the greater the selectivity, the higher the overall ranking. But how valuable is this selectivity measure? Do you really care who *didn't* get in? Isn't the quality of the students actually admitted what matters to you? The number of applicants turned away by a school is a statistic that is easy to collect, but it is at best an indirect measure of quality.

Do the same double click on the reported quality of admitted students, the ones who *did* get in. SAT and ACT scores are standard measures used to compare one school to another. But what do high test scores really mean? Do you know how many times

"My classmates are smart, but they're kind of competitive."

the admitted students took the test, or whether they got help in test-preparation programs? (Remember, that's the strategy we talked about in chapter 4—doing all you can to boost your test score.) The high test scores at a prestigious school may reflect not just intelligence but also advantages in preparation, such as having the money to take expensive prep courses or to hire personal tutors.

Even if a school's students really are super smart, is that necessarily good for you in your quest for HSJ skills? What if your fellow students are brilliant but hypercompetitive? What if they refuse to join you in study groups? What if they spend their time in class trying to impress the teacher with smart comments, rather than contributing to useful group discussion? If that's the case, then having such intelligent classmates could actually be a disadvantage when it comes to real learning.

So be careful of relying on numbers that don't tell the whole story. And be especially careful of numbers that come from surveys of students and faculty members, because . . .

The "Experts" May Not Be

Many rankings include data from surveys of students. Some also incorporate the opinions of college administrators and faculty members, who are asked to rate peer institutions. At first glance, this kind of data looks both relevant and trustworthy. After all, who can better judge the quality of a school than the "customers" who actually study there? And who better to give informed but unbiased opinions about a school than its professional "competitors" at other schools?

In fact, this kind of survey data should be read very cautiously. Can you see why? Think about student surveys. It's true that students have firsthand knowledge of their school, and they can certainly judge what they like and don't like. If the students at a school are uniformly dissatisfied, that is something to worry about.

But what if a school gets rave reviews from its students? Is there any reason to be skeptical? What if the students, for instance, are happy not because they're learning a lot but because grade inflation means that almost everybody gets A's? What if they are satisfied with their experience because they don't know what they're missing at other schools? Or what if they have figured out that saying good things about their school will improve its ranking and benefit them when they graduate and look for jobs?

You likewise need to view cautiously surveys asking academic administrators to evaluate other schools. The best source of information they are likely to have (other than last year's ranking) is the scholarly productivity of the faculty at these other schools. This kind of productivity, as measured by research publications, may be a good indicator of the intelligence and diligence of a university's professors. However, it doesn't guarantee that the students there are getting a good education.

In sum, rankings can be a useful starting point in your analysis of schools. But you have to know what you're looking for, and you have to double click on the data beneath the rankings. **Don't trust numbers that don't tell the whole story, and don't place too much weight on the opinions of others.**

BUILDING YOUR OWN "RANKING"

The thing to do, in fact, is to build your own ranking. It's not as hard as you might think. When you're applying to a college, it's natural—and probably accurate—to assume that you're just one of thousands, or even tens of thousands, of people doing the same thing. The school's selectivity statistics may make you feel that the burden is entirely on you, that the application process is all about proving *your* worthiness to be one of the lucky few admitted.

If that's your mind-set, you'll keep your head down during the application process. You may be interested in what the school has to offer, but you'll be inclined to limit your study mainly to the materials you've received by mail or found on the Web site. You'll probably look at the rankings, and you might even buy a college guide. But those sources will have many of the limitations we've been talking about.

Here's a tactic, though, that you may not have considered: **Pick up the phone.** That's right, just call the place. Now, you probably don't

want to call the admissions office. They're swamped, especially during application season (fall and winter). And the fact is that they couldn't tell you everything you need to know about whether the school is the right place for you, even if they had the time to talk. The admissions officers don't actually work in the part of the school that you'll experience if you're admitted.

The people you need to quiz are in the academic departments, specifically the one that offers your intended major. These are the people who create the learning environment in which you'll build HSJ capability. Your phone call, then, should go to the secretary of the department that you think you're most likely to be in. (If you're not sure of your major, make your best guess.)

Do your homework first, by studying the department's Web site and maybe even talking with a graduate of that department. Then place the call. This will be a great chance to practice your people skills. Say something like, "Hello, my name is Eager Beaver. I'm applying for admission, and I'm very interested in your electrical engineering major. I'm impressed with what I've seen on your Web site, and I'd like to know a little more. Can you tell me, for instance, about the placement record of your graduates?"

Hello, my name is Eager Beaver

What happens next will reveal more than any statistic you can find on a Web site or in a ranking. By way of warning, you should know that the secretary won't consider talking to you to be part of his or her job; even if you've been admitted, you're not a current student yet. But **the way the secretary responds will show, to a significant degree, how students are treated in that department.**

You might be referred to someone else. That's not necessarily bad; it could be that the secretary knows an expert who can help you. But you'll sense it if you're getting the runaround. You'll also be able to tell whether the department cares about what happens to its students after they graduate. If they don't track student placement (in other words, who has succeeded at getting a job or getting into graduate school by the time they graduate), that's not a good sign. It's also not a good sign, of course, if the department tracks the numbers but placement rates are low.

THE IMPORTANCE OF PLACEMENT

If you do get placement statistics, look for a couple of things. Probably the most telling statistic is the percentage of graduates who are seeking a job but don't have one by the time they graduate (this number may show up under the label "Seeking but Unemployed"). If that number is big, more than about 25 percent, watch out. Every school graduates some students whose unpreparedness for what comes next is their own fault, either because they failed to study hard or they neglected to make good long-term plans, or both. **But if the number of graduates who can't find a job or a graduate school opportunity is large,**

it's a signal that the school may not be doing all it should to prepare students for life after college.

Another thing to check is what salary graduates are being paid; with a quick search on the Web, you can find out whether the average salary for the department's graduates is higher or lower than the national aver-

age. (If you're an aspiring electrical engineer, for example, search "starting salaries for electrical engineers.") Also ask whether the graduates of the department are getting jobs or going on to graduate programs that are related to their major. In other words, are the electrical engineering majors going to work as electrical engineers or winning admission to graduate programs in electrical engineering, or are they being forced to find work in other fields? Take a look both at the overall statistics and also at special relationships that the school might have with particular companies and graduate programs; if the department has such relationships, they'll be glad to tell you. Schools that take an active role in getting their students placed tend to nurture such special connections.

ATTENDING CLASS

Something else to ask the department secretary when you call is whether you can visit the campus. (You need to do that, by the way, before committing to a school, even if it means buying an airline ticket.) You could say, "I'd like to attend a class and meet some students and perhaps even a faculty member." Here again, the reaction you get will be telling. Ideally, the secretary will suggest several good classes. If you can, arrange to attend not only a class in your major but also a General Education class. Because GE courses are required for all students, they tend to have big class sizes; the GE class, therefore, will be a good test of the college's commitment to personalized instruction. If you find yourself among hundreds of other students, that's a reason for concern. There are some professors who have the personality and skill to captivate groups of this size, just as there are some athletes and musicians worth seeing even from a stadium's cheap seats. But such teachers are exceptional. Other things being equal, you want to see smaller class sizes.

As you sit in each class, watch what happens. Pay particular attention to the way things are taught. Does the instructor just lecture, or are the students actively involved? If the students do interact with the instructor and with one another, is the spirit of those interactions friendly, or is it competitive and sometimes even disrespectful?

Here's another good test: Does the instructor act like the all-knowing expert, or is he or she open to learning something from the students? That might sound like an unreasonable expectation, but it's not.

I remember a day when my constitutional law professor, Rex Lee, was leading a discussion of a case he had actually argued before the U.S. Supreme Court. (As the U.S. Solicitor General under Ronald Reagan, Professor Lee appeared before the Court fifty-nine times.) My fellow first-year law students and I sensed the privilege of learning about the case from the person who knew it better than anyone in the world.

But the really unforgettable moment came when a curious student asked what the rest of us considered an off-the-wall question, one that wasn't obviously relevant to the case. Professor Lee stopped. He smiled,

put his hand to his forehead, and said, "That's a good question. I've never thought about it before." For several spellbinding minutes he reasoned out loud, exploring a question for which he didn't already have an answer. The rest of us envied our brave colleague, who got to talk with Professor Lee as though they were law partners. Such humility in an expert is rare, but not in the best teachers.

When you're in class, also observe carefully *what* is being taught. Is it all just facts and theories, or does the instructor show the practical side of the things being discussed? Can he or she relate what is being taught to current world events? Better yet, do you get to explore the application in your own life, the way George Washington would have done?

SIZING THINGS UP

You can learn important things about whether the school is the right one for you not just in the classroom, but outside as well. The department secretary may help you set meetings with some professors and students. But even without that help, you can meet a lot of people just by walking around the campus and saying hello. Go all over—to the bookstore, the library, the dorms, the cafeteria. Don't worry about impressing (or annoying) anyone. You may be a stranger, but remember that at a large school almost everyone is a stranger to most of the people he or she meets, even when the person has been at the place for years. What you want to

find out is precisely how the people on campus treat someone they don't know, someone they don't have to be nice to.

One of the things you'll notice is the size of the campus. Some colleges enroll only a few hundred students, while others have tens of thousands. You'll want to decide what size feels best to you.

Another thing to consider is the school's relative emphasis on undergraduate education. At some places, such as community colleges, teaching college-degree seekers is all they do. At most universities, by contrast, college-level instruction is just part of the equation. Particularly at large research universities, much of the faculty's time is spent mentoring graduate students and performing research into things like cures for cancer and other ways to improve the quality of human life.

This difference could be very important to you. If you hope to go to graduate school yourself, a research university could be just the place to get your college degree. The faculty will teach a host of advanced subjects with a high degree of expertise. Even if they don't bring their discoveries directly into undergraduate classrooms, they do bring a spirit of inquiry and openness to new ideas; their research can invigorate their teaching. Some of them might even be willing to involve you in their work.

A small school may offer greater intimacy with students and professors, but might have more limited academic offerings and less national recognition. A large school can be exciting and may offer a broader array of majors and courses. You'd need, though, to be the kind of person who feels comfortable in crowds.

There's a potential cost, though, to this research activity. Undergraduate education may take a backseat to research and to the mentoring of graduate students, who are typically more qualified to help in the research. You need to consider both the benefits and the potential costs of being an undergraduate student in such an environment.

the feel of campus

Unless you plan to attend one of the Church-sponsored schools (BYU, BYU–Idaho, BYU–Hawaii, or LDS Business College), be sure to visit the Church's institute of religion near the campus of the school you're considering. Modern prophets have taught the critical importance of studying the gospel as we pursue higher education.[3] The institutes have been created to help you do that along with others who share your faith and desire for learning. The institute near your school will be a source of spiritual and social strength throughout your time at college. And the institute director will be a great mentor to you in both your spiritual and your secular studies. You should definitely **make the institute part of your first visit to campus, as well as every semester you're in school.**

You'll find as you walk the campus that it has a "feel" about it. Most people don't go to work in higher education for the money. Many of the professors and administrators could make much more someplace else. They chose a career in higher education for intangible reasons, things that are hard to measure but easy to feel: learning, discovering, teaching, collaborating with gifted colleagues and students. The relative emphasis on these activities differs from one campus to another. Some are teaching oriented, while others are more focused on research or athletics. Whatever the emphasis, though, the motive is excellence and the work requires personal sacrifice.

That's why the feel of a college campus is so strong and why it's important that you like that feel. If you're wise, you'll give special credit

in your personal ranking to a school that, whatever its size or prestige, feels optimistic, friendly, and attentive to students like you. It will feel like a place where you can develop not only analysis and people skills but also moral sense.

THE POWER OF PEOPLE

The people you meet in college and later in graduate school will change your life. That won't be true of every professor or classmate, but a precious few of them will have tremendous impact. They may even change who you are.

For me, Professor Bonner Ritchie was such a life-changing person. In the fall of 1986 I was a student in his organizational behavior class. Bonner (he was happy to let students call him by his first name) didn't fit my image of a business school professor. He was freethinking, questioning of convention, even skeptical of "the numbers" that I had come to trust without reservation. Ironically, Bonner got his PhD from the same place that Grandpa Eyring did, the University of California, Berkeley. But Bonner was at Berkeley in the 1960s, when that campus was known for its hippies. Even twenty years later, I could easily imagine Bonner's days as a graduate student at Berkeley, studying squishy people skills.

In late October 1986, Bonner missed a Monday class. We had a substitute, but Bonner's unexplained absence supported my hypothesis that he didn't take our MBA program seriously enough. When, at the beginning of our next class, he reported having been in New York and seen two World Series baseball games, my hypothesis was confirmed beyond doubt; I could barely conceal my contempt. Yet Bonner seemed unashamed. He took a chair at the front of the class and, leaning back comfortably, began to talk about the baseball games.

It was the year that the Boston Red Sox played the New York Mets for the world championship. Now, to appreciate Bonner's story, you have to know about something called "The Curse of the Bambino." If you're a baseball fan, you remember Babe Ruth as the home-run king of the New York Yankees. But if you're a *really serious* baseball fan, you know that Babe Ruth, the Great Bambino, played for the Boston Red Sox before he became a Yankee. In fact, from 1915 to 1918, Babe Ruth helped the Sox win three World Series titles.

But then the owner of the Red Sox unwisely sold Ruth's contract to the New York Yankees. The Bambino turned the Yankees into the same kind of perennial champions that Boston had been. The Red Sox, on the other hand, didn't win another World Series in the next sixty-eight years. Superstitious Sox fans saw a connection between the ill-fated trade of Babe Ruth and this painful championship drought; they named it "The Curse of the Bambino."

In 1986, on the very weekend that Bonner went to New York, the Red Sox were on the verge of breaking the Curse. The underdog Sox came into Game Six with the Mets, on Saturday night, ahead three games to two and needing to win just once more. In the tenth inning, they were leading by two runs, with a single strike between them and victory. The stadium scoreboard ran a congratulatory message from the Mets to the Red Sox.

As Bonner spun his yarn, something began to happen to me. I'd actually watched this game, glancing at a TV screen as I did my homework.

Along with millions of others, I'd seen the Mets score two more runs to tie the game and then win it on a ground ball to first that spun forward and bounced low under the first baseman's glove. I also had the TV on when the Mets decisively won Game Seven and clinched the Series.

But Bonner was describing something far more important than a mere baseball game. He talked about riding the subway home from Game Six at two o'clock in the morning. Everyone on the train, even the Boston fans, seemed to believe that the Red Sox would lose Game Seven. That night in New York, he was witness to an organizational behaviorist's version of a Greek tragedy.

A sixty-eight-year championship drought. Redemption and glory in the palm of the hand. An amazing rally. An unthinkable error! Fate! Destiny! The Curse of the Bambino.

For the first time, I saw Bonner and his academic subject in a powerfully positive light. He didn't draw firm conclusions from the game. In fact, he tried to get our help in making sense of what he had experienced. It was clear, though, that he perceived dimensions of the game that I had never imagined. The players were members not only of a team but of a vast, informal organization, one encompassing umpires and fans and players from decades past. **The game was a parable of the way people's perceptions can affect them and the organizations they're part of.** I could see, for example, how the employees of a failing business might succumb to the mythology of a "curse." There were lessons in Bonner's story even for numbers-driven MBA students.

Bonner's epic tale of the '86 World Series sparked change in me. For one thing, I learned that I'd misjudged him. He had been in New York not for baseball, but on a consulting assignment for one of the world's largest corporations. His clients had invited him to the baseball game. He sat in their company box along the first baseline, where he was an eyewitness to the error that seemed to seal the Curse. He couldn't resist thinking about the psychological factors at work in the ballpark; even at a World Series game, he was applying his professional skills. His profession, I realized, was also his personal passion.

As you can see, when you choose your college, you are not just choosing a place to learn. You are also choosing a place to meet the Rex Lees and Bonner Ritchies who will change the way you think and even who you are. So in your decision-making process, study not just *what* a college has to offer, but *who* it has to offer. You're unlikely to meet your Rexes and Bonners when you first visit a campus. But remember, Heaven has a place for you at a particular school. That place has not only a unique set of learning opportunities but also a unique group of people for you to meet and befriend. If the school you're visiting is

Bonner blessed me with his passion for understanding people; I've spent the twenty-plus years since he told his story trying to enhance my own people skills. And Bonner has become my lifelong friend and colleague. He retired from the university, but he still travels the world, sharing his insights into people. He goes often to the Middle East, where his conflict resolution skills are highly valued. He passed through Tokyo when I was living there several years ago. We arranged to meet and spend an afternoon talking about people and organizations. Just as in the days when I was formally Bonner's student, I could feel his contribution to my people and analysis skills and to my moral sense.

the right place for you, you're likely to encounter instructors and students and office staff members who seem like good people, people you want to get to know better. If that happens, you may have found the number-one school in your personal ranking.

[1]Frank Zang, "School Spirit," *Horizon Air Magazine,* September 2007, 104.
[2]National Center for Education Statistics, *Digest of Education Statistics,* "Degree-granting institutions, by control and type of institution: Selected years, 1949–1950 to 2007–2008," Table 265, http://nces.ed.gov/programs/digest/d08/tables/dt08_265 .asp.
[3]See President Thomas S. Monson's statement on the Institutes of Religion home page: http://institute.lds.org/.

BEING YOUR OWN GENERAL CONTRACTOR

Have you ever known a family who built their own house—not professional home builders, just ordinary people? You probably admired their courage. You may have wondered where they learned everything they needed to know. Perhaps you thought, "I could never do that."

Well, if you want a good college education, you're going to have to be your own builder, the "general contractor" who oversees the whole project. It's not enough to choose a major and get good grades. There's more to it than that, as I learned when I graduated. **A good college education goes beyond a good transcript, just as a house is more than the wood and wires and pipes that go into it.** A college education, like a house, is a complex structure with many

parts. And there's no one but you who can ensure that the whole structure is sound. That means you'll need to make a lot of high-stakes judgments as you get your degree. The task will also require inspiration, much like the building of Nephi's ship.

"Wait a minute," you say, "I've gone to all the trouble of choosing the right school. I found a great department where the people are friendly and helpful. I've even talked with the school's academic advisors and career counselors; they helped me map out an eight-semester graduation plan, one that shows when I'll take each of my courses."

All of that is great. Your graduation plan will be very helpful, as a blueprint is for a home builder. But the plan will almost certainly need to be modified as you go, especially if you've chosen a major without being really sure of how you'll use it after graduation. Also, your graduation plan doesn't show some of the most important elements of your education, such as internships and extracurricular activities.

Though many people at the school will help, when it comes to acquiring HSJ capabilities and preparing for your future, you have to take personal responsibility. To appreciate this responsibility, think of things from the standpoint of a professor. In a classroom of, say, thirty electrical engineering students, no two have exactly the same objectives. Some plan to go straight to work; others are going on to graduate school in engineering or law or business. Some students hope to manage teams of other engineers and maybe even start their own companies; others want to focus just on the task of designing things. There is no way to satisfy the HSJ learning needs of all of the students in a particular class or a given major, no matter how much time and talent a professor brings to the job.

The same thing is true of the academic advisors and career specialists whose job it is to help you build your education. Even if your school has enough of them to give the students all the time they need (which is unlikely to be the case), in the end only you can answer the important questions about what to study and how to prepare for life after graduation. You are unique, and so you need to take personal responsibility for your learning. Building a solid education isn't easy, but you can do it. The seven rules of educational "general contracting" outlined in the following chapters will help.

CHAPTER SEVEN

GENERAL CONTRACTOR'S RULE #1

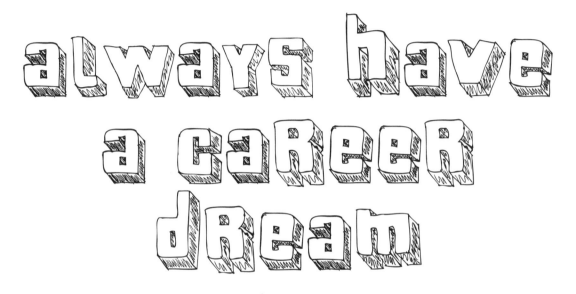

always have
a career
dream

I, Nephi, crept into the city and went forth
towards the house of Laban. And I was led by the Spirit,
not knowing beforehand the things which I should do.

1 NEPHI 4:5–6

he first thing you'd do if you were building a house would be to decide where you want to live. Is it an exclusive neighborhood of mansions an hour from Manhattan, the kind of place where a Wall Street banker or lawyer would live? A subdivision of doctors' houses close to a hospital? A tree-lined street of homes within walking distance of a college campus, ideal for a professor's family? Or perhaps a big ranch house full of children who help with the chores and study at home?

It's hard to know, when you're young, what you want to be when you grow up. In fact, it's hard for most of us who *have* grown up to be sure. There may be people who know from a young age what career they want; some of them may even turn out to be right. But for the majority of us, either we don't know for sure or we start with a dream that we end up changing before finding the right thing. The process requires a lot of difficult HSJs.

Yet the most dangerous thing is to have no dream at all. The only way to know whether a particular career path is right for you is to start down it. The sooner you make your best guess, the sooner you'll begin to learn who you are and who you're not. Waiting to decide, by contrast, teaches you nothing. You can't simply wait for your career doubts to leave you; you have to venture out and leave them behind.

That is the principle Oliver Cowdery learned when he tried, unsuccessfully, to translate the Book of Mormon. He thought the words would just come to him as he read. But the Lord taught him this: "Behold, you have not understood; you have supposed that I would give it unto you, when you took no thought save it was to ask me. But, behold, I say unto you, that you must study it out in your mind; then you must ask me if it be right, and if it is right I will cause that your bosom shall burn within you; therefore, you shall feel that it is right" (Doctrine and Covenants 9:7–8).

ne particularly common mistake is choosing a college major before thinking seriously about what kind of career you're targeting. As an incoming freshman you might reason, "It's too hard to be sure what kind of job I want. I'll pick my major now and decide about a job later." This sounds like a reasonable sequence of events; by choosing your major, you may feel as though you've made at least the first half of your decision about what to be when you grow up. You'll wait to address the question of what job to pursue when the time comes, just before graduation.

This can be especially tempting if you've chosen a broad, professional-sounding major like business or communications. These majors focus on the world of companies, and so you might naturally assume that someone graduating with a degree in business or communications will automatically be employable. That, however, isn't the case. Lots of students graduate in these fields without any idea of what kind of organization they want to work for; as a result, they are unlikely to have taken courses outside of their major that set them apart from the crowd.

The highly sought-after business and communication graduates, by contrast, will have answered the question, "The business of *what?*" or "Communicating *what?*" For example, suppose you're a wise business major who has decided to focus on something specific—say, the business of *health care*. As you study business, you'll be thinking about hospitals and nursing homes and physical therapy centers. In addition to your business major courses, you'll take classes in subjects such as biology and nutrition and exercise science; these science courses will broaden your analysis skills beyond just business. You might even enhance your people skills and moral sense by taking classes in psychology and

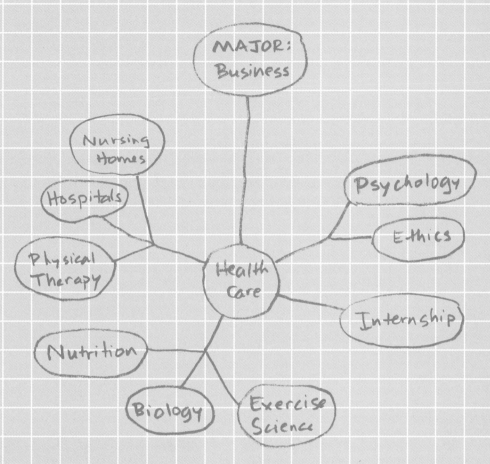

ethics; that will prepare you to interact with health-care patients and to tackle ethical dilemmas such as when to end life-prolonging measures for the terminally ill. In addition, you'll perform at least one internship with a hospital or nursing home or medical insurer. Because of your focus on health care as a career, your résumé will come to the top of the stack in interviews with health-care companies. You'll be recognized as being ready to contribute to the organization right from your first day on the job.

WHAT YOU THINK ABOUT IN THE SHOWER

"All right," you say, "I get your point about having a career dream from the beginning. But how do I come up with that kind of dream?" It's a good question, one that I had when I was preparing for college. My dad helped me answer it. He taught me that **your guess about a career should take into account what you think about when you're not required to think about anything.**

Dad learned this lesson from his father, my Grandpa Eyring. Grandpa encouraged each of his three sons to major in physics. Actually, it was pretty strong encouragement—he told them that majoring in physics was the price of room and board at his home, where they all three lived while attending the nearby University of Utah. Though Grandpa was a chemist, he felt that physics, even more than chemistry, was the best preparation for a career because it explains the fundamental, unchanging principles of our physical world.

Dad dutifully majored in physics, but not with much enthusiasm. He found the math particularly challenging. When struggling with knotty math problems, he frequently sought Grandpa's help with homework, as anyone living under the same roof as a math genius would. Dad, who goes by Hal, often told the story of how one day Grandpa confronted him on his lack of personal effort. They were standing together at a blackboard in their basement (that was Grandpa's idea of a game room).

Portrait of Henry by Alvin Gittins, 1969. The original hangs in the lobby of the Henry Eyring Building at the University of Utah.

Suddenly Grandpa stopped. "Hal," he said, "we were working this same kind of problem a week ago. You don't seem to understand it any better now than you did then. Haven't you been working on it?"

Dad admitted that he hadn't been studying the problem, and he got this response from Grandpa: "You don't understand. When you walk down the street, when you're in the shower, when you don't have to be thinking about anything else, isn't this what you think about?"

Again the answer was, "No."

It was a painful moment for Grandpa, who hoped that all of his sons would become scientists. Finally he said, "Hal, I think you'd better get out of physics. You ought to find something that you love so much that when you don't have to think about anything, that's what you think about."[1]

Grandpa understood that making high-stake judgments requires more than just analysis skills and people skills and moral sense. It also requires focused attention. **The people who make HSJs well think about them not just at work but also when they don't have to**, such as when they're in the shower. They even think about them subconsciously, waking from sleep with new insights.

The good news for Dad was that, knowing he wasn't cut out to be a physicist, he started looking hard for something he could put his whole heart and head into. In time, he discovered that he loved teaching. He especially liked teaching about the way organizations work—the way leaders lead, for example. That was something he enjoyed pondering in the shower. Having found the thing he enjoyed thinking about even when he didn't have to, he became very successful in it. And it turned out that his physics background, especially the study of math at the blackboard with Grandpa, prepared him for success as a university professor of business.

A HIGH, BROAD TARGET

As you try to translate the thing you think about in the shower into a career dream, several things may help. First, aim higher rather than lower. Don't let fear or laziness keep you from dreaming of jobs that may seem beyond your abilities. You don't know yet what you're capable of; you're likely to surprise yourself. And **life tends to have more tough breaks than lucky ones. That's why you should set your sights high.**

Let's suppose, for instance, that you start dreaming about being a surgeon. With hard work and good fortune, you'll become one. Suppose, on the other hand, that things change: your grades might not be good enough to get into medical school; you might need to start work to support your family; or maybe you'll just decide that being "on call" nights and weekends isn't for you. If something like that happens, you'll still be in a position to find a good career. For example, your pre-med education could give you the option to work as a physician's assistant (PA), or to get a graduate degree in a field less demanding than medicine. The converse, though, isn't true: It's unlikely that you'd plan to be a PA and wind up as a surgeon. So, aim high.

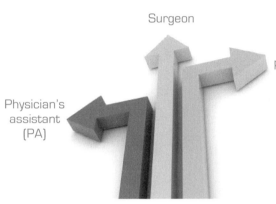

Surgeon

General practitioner

Physician's assistant (PA)

Another way to make your career guess a good one is to keep it broader rather than narrower, especially at the beginning. For example, **you don't have to know in the first year of college whether you're going to be a doctor or a dentist. Either way, your immediate priority is to get good grades in chemistry and biology.** You'll learn more about the differences between medicine and dentistry as you go, especially if you do some good internships (something we'll discuss soon).

Your dream can change—but not if you don't have one to begin with. So that's our first rule as you begin constructing your college education: Always have a career dream.

---

[1]Gerald N. Lund, "Elder Henry B. Eyring: Molded by 'Defining Influences,'" *Ensign*, September 1995, 10.

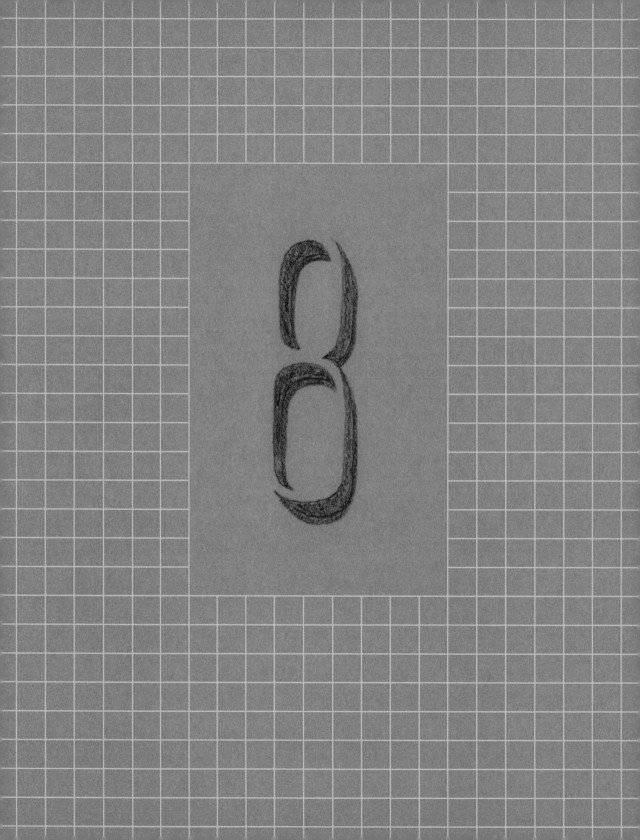

CHAPTER EIGHT

GENERAL CONTRACTOR'S RULE #2

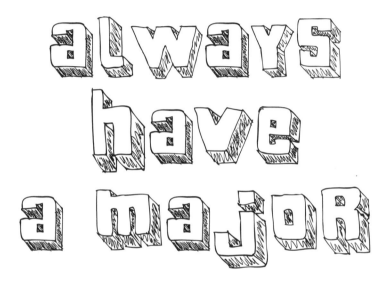

always
have
a major

Behold, you have not understood; you have supposed that
I would give it unto you, when you took no thought save it was to ask me.
But, behold, I say unto you, that you must study it out in your mind;
then you must ask me if it be right, and if it is right I will cause that your
bosom shall burn within you; therefore, you shall feel that it is right.

DOCTRINE AND COVENANTS 9:7–8

aving made your best guess about a career, you're ready to choose a major. Your major is like the basic blueprint for a house. Of course, you'd never start building a home without a blueprint.

You may meet some folks, though, who will say there's no need for a freshman to have chosen a major; they'll tell you that there's plenty of time, that you can wait until your second or third year to make the decision. Some people might even say that it's a mistake to choose a major right away, before you've explored the broad offering of General Education courses. They'll warn against locking yourself into something when you're not prepared to make an informed choice.

There's something to be said for taking your time and gathering

information. The risk, though, is that waiting to declare your major could cost you both time and money. Especially if your major has many required hours (something we'll discuss in a moment), waiting to get started could mean taking more than four years to graduate. And many people end up changing their majors, no matter how long they took deciding the first time. That is why it is so hard to finish college in four years.

The truth is that choosing your major is a complicated, high-stakes judgment, one of the most important you'll make at this stage of your life. But you don't need to be afraid of it—if you're thoughtful and prayerful, and if you start the process as soon as you can, ideally even before you arrive on campus. If you make your best decision early and then change majors later, you'll find that the initial courses in many majors satisfy GE "elective" course requirements. You might also decide to turn your first major into a "minor" or an "emphasis," which means that the courses could count toward your graduation plan.

You should never be careless in selecting or changing your major; you need to "study it out" and seek a spiritual confirmation. But you needn't be afraid of committing to act. In fact, waiting to decide will almost certainly be more costly than moving ahead quickly, so long as you move ahead thoughtfully.

Even if the courses from your abandoned major don't serve you in GE or a minor, you're likely to be glad you took them. The early courses in any major will expose you to the ideas in that field that are most broadly applicable and fundamental. These courses will make you more knowledgeable than most people are about that field. You'll have paid a relatively small price to be forever familiar with the basics of, for example, computer science or biology.

ACTING AS IF YOU KNOW

The reason for declaring a major as soon as you can is the same as the reason you should always have a career dream: **Acting as if you know where you're going and beginning to move down that path is the best way to find out whether you're right.** Let's suppose, for instance, that you like politics enough that you think about it in the shower. There's a major that could help you prepare for a career in politics—it's called political science. As a major in political science, you'll study things like the U.S. Constitution and the process of running for public office.

You don't have to be absolutely sure that political science is for you. Even without a strong spiritual confirmation, you can just try it for now.

Be sure, though, to act as though you love it. In addition to studying hard for your classes, subscribe to a publication in the field. (*Foreign Affairs* is a good one for political scientists.) Read political blogs. Get involved in local politics. Meet some elected officials and lobbyists; volunteer to work for them.

If you like all of this, you may be a political scientist. If not, you can prayerfully try something else. In that case, you'll have the benefit of better understanding what you *don't* like. For example, while pretending to be a political scientist you may have found out that you don't like the messiness of politics, the need for constant compromise and infinite patience. That might steer you in the direction of something more mathematically precise, such as accounting. Your second guess about a  major will be better than the first because of what you have learned. The process is one of trial and error, and **the sooner you start making educated guesses, the sooner you'll hit on the right answer.** From this perspective, you can see that the worst major is "Undeclared."

Learning to think like a geologist (or whatever you choose to be)

As you explore your major, remember not only to think a lot *about* your chosen field of study (in the shower and other places), but also to think *like* the experts in that field do. My geology professors helped me do both of those things. When I was in elementary school, the geologists at BYU–Idaho, where Dad worked after leaving Stanford, let me tag along when they took the college students to the field. I went into mines with Glenn Embree and up the Teton Mountains with Ed Williams. We brought home some terrific rocks and fossils, and I started thinking about them a lot, even in the shower. I became a rock hound. It was partly because of this love for geology that I chose it as my major.

But when I was in college myself, I learned that there is more to geology than just loving rocks. I learned that geologists have a particular *way* of thinking that helps them do their work. For example, a good geologist has a unique view of time. Most geologic events—the creation of a mountain, for instance—take millions of years. Good geologists must be able to see that super-slow process unfolding as though it were a sixty-second video clip. They learn to imagine silt on the ocean floor being compacted into rock, then thrust thousands of feet into the air, and finally sculpted into towering peaks by rain and glaciers.

Geologists also have a saying, "If it *did* happen, it *can* happen." This saying helps them suspend their disbelief when they encounter something unimaginable, such as a fossilized sea coral on the top of a mountain. The

geologists who first unraveled this mystery had to get over the gut reaction, "This can't have happened; there can't be a coral fossil on a mountaintop." Only when they accepted the fact that it actually did happen were they able to conceive *how* it might have happened. Believing that the coral had some natural way of getting from the sea to the mountains led them to discover the secrets of earth movements and mountain making. To understand geology, in other words, they had to learn to think like geologists.

In your major you'll learn lots of important facts and figures. But you'll be really successful in your field only if you learn the *way of thinking* that ties these facts and figures together and makes them useful. That's the real meaning of analysis skills. A good financier, for example, knows the mathematics of calculating interest rates. But a great financier, such as Warren Buffett, understands not just how to calculate an interest rate but how to estimate the risks and the potential return of an investment. He's been making high-stake judgments about that since high school, when he had to decide how much to pay for used pinball machines that he put in barbershops. He mastered the art of thinking like a financier. That's why, when he invests in troubled banks and companies during a market meltdown, financiers around the world take comfort.

George Washington is another good example. Some political scientists might have advised George Washington that he had the right at

Valley Forge, based on military tradition, to simply take from surrounding farms and towns the food he needed for his starving troops.[1] But Washington, a truly great political analyst, knew that he couldn't win the war without the goodwill of all Americans; he knew from the moral training of boyhood that he couldn't use his army to steal food. And he had the people skills and moral authority to convince his men of this. They went hungry; many died. **But the sacrifice of Washington and his troops won the hearts of their countrymen, who rallied behind them in the cause of independence.** It wasn't just what Washington knew about political science that mattered, it was the *way* he thought about it that made the difference. Like Washington, you can learn not just facts and figures of your field, but also the unique way of thinking that will allow you to make high-stakes judgments.

Go forward, be prayerful, study it out, and choose a major. You'll be glad you did.

---

[1] James Thomas Flexner, *Washington: The Indispensable Man* (Back Bay Books, 1994), 109–10.

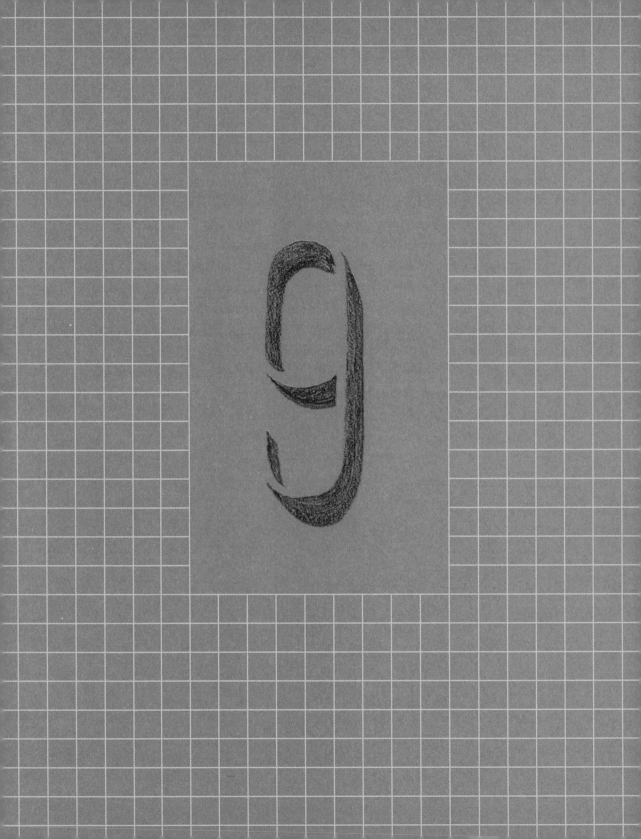

CHAPTER NINE

GENERAL CONTRACTOR'S RULE #3

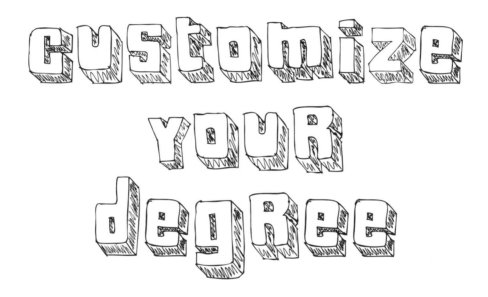

customize your degRee

Now I, Nephi, did not work the timbers after the manner which
was learned by men, neither did I build the ship after the manner of men;
but I did build it after the manner which the Lord had shown unto me.

1 NEPHI 18:2

ven after you've identified the subject you love, you'll still need to be thoughtful as you pursue your degree. You should think of your major as a generic house blueprint, one you downloaded from the Web for free. It will require customization to meet your individual needs. We've talked, for example, about the value of adding science courses to a degree in business or communications.

Another thing to consider is that most majors leave the choice of many elective courses to you. In fact, the electives you end up choosing may outnumber the required courses you take. That puts the burden on you to **know which elective courses will help you get where you're going.** For example, an economics major who intends to get a graduate degree in that field would be well served to take elective courses on the history and theory of economics as a foundation for advanced study. On the other hand, one thinking of going to law school and becoming an advocate for the poor would benefit from courses that explore the causes of poverty and economic policies for creating jobs and wealth.

As you choose your electives, remember your general contractor's responsibility to design and build for your unique future. Your professors are specialists; each one is expert in a relatively narrow aspect of your major. They have limited opportunity to think about the whole bundle of courses that make up your major. Nor are they given much time to go out and study the connection between the courses they teach and the needs of the organizations that might employ you. That's true not only at universities, where professors are required to do research, but also at community colleges, where teaching loads are very heavy. **The research and teaching burdens professors carry make it hard for them**

to ensure that your courses are connected tightly to the changing workplace that you're headed into. That means the responsibility is yours.

Be especially sensitive to the fact that many majors presume you're going on to graduate school *in that same field*. For example, a bachelor's degree in geology is more likely to give you the courses that provide the foundation for a master's degree in geology than it is to prepare you to work immediately as a geologist. In other words, the assumption of the designers of these degrees is often that you'll get both a bachelor's and a master's degree (and maybe a PhD), rather than seeking work with only the former.[1] The bachelor's degree, therefore, may not fully prepare you for your profession. You might be able to find work with only a bachelor's in geology, for example, if your grades are very good and the demand for geologists is high. But, to be sure of getting a job in geology—and in many other professions—you probably need a master's degree. (You can read more about postgraduate education online at majordecisionsforcollege.com.)

BLUEPRINT MODIFICATIONS

That's where I got myself into trouble. I knew that I didn't want to get a master's in geology; I wanted an MBA, a broad master's degree that would give me the option of working for more than just oil or mining companies. I also knew that the good MBA programs require several years of full-time work experience. The smart thing for me, given the low probability of getting into the most prestigious business schools without full-time work experience, would have been to take at least a few courses in fields such as accounting and information technology. Those courses would have made me more attractive to the oil companies, who weren't drilling for oil when I graduated but might have been interested in an undergraduate geologist with some business skills. For example, I could have helped an oil company find ways to run its refineries or gas stations more efficiently. Or, if my non-geology training had been good enough, I could have gotten work with a company outside of oil and mining and other geology-related businesses. That would have allowed me to find good employment even during a time of low oil prices.

In other words, I should have modified the generic geology blueprint to include a *mixture* of courses complementary to my education and career goals. My analysis skills were good, but they were narrowly focused on science. And I had taken very few courses in things like the humanities that would have added to my people skills and moral sense. As it turned out, I was fortunate to get into a good MBA program without work experience. But a blueprint change to my geology major would have given me more options.

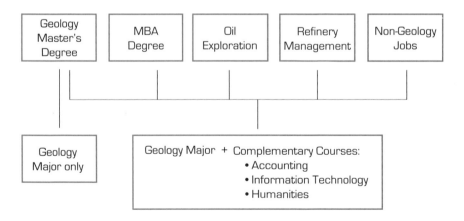

MAKING YOUR MAJOR "WORK"

Depending on your major, the need for customizing your blueprint could be even greater than it was for me. There are many majors that don't prepare you well for a job outside of the classroom even when the economy is hot and the demand for college graduates is high. In fact, some majors don't give you many career options even when you add a master's degree in that same field. You can learn a lot in such a major, but it may not be enough for broad employability unless you modify it.

For example, a degree in history, one of my favorite subjects, can give you great insights into the way the world works. Really studying and understanding history is a great way to develop HSJ skills; historians get to explore the world's best and worst examples of analysis skills, people skills, and moral sense. The same thing is true of dedicated students of psychology and philosophy.

The problem, though, is that your first job out of college is probably going to require you to do some technical, hands-on things. In fact, in almost any career, you'll need a certain amount of technical training, not just at the beginning, when you're low in the organization, but even when you're a senior specialist or running the whole show. For example, in most jobs you'll have to create budgets and write project proposals. That will require that you know how to use spreadsheets, read financial statements, and write for professional audiences. The good news is that, in most majors, you can easily modify your major blueprint with courses that supply those kinds of technical skills.

Remember, *all* majors need customization to a person's unique needs. Unless you're dead set on getting a master's degree in the same

You might say, "Yeah, I'm majoring in philosophy, but I'm going to law school. I don't need to know that business kind of stuff." Well, it's true that philosophy is great training for law. But you'll be a better lawyer if you also know spreadsheets and financial statements. And what if you graduate with your law degree and want to change to a different profession? Or what if you decide not to go to law school after all? You'll be wise to modify your blueprint to make it more practically useful in case things turn out differently than you planned, as they did for me when I graduated from college.

field of study as your bachelor's, your major is very unlikely to give you everything you need. That's true even if the major has a more practical sound to it. You might reasonably assume, for example, that a degree in communications will better prepare you for a high-paying job than one in English. But remember that both degrees probably have been designed with the assumption that you'll continue your education after college. Most communications courses will provide a foundation for a graduate degree more than a foundation for work, just as English courses do. But with the right kind of modifications, a degree in either communications or English could prepare you for high-paying employment. From an HSJ standpoint, there aren't necessarily good majors or bad majors. Many majors can prepare you for a successful career in the workplace or the home. But, unless you plan to become a university professor, almost every major needs to be customized.

add a minor to your major

One of the best ways to customize is to broaden your education by adding a minor to your major. A minor is a collection of about half a dozen courses. It's designed to expose you to the basics of a field, enough to show a prospective employer that you know more than just one subject. For me, as a geology major, a minor in business or economics would have been a great choice. The communications major we talked about earlier, the one with an interest in health care, might consider a minor in something like health science or biology.

Getting a minor may take an extra semester or even two. But it doesn't have to, if you choose it soon enough and plan your schedule carefully. And even if it does push your graduation date back a bit, a minor that prepares you for a successful career is well worth the investment of time and money. I learned that the hard way. You can get it right the first time.

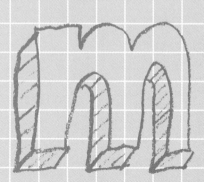

A "MAJOR" CAVEAT

Though you shouldn't fear making an early commitment to a major, there is something that *should* concern you, even if you're quite sure about your decision. That is how many credit hours your major requires.

One of the confusing things about college is that there are two numbers to watch when planning your path to a degree. The first of those numbers is the *total of all credits* required for graduation, usually between 120 and 128 (or 15 to 16 credits during each of eight semesters). But you'll rarely meet a bachelor's degree holder who graduated with the minimum number of total credits required. The reason is that you also have to complete the courses required by your major; for most bachelor's degrees, that number will range from 45 to 75 credits. Few people have these major credits completed by the time they hit the total credit requirement (let's say it's 120), and so they have to keep going for an additional semester or two.[2]

That's why you're likely to get a confusing answer when you ask college students how far they are from graduating. "Well," they'll say, "that depends." They'll then explain that the credits they've earned technically give them junior or senior standing, but that they are in fact more

than just a year or two from graduating.

You might wonder, "What's wrong with these people? Why should it be so hard to get 50 or 60 major credits before hitting 120 total? Do they just go crazy with bowling and archery classes?"

The answer, unfortunately, is no. It's true that you need to limit your elective courses if you want to graduate in eight semesters. But that won't be enough.

Remember that, in addition to completing your major requirements, you'll also have to take General Education courses, probably 30 to 40 credit hours' worth (let's say 40). If you're wise, you'll also add a minor, which will tack on another 20 credits or so. Totaling all of that up with a major of, say, 60 required credits, you're looking at 120 hours.

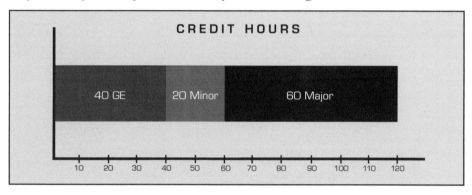

"All right," you say, "so I won't be taking bowling at college. But with careful planning and a little discipline I should have no trouble finishing my degree in four years."

That may be true—*if* you never change your major, or if you change soon enough that you can turn the courses you've taken into a minor without going over the required credits for that minor. But suppose you change your major twice, something that's not uncommon. Or suppose that your major requires not 60 credits but 70 or 80; then changing your mind even once could mean taking more than four years to graduate. It might also preclude you from picking up a minor at all.

Because the risk of things like this happening is fairly high, and because they could cost you so much time, let's take a minute here to play out one of these scenarios. The insights you gain could save you months or even years of extra study.

Let's suppose, for instance, that you think you want to be a doctor. You choose biology as a major, knowing that medical schools will require some biology; you also enjoyed that subject in high school. The biology major, though, requires 70 credits. With 40 credits of required GE, you'll have only 10 left over, not enough for a minor if you want to graduate with just 120 credits, or in eight semesters. Knowing that medical school and the residencies that follow are likely to take at least seven years,[3] you don't want to spend more than four years in undergraduate work. So you decide to skip the minor and give yourself a cushion of 10 elective credits.

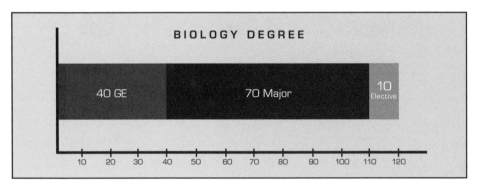

Think, though, of the things that could happen. **What if you find out in your third-year cadaver lab that you don't have the stomach for medicine?** Or what if you make it nearly all the way through college but don't win admission to medical school? You'll have a lot of biology courses on your transcript, probably more than you need for a minor and too many to allow for a change of majors without going over the 120-credit limit.

The bad news is that if you're not going to be a doctor, a bachelor's degree in biology won't be very valuable in the workplace unless you go on for a master's or combine it with something practical like business or health-care management. Your options for graduating with a marketable bachelor's degree might look something like the following:

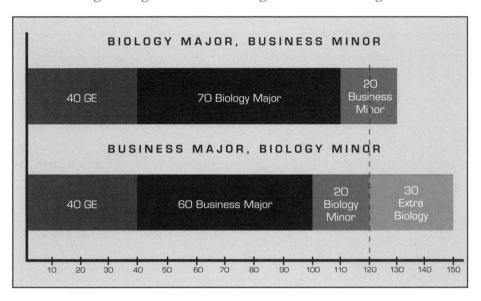

So, **look hard at the number of credits required by your major before you commit to following it all the way through. If the number is large, you'll want to be quite sure that this major is for you.** In fact, whether the major is large or small, be an Eager Beaver and get the full list of courses required—not just the course numbers, but the actual names. Ask to visit with a knowledgeable member of the faculty, ideally a current or former chair of the department that offers the major. In the case of courses whose names don't reveal their purpose (which may be most of them), ask what they are designed to prepare you to do.

In particular, note how often the answer comes back, "You'll need that for graduate school." If you're not planning to get a graduate degree in that field, a few such courses could still be valuable; they're likely to enhance your analysis skills. However, **you want the majority of the courses in your major to be significantly related to your future education and career plans.** If the major you're considering fails that "majority" test, you should probably convert it to a minor.

For example, a future doctor doesn't necessarily need to major in biology; a minor, along with a few other medical school prerequisites, may be enough. Instead of plowing through 70 credits of biology, you might minor in biology and major in something related to medicine that requires fewer credits, such as exercise physiology or psychology.

AN "ASSOCIATED" CAVEAT

Here's another word of warning about your major: As you pursue a bachelor's degree, don't lose sight of the requirements for getting an associate's degree. A lot can happen in the four years (or more) it will take you to get your bachelor's degree. For instance, you could get married or face a financial setback requiring you to drop out of school for a time. Or you might just decide that a four-year degree isn't for you.

In that case, you don't want to be left with no diploma to certify the effort you've made and the things you've learned. One way to avoid that problem is to make sure the courses you take during your first two years of college fulfill the requirements for an associate's degree. Not all bachelor's degrees have a related associate's degree, but your college is likely to have one in "General Studies" or "University Studies," if not one in your specific major. **As you create your four-year**

graduation plan with your college counselor, try to identify the associate's degree you might be able to get while taking your GE courses and the entry-level courses required by your major.

You may find people who tell you not to even think about an associate's degree; they may say that you have "too much potential" to settle for anything but the bachelor's degree. Well, you do have the potential to get a four-year degree, and maybe even to go on to graduate school. But intelligent students, the ones with real potential, understand the value of insurance policies and safety nets in life. Nearly half of all students who start a four-year degree fail to finish.[4] Notwithstanding your commitment and capability, you could be one of them, and it only makes sense to be prepared to make the best of such an outcome.

Think of college like a marathon. It's a long race, and not everyone will finish. But there's a lot to be said for completing a half marathon. You can dream of completing the full race while keeping an eye on the finish line for the half marathon, or the associate's degree.

By paying close attention now to the finish line, you can customize your degree to take the best advantage of all your possibilities.

---

[1]The graduate-school orientation of the bachelor's degree dates back to at least the early 1900s, when the elite Association of American Universities began "effectually accrediting other institutions by listing those whose bachelor's degree holders could be deemed ready for graduate study" (Arthur M. Cohen, *The Shaping of American Higher Education: Emergence and Growth of the Contemporary System,* [Jossey-Bass, 1998], 108).

[2]The average time to graduation is 55 months, or 10 months longer than a student who graduated in eight semesters would take; that suggests roughly two extra semesters (see National Center for Education Statistics, *The Condition of Education,* "Time to Bachelor's Degree Completion," 2003, http://nces.ed.gov/programs/coe/2003/section3/indicator21.asp).

[3]According to the Bureau of Labor Statistics, you should expect to take seven to twelve years in medical schools and subsequent training (see the Bureau's Web site, http://www.bls.gov/k12/help06.htm).

[4]National Center for Education Statistics, *The Condition of Education,* "Postsecondary Graduation Rates," 2009, http://nces.ed.gov/programs/coe/2009/section3/indicator22.asp.

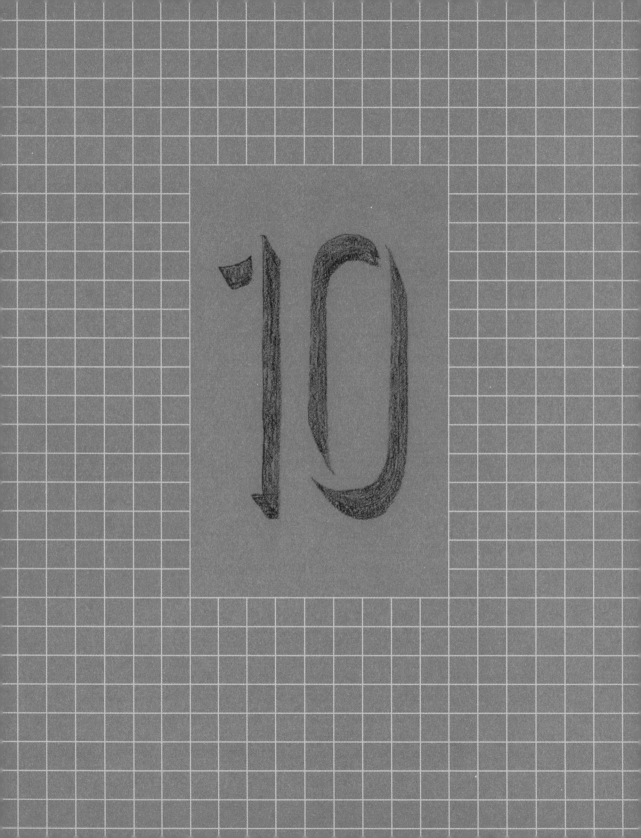

CHAPTER TEN

GENERAL CONTRACTOR'S RULE #4

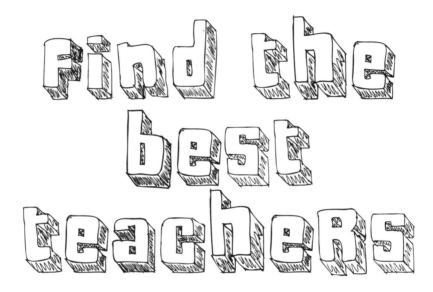

Find the best teachers

And also trust no one to be your teacher nor your minister,
except he be a man of God, walking in his ways
and keeping his commandments.

MOSIAH 23:14

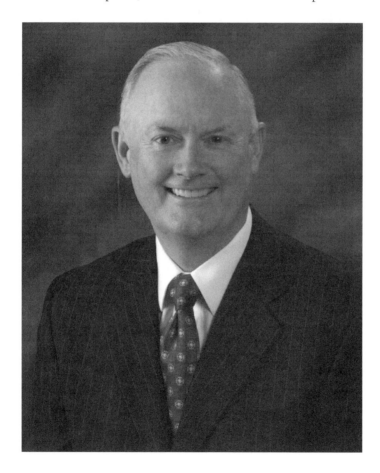

ne of my mentors, Kim Clark, president of BYU–Idaho, remembers the day he got a piece of advice about college that changed his life. Before he registered for his General Education courses, he went to talk with his uncle, a university professor. President Clark asked what courses he should take that year. His uncle replied, "Don't take courses. Take professors."

That's sound advice. Your professors are like the subcontractors who provide the essential components of the house: the electrical wiring, the plumbing, the finish carpentry. The quality of your educational "house" will rest heavily on their skill. You may have the right major and all of the right complementary courses. But if your classes are taught poorly, your college education could resemble a house with lights that flicker and pipes that leak. There could be gaps in your HSJ skills like the gap between a baseboard and a crooked wall.

bRinging the law to life

A great teacher can not only engage and enlighten you but change your life. That was true of Jim Gordon, one of my law professors. I didn't actively find Professor Gordon; he was the teacher of my required course in legal contracts. But I knew from the first day of class that he was one of the best teachers I'd ever seen. For one thing, he was unusually entertaining. He began most classes with a monologue of jokes, many borrowed from the famous comedians of the day; this monologue grabbed our attention and got us ready to contribute to the class discussion that was soon to follow. Professor Gordon had other stand-up comedy gifts: Once, slipping off his shoes, he climbed up on the long table at the front of our law school courtroom and moon-walked across it.

Professor Gordon was also enthusiastic about what we were learning. In our legal writing class (another required course) he found a way to get us excited about such traditionally unpopular subjects as grammar and footnote formatting. Once, having read to us a writing sample from a case in which the judge had needlessly repeated himself, Professor Gordon shouted, "That's redundant! Not only that, it says the same thing twice."

Most important, Professor Gordon taught us to think like lawyers. In his securities class, an elective course that I took because he was teaching it, he challenged us to question our assumptions and look at issues from all possible angles, not just the most obvious one. That lawyerly technique is one of the most important analysis skills when it comes to making HSJs. Professor Gordon warned us, for example, not to trust an investment just because it bears the name "security." He showed, using one historical case after another, how a security, such as a stock, is worth nothing more than what someone else is willing to pay for it. Professor Gordon's warnings rang in my ears during the infamous dot-com bubble of the late 1990s, when start-up companies with nothing more than a Web site sold billions of dollars of stock to greedy buyers and promptly went bankrupt. That warning helped me avoid the market crash with my personal financial investments.

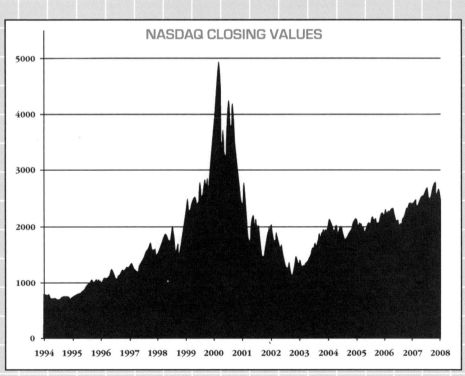

NASDAQ CLOSING VALUES

TEACHING HURDLES

As you learned in high school, great teaching is a gift that not everyone has. In fact, in college there are forces at work that sometimes make it hard for even naturally gifted teachers to perform well in the classroom. One, which we talked about when you were choosing a school, is class size. Some college classes are too big for anyone to teach well.

Professors at universities also face pressures outside of the classroom that can detract from their teaching. For example, young professors teach at the same time they're trying to establish themselves as researchers. If they fail to produce enough scholarly publications, they won't win tenure, which is the guarantee of continued employment at the university. (You'll sometimes hear this described as the mandate to "publish or perish.")

Notwithstanding their teaching responsibilities, the success of these young university professors in getting tenure depends primarily on research productivity. Really poor teaching could be a problem for them at tenure-decision time. But the converse isn't true: Even great teaching won't compensate for poor research. When faced with the choice, then, untenured professors need to invest their discretionary time in research rather than teaching-related activities. That research could benefit you, as the professor brings leading-edge concepts and a spirit of inquiry into the classroom. But you can see how it might also come at your expense.

Even tenured professors may put research activities ahead of teaching. Some of them give teaching responsibilities such as grading papers to graduate students so that they can spend more time on their research. Tenure, which exists not only at research universities but at many small colleges, means that a professor who has achieved this status can't be

dismissed for sub-par teaching. Of course there are minimum standards, and the majority of professors give teaching their best as a matter of principle and pride. But really good teaching is more a personal choice and a sacrifice than a job requirement for tenured professors. They need not feel threatened by anything but unusually poor course evaluations. It would probably surprise you to know how much less attention many pay to RateMyProfessors.com than you and your classmates do. **Both the research-driven process of winning tenure and the job security that results from it mean that you've got to be picky about your professors.**

NON-TENURE-TRACK TEACHERS

Many of the teachers you'll see listed when you register for classes are neither tenured professors nor assistant professors trying to win tenure. A significant percentage of the course "sections" (classes offered at a particular time by a particular teacher) will be taught by part-timers, graduate students, and full-time professors who are not on the tenure track. Taking a course from one of these non-tenure-track professors isn't necessarily a bad thing. It's true that many of them will have less classroom experience. It's also true that universities and colleges tend to hire them because they are less expensive than tenure-track professors. However, as in the case of professors who have research responsibilities, you can't judge the quality of a teacher by the category he or she falls into.

In fact, some of the nontraditional faculty members may be among the best teachers. For example, a part-timer (often called an "adjunct" professor) may be employed outside of the school in a company of the kind you want to work for after graduation; the insight that professor might give you into real-world application of the things you're learning could be invaluable. Likewise, a graduate student, though less experienced in the classroom, may actually be a more effective teacher because he or she remembers what it was like to be in your

> *Regardless of employment contracts and relative emphasis on teaching versus research, every college and university has good teachers, just as every high school does. The best teachers at the college level are very, very good. A key part of being the general contractor of your education is finding those teachers.*

shoes, having been there not too long ago. And non-tenure-track profes-sors may have the advantage of a passion for teaching that they are able to spend full time developing. They might bring unique teaching meth-ods, such as case studies or group projects, into the classroom.

You won't always be able to handpick your teachers. Some of the courses you need for your major will be taught by only one professor, who is the department's specialist in that area. But the good news is that, based on things we've talked about, you will have chosen a school and a department in which student learning is a priority. So even when you don't have a choice of professors, the one you get will be pretty good.

You'll discover that many courses are taught by more than one pro-fessor each semester; that will be true, for instance, of GE offerings, where many sections of each course are offered. You'll also be able to choose among elective courses both in GE and in your major. In those cases, you might decide to "take" a great professor, not worrying so much about the subject matter of the course. The quality of what you learn from that professor could make the particular course content of secondary importance, as I found to be the case with everything Profes-sor Gordon taught.

MAKING THE MOST—BUT NOT TOO MUCH— OF RATEMYPROFESSORS.COM

Now, you probably think you know how to find the great professors at your school. Even if you're not in college yet, you may have heard from friends who are there to never sign up for a course without check-ing RateMyProfessors.com. It's true that you should make the most of

the opinions of your peers who know a professor from firsthand experience. But be careful. Sometimes a professor gets a bad rap—or a good one—for the wrong reasons. I learned that when, as director of an MBA program, I interviewed students at graduation time. Before getting a diploma, each of them was required to complete a survey in which we asked them to name their most valuable and least valuable courses over the past two years.

I found something surprising in those interviews. Often there was a big difference between what the students said as they were graduating and the written course evaluations they had done at the end of each semester. That was especially true of the first-year courses, taken when the students were less experienced (and most overworked). **Some of the courses that got bad evaluations the year before turned out to be among the most appreciated by graduation time.** And the converse was also true; many courses that were liked as they ended were, at graduation, rated "least valuable."

I couldn't understand this at first. But as I explored the discrepancy, I discovered that the students' views had changed as they matured. When they were young, stressed-out, first-year students, they appreciated professors who let them off easily. That's a temptation you'll face as a college student. When the pressure is on, you may actually prefer the professors who, by asking less of you, are giving you less of what you've paid for in your education. If you think about it, that would be like telling the finish carpenter on your new house, "You know, you're taking an awfully long time and making a lot of dust. Can you wrap things up early so I can move in? I don't mind if you're not finished; I'll pay you the full price anyway."

With a bit of hindsight and experience, my MBA students realized that they hadn't learned much in their easy courses. That became clear especially as they performed summer internships, where their employers expected them to

"I LOVE THIS CLASS."

have more than a passing understanding of the subjects they had been taught. When it came time to deliver on what they knew, the students suddenly felt a new appreciation for the tougher professors, the ones who pushed them and, in so doing, gave them their money's worth.

That means you need to do an analytical double click on the comments you find on RateMyProfessors.com. In particular, be careful to distinguish between statements like, "This guy doesn't care about his students," and, "The workload was completely over the top." The former complaint is one you probably want to take seriously; the latter may not be. Very often, the professors who care the most, and who are putting the most into the course, are the ones who demand the most from you in return.

The safest way to find a great professor is to get your own information, just as you did in choosing a school. Talk directly to people who have taken a class from the professor. Better yet, attend the class yourself. You could even visit the professor during office hours.

YOUR PROFESSOR AS A MENTOR

In a few cases, you may be able to develop a relationship with a favorite professor that goes beyond the classroom. Particularly if you are the kind of student who does more than is required and is motivated to learn, as opposed to just seeking a good grade, your professor may take a personal interest in you. If that happens, the professor could be an invaluable source of insight not just into a particular academic subject, but into the process of getting a good education and finding the right career. The professor also might become a valued recommender for graduate school and full-time employment.

You're most likely to cultivate this kind of relationship if you're aware of what the professor might be glad to get in return. Of course, he or she will find satisfaction in merely helping you develop. However, you could provide additional benefits if you thought about the professor's other objectives. Those probably include helping students who are struggling in class and taking up a disproportionate percentage of the professor's office hours. You might offer to work with those students,

drawing from your knowledge of the subjects they struggle with. In fact, you'll find that teaching others is the best way to increase your understanding of a subject.

You might also make a special study of the professor's research interests. You could start by reading his or her published papers. Then you might ask whether there is a current research topic on which you could be of help. Even if your work as a research assistant were unpaid, you could find the learning well worth the time invested. In fact, if you are thinking about becoming a professor yourself, you'll need not only a good graduate school recommendation but also some experience with academic research. **Being an undergraduate research assistant wouldn't be easy, but it could be the highlight of your college experience and produce an invaluable relationship.**

THE GREAT TEACHER

Remember that the connection between a teacher and learner is unique to the two of them, just like the connection between two friends. Even the most popular teachers aren't liked by every student, and once in a while a generally unpopular teacher turns out to be someone's favorite. Just as every teacher teaches differently, every learner has a unique learning style. Look for teachers whose style works for you, even if they're not everybody's hot chili pepper.

One common quality to look for, though, is described by President David O. McKay, who was a schoolteacher and a principal before being called as an Apostle: "The successful teacher is one who, with a spirit of discernment, can detect to a degree at least, the mentality and capability of the members of his class. He should be able to read the facial expressions and be responsive to the mental and spiritual attitudes of

those whom he is teaching. The Great Teacher had this power of discernment in perfection, as is well illustrated in His conversation with the woman of Samaria, whose interests He not only interpreted, but whose soul He also read by virtue of her past deeds."[1]

All of my great teachers have had the gift of discerning my learning needs. And all of them reminded me of the Great Teacher. Look for that kind of teacher, and when you find one, hang on; take as many courses from him or her as your graduation plan allows.

[1]David O. McKay, *Gospel Ideals: Selections from the Discourses of David O. McKay* (Improvement Era, 1953), 439.

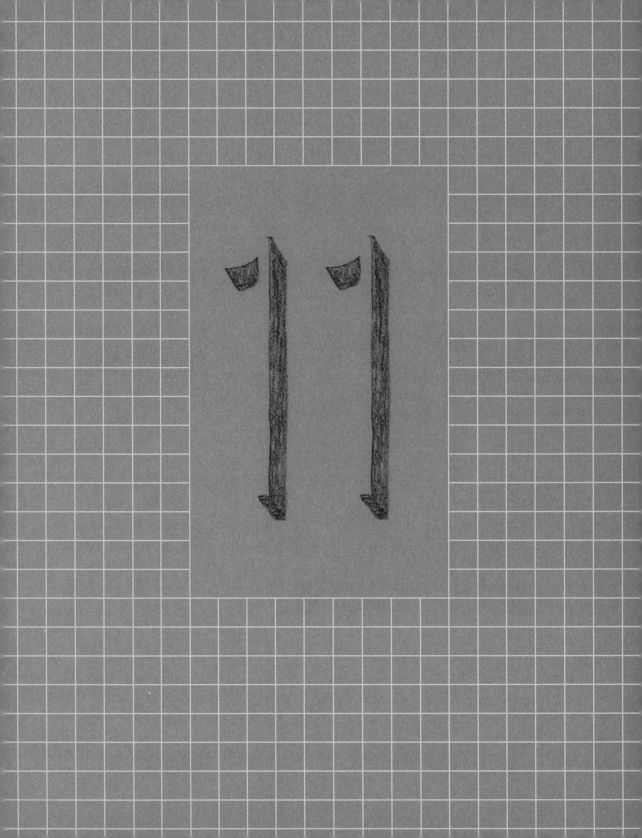

CHAPTER ELEVEN

GENERAL CONTRACTOR'S RULE #5

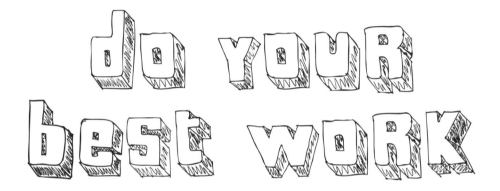

do your best work

Know ye not that they which run in a race run all,
but one receiveth the prize? So run, that ye may obtain.

1 CORINTHIANS 9:24

ven a layman can tell a well-built house from a shoddy one. It's particularly easy to distinguish between the work of professional builders and that of amateurs. The same thing is true of a college education. You have just one shot at college. Many of your HSJ skills, especially people skills and moral sense, will come in the workplace, over time. But college lays the essential foundation, especially when it comes to analysis skills. If you give college less than your best effort, you're likely to leave with lasting deficiencies that will be hard or even impossible to make up.

I still remember, with sadness, interviews with MBA applicants who tried to explain why their undergraduate GPAs didn't reflect their true capabilities. I felt like a building inspector, hearing excuses about why a house wasn't "up to code." Some applicants would say, "I goofed off my freshman and sophomore years, but since then I've gotten good grades."

Others would explain, "I know that my GPA is below average, but I worked thirty hours a week to put myself through school. Just imagine how well I could have done if I hadn't worked."

Occasionally there was evidence that these excuses were valid: A candidate's subsequent achievements demonstrated that the lackluster GPA wasn't indicative of his or her real abilities. But even in those cases, I felt lingering doubts. C and D grades on a transcript are a red flag when you don't personally know the candidate you're talking to. And there's almost always another candidate with a better GPA. **When grades are the only thing separating two otherwise equally qualified people, it's hard to justify taking a chance.** In most of these situations I ended up saying something like this: "I wish I could imagine how you might perform if you had college to do over again. But we have other candidates who have proven what they can do."

YOUR BEST SHOT

To avoid this kind of conversation with a prospective employer or graduate school admissions officer, make sure that your college record reflects your best effort and ability. **As a general rule, you need to allocate at least two hours of out-of-class study time for every hour you spend in class. For example, if you are taking fifteen credit hours, you'll want to spend at least thirty hours each week doing homework.** That means a commitment of at least forty-five hours per week to school. But remember that the serious students will be giving it more time than that. If you hope to earn A's and B's, you need to be realistic about what it will take for you to perform at that level, given the time and effort that others are investing.

To begin with, don't enroll in any class unless you're prepared to give everything it takes. If you plan to spend the first year at college partying, stay home and party until you've gotten it out of your system. Likewise, if your schedule is so heavy that you don't have a good chance of getting an A or a B in a class, either change the schedule or drop the class.

be a focused student

Be especially careful about working your way through college. Your parents may have done this, and limited financial resources may make you feel that you need to do the same thing. But times have changed since your parents went to college. Student loans are easier to come by these days. More students are borrowing money, foregoing part-time jobs,

and dedicating themselves to their studies full time.[1] Because many college professors grade on a curve, you'll get an A only if you can beat the students who are studying full time. If part of your time is off the table because of a job, you're at a disadvantage. You may be better off dropping the job and picking up an additional student loan. Or, if you feel uncomfortable adding to your student debt, you may want to drop out and work for a semester—full time—and then come back to school. If working while you go to school is unavoidable, take only as many classes as you can handle at a high level of performance.

The same thing goes for extracurricular activities. You can learn a lot leading a service club or an intramural athletic team. In fact, it may be easier to develop people skills and moral sense in extracurricular activities like these than in the classroom. Some graduate schools and employers will be justifiably impressed by this kind of activity on your résumé. Remember, though, that the primary measure of your success at college is classroom performance. Don't let extracurricular activity compromise your formal learning or your transcript, which is the most-trusted manifestation of what a new college graduate is capable of.

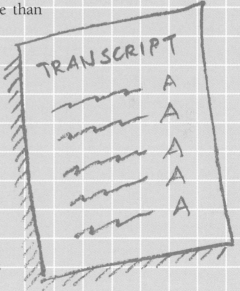

Now, you may have read all of this and thought, "I wish you'd told me this before I started college. I've gotten some lousy grades. What should I do?" The answer is that if you have low grades (C's or D's) that don't represent what you can really do, you should consider retaking the classes. You might want to do that even if you've gotten a mediocre grade (a B- or C+) in a subject that you really need to know in your chosen profession. For instance, if you hope to be a pharmacist and you got a C+ in organic chemistry, you probably ought to retake it. Even if your school averages the new grade in with the old one, rather than replacing the old with the new, you'll have shown what you can really do. And you'll be confident that you've mastered the subject. Be your own building inspector throughout your college experience, making sure as you go that when you graduate your degree will be up to code.

STAYING AHEAD OF THE GAME

Almost all students who have performed below their abilities in college courses will tell you that they made the mistake of getting behind. At the beginning of the semester, the pace seemed all right, maybe even a little relaxed. But before long things started moving faster, and by the end of the semester there was just no catching up. It's a common experience, reminiscent of the great *I Love Lucy* episode where Lucy and Ethel are working on a chocolate candy assembly line that keeps picking up speed.[2] Before long, rather than wrapping every chocolate, they are stuffing most of them in their mouths (and other places).

The key to performing well in college is staying ahead of the game. You

don't necessarily have to spend more time than the other students; you just need to invest that time in advance. It begins with class preparation. Be Eager Beaver. Prepare for every class by reading all of the assigned material in advance; make note of questions you want to find answers to in class.

Never miss a class. Sit near the front and, if the professor invites participation, be prepared to raise your hand at least once every day. Try to make comments that take the class discussion in the direction the professor seems to be going; avoid attempts to impress others or dominate the discussion.

Take notes not only of the important things that are said but of insights or questions that come to you. In law school, I learned from classmates to take notes with a vertical line down the center of the page. On the left we noted key statements by the professor and other students. On the right we made notes to ourselves, things like, "This is important!" or "Find out more about this." We set aside time after class to consolidate our notes and follow up on the things we had written in the right-hand column. Later, when it came time to prepare for exams, we focused on that column.

In fact, we treated every day as an exam preparation day. Of course,

there was still an intense week or two of "cramming" at the end of the semester, but we'd been thinking all along about the questions likely to be posed on exams. The same thing was true of assigned papers: Rather than waiting to start writing until a few weeks before the deadline, we began our researching and outlining immediately. **You'll have no trouble in college or graduate school if, instead of thinking, "I wonder when I'll have to start working on this assignment," you say, "I wonder how soon I can start."**

SEEKING GUIDANCE

Another key to building a great college education is to understand what is expected in each course. Most courses are designed so that the rules are clear and success is largely a matter of working hard and staying ahead of the game. Those rules are captured in the syllabus, which is the most important document you'll read in the course, the professor's statement of what will be taught and what is expected of you. Be sure to fully understand the syllabus from the beginning, and refer to it often throughout the semester.

Occasionally, even your best efforts will leave you feeling that something is missing, that you just don't have a grasp of the subject or of what the professor is trying to help you accomplish. If this happens—as it probably will at least once in your college career—look for opportunities to go the extra mile. Join study groups. Attend special tutorial sessions that the professor may hold. Seek out teaching assistants or labs where help may be offered, including the university tutoring center. Remember the great gospel principle, "It is by grace that we are saved, after all we can do" (2 Nephi 25:23).

If, after all you can do, you're still struggling, seek feedback from your professor. Because you'll have come prepared for every class, sat near the front, and made regular efforts to contribute, your professor will know you and your good intentions. He or she will want to help you and may

> *Use the syllabus to determine not just what the professor wants you to do but what he or she hopes you will learn. Be aware of what it will take to earn a good grade, but don't let the accumulation of points take precedence over real learning. A perfect grade is less valuable in the long run than a great learning experience. If you pay the price to learn, the grade will take care of itself and you'll get the education you need.*

have insight into things you could do differently. Maybe you're focusing too much on facts and figures and failing to see the bigger picture. Maybe you're investing too much time in activities that don't matter as much as others. Perhaps you have trouble appreciating viewpoints different from your own. Your professor, who will probably know you better than you think, could provide guidance that will prove valuable not just in the class but throughout your life.

As you approach your professor, though, try to imagine and keep in mind what happens to him or her during office hours. Very few students who come for help have done everything they can for themselves, as you'll have been careful to do. Some bring questions they could have answered by doing the "extra" reading or by asking a fellow student. Others are looking for leniency with deadlines or the chance to do makeup work.

Worst of all, many of your classmates come to the professor's office to wrangle over grades. Sometimes these students are on the brink of failing the class. More often, though, they are the competitive students who need an A to maintain a scholarship or to win graduate school admission. They tend to argue over any point that might move them up a grade. This kind of conversation is the bane of all professors, the one thing about an otherwise great job that even the most saintly teacher can hardly bear.

Grading requires quantifying things that are difficult and even impossible to quantify. Doing it well is tremendously time-consuming. And, in the case of final grades, it must be done under tight deadlines, often requiring night and weekend work. All the while, the professor labors with the unpleasant vision of students coming to dispute their grades.

So, as you seek your professor's help, do so without concern about your grade. Some grading systems really are ambiguous, and you may in fact need special guidance to improve your performance in the class. But seek that guidance in the spirit of true learning. Come to your professor's office having done all you can for yourself, and be open to whatever counsel you receive. Remember that there is much more at stake than a grade. You could learn eternally valuable things about yourself. And you could win a lifelong friend and mentor.

---

[1]C.C. Wei and L. Berkner, *Trends in Undergraduate Borrowing II: Federal Student Loans in 1995–1996, 1999–2000, and 2003–2004* (NCES 2008–179rev), National Center for Education Statistics, Institute of Education Sciences, U.S. Department of Education, Washington, DC, figure 1-A (page 7 of report), http://nces.ed.gov/pubs2008/2008179rev.pdf.

[2]This hilarious clip can be viewed on YouTube: <http://www.youtube.com/watch?v=4wp3m1vg06Q>.

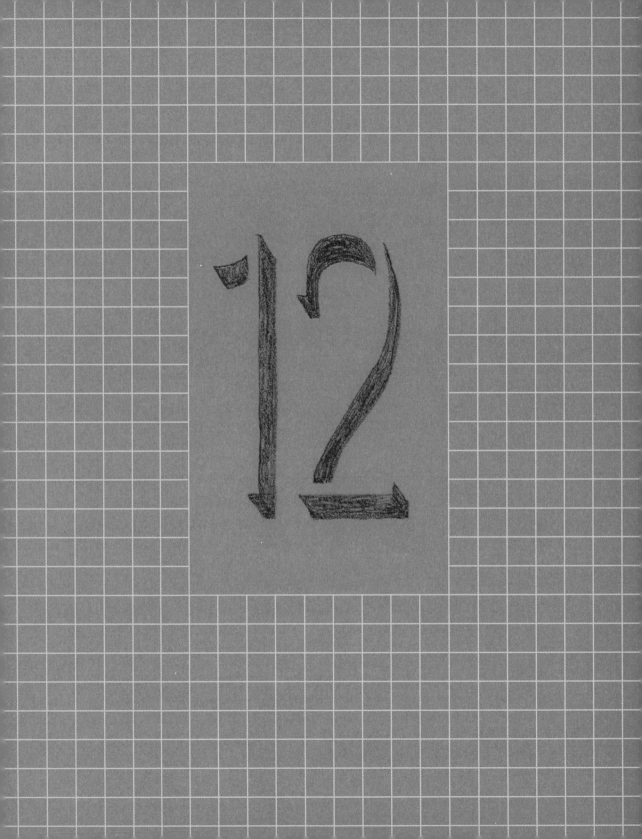

CHAPTER TWELVE

GENERAL CONTRACTOR'S RULE #6

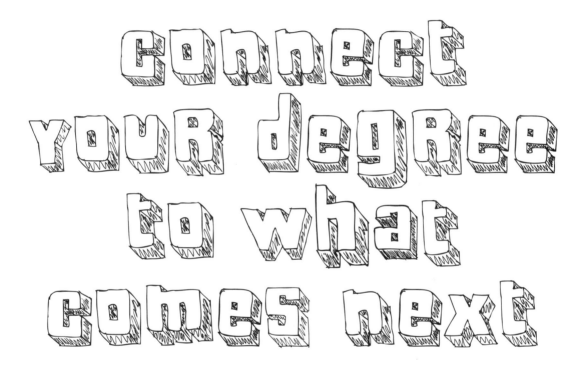

Connect your degree to what comes next

Prepare ye, prepare ye for that which is to come.
DOCTRINE AND COVENANTS 1:12

e've already talked a lot about your personal responsibility to ensure that college prepares you for what comes next, even if oil is selling for just eight dollars a barrel or, for any other reason, graduates in your field are having trouble finding work. You have to be sure that your college education connects either to the workplace or to graduate school, just as a general contractor has to arrange for power and water and gas hookups for a house. A college degree that doesn't prepare you for what comes next is like a finished house with no lights, water, or heat.

It's possible to start making these connections while you're still on campus. You might look for student societies in your field, where outside professionals are invited to come and speak about what they do. You may also find student-led organizations that give hands-on work experience. For example, my daughter Emily, an English major, had great practical experiences writing for the student newspaper. In some ways, it was even better than working for a commercial newspaper, because she was given a lot of responsibility very quickly. The student paper was run to high standards, and her experience there prepared her well for a professional writing career.

Though campus extracurricular activities can be useful, probably the most effective way to connect your education to life after graduation is to do off-campus internships. (These also go by the names "externships" and "co-ops.") An internship helps you test what you're learning and put it into real-world perspective. During the internship you'll discover the gaps in your HSJ skills. You'll also get a better sense of whether you like what people in your field do for a living. As a result, you'll go back to college with clearer learning goals.

For example, Emily followed up her semester on the school newspaper with an internship at a magazine publishing company. She was pleasantly surprised by the difference between newspapers and magazines. At the magazine company she was given responsibility for articles that included lots of photos and illustrations. She discovered a passion for the layout of both printed words and associated graphics. She also came to appreciate the lengthier publication cycle of magazines. At a newspaper, deadlines are tight: It can seem that anything that isn't due tomorrow is due today. That leaves little time to polish a piece of work. Magazine contributors, by contrast, have greater leeway in the publication schedule. Emily enjoyed having days and sometimes even weeks to get an article just right.

Having learned of these important differences and her own preferences, Emily changed her plans when she returned to school from the internship. She continued to work for the school newspaper, as it provided the closest thing she could find on campus to magazine publishing. But she changed her major from English to communications, which

allowed her to pick up courses in graphic design and visual media while still developing her writing skills. And she looked for opportunities to write features for the newspaper that included magazine-style layouts. She also learned to create her own Web sites, opening up career opportunities in digital media. Her internship, in other words, didn't just help her identify her preferred profession. It allowed her to change her education plan in time to prepare for that profession.

A FREE LUNCH

I did one internship—that summer after my freshman year when I worked in an oil company office with Doyle the draftsman. The perspective I got of the actual practice of geology helped me choose my later courses and focus my learning. But I should have done at least one more internship, maybe two. If I had, I'd have been better positioned to get a job at graduation. I might even have found an internship that led to a full-time job offer before graduation.

henry christian

My son Henry Christian (we call him H.C.) has discovered the benefit of multiple internships. He did his first one the summer before starting college. His uncle offered him a job at a financial investment firm, where H.C. spent three months building spreadsheets and studying companies that the firm was thinking about buying. His analysis skills were stretched to the limit and beyond. He worked the long hours—sometimes twelve hours a day—that the full-time members of the firm did. And he was paid nothing. The only compensation he got, other than great learning experiences, was a free catered sandwich each day.

When H.C. mentioned this apparent unfairness to me, I reminded him that he wasn't doing the internship to make money; he was doing it to learn and to get a credential. "That's the same reason you go to college," I pointed out. I reminded him that you don't get paid to go to college; in fact, *you* pay for the privilege. And there are no free sandwiches.

H.C. began to reap the benefit of his unpaid internship that fall, when he went back to school. The things he had learned during the summer gave him real-world perspective on his studies. For example, the income statements and balance sheets his accounting professor introduced that first semester looked familiar to him, thanks to his struggles with accounting statements the summer before. He was excited when he learned things in the classroom that would have saved him hours if he'd known about them when he was working late nights at the investment firm. His experience of struggling to understand a problem on the job made the answer really stick when it was presented in class.

The benefits of the first internship became clearer the next summer, when H.C. got a position with a consulting firm in Boston. Not only was he paid this time, but his weekly salary was the same as what new college graduates were making. Because of his experience from the year before, he was ready to carry more responsibility in this second internship. Assigned to support a senior consultant, he gradually demonstrated his ability to manage his own work. In time he was trusted to attend meetings with the firm's clients and even orient a newly hired consultant. His people skills grew.

In both internships, H.C. worked with people of high moral character. He saw the difficult decisions that must be made in the world of work. He returned to school with insights into moral sense that changed what he saw in his textbooks and classroom discussions.

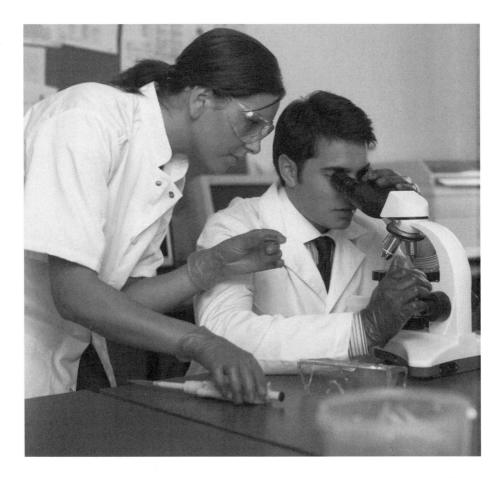

Instead of backpacking or surfing during your breaks from college, give serious thought to two or even three internships. It doesn't matter what they pay you or how much rent *you* might have to pay to live in a big city like Boston or New York. In fact, **a good internship is even worth taking off during fall or winter semester if**

that's the only time you can get it. The investment may be worth as much as or more than what you'll be paying each semester for tuition.

One day you'll graduate from college. You'll be grateful then if you've prepared yourself well to move right into what comes next.

GENERAL CONTRACTOR'S RULE #7

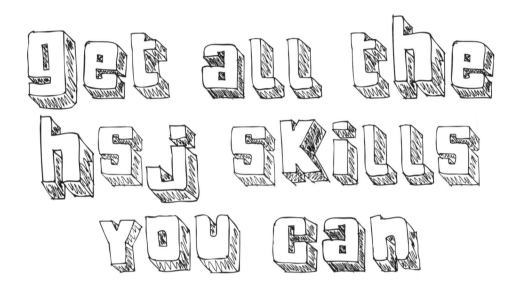

get all the hsj skills you can

O, remember, my son, and learn wisdom in thy youth.

ALMA 37:35

ollege, as we've discussed before, isn't really designed to give you all the HSJ skills you'll need for a successful career. Ideally, you'll go on to graduate school; if your education is a house, graduate school puts the second story on it. That's where you learn most of the analysis and people skills, as well as some of the moral sense, required to make HSJs.

But remember, you're Eager Beaver. You can find HSJ learning opportunities even as an undergraduate. One way to do it is to find courses that teach analysis skills, people skills, and moral sense. The analysis skills courses will have titles like Logic, Argumentation, Quantitative Reasoning, and Statistics for the Real World. People skills courses might be called Rhetoric, Communication, Organizational Behavior, or Leadership. You could learn something about moral sense in courses with names like Ethics, Philosophy, and Power and Influence.

You'll want to choose these courses carefully, though. In particular, be aware of the difference between a course that is merely *about* analysis skills or people skills or moral sense and one that really lets you *practice* those skills. For example, much of the time in a college ethics class is likely to be spent in lectures about the theories of such philosophers as Socrates and Aristotle and Immanuel Kant. Their ideas about right and wrong and "the good life" are useful, to a point.

WALKING THE TALK

You, though, are trying to build actual capabilities. You need to do more than merely study different theories of moral sense; you need to *practice* making moral judgments. A course that, from beginning to end, presents lectures on the lives and theories of the great philosophers won't allow you to develop and practice a moral philosophy of your own. That would be like taking a survey course on all the major architectural styles and hoping at the end of the semester to be a qualified architect. What you need, in addition to theory, is the opportunity to practice making HSJs.

And so, along with courses *about* analysis skills and people skills and moral sense, look for courses that let you practice making decisions, regardless of the subject matter. Such courses could include one in history, if the professor invited you and your classmates to think about, say, how India and Pakistan could have been divided in 1947 with less bloodshed. You

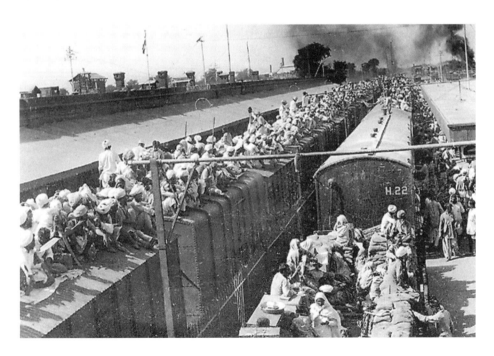

Someday, when your boss assigns you to write a memo on an important issue, you won't want to ask, "How much time should I spend on this?" or "How long does the memo have to be?" (The answer to both questions is, "As long as necessary, but no longer.") Always look for professors who put the responsibility for your learning on you, both in and out of the classroom.

could also develop HSJ skills in a human biology class, if you were part of a team challenged to decide whether a comatose patient should be kept on life support.

As you can see, the style of a professor's teaching may matter more than what he or she teaches. Lectures, no matter how interesting, are less valuable than the opportunity to discuss and decide things. And a professor with high expectations is more valuable to you than one who makes things easy. Don't be put off when you hear that a professor is demanding, or when, having enrolled in the course, you find that the syllabus doesn't tell you exactly what it takes to get an A. The very process of figuring out what constitutes A-level work is a high-stakes judgment.

FIELDWORK

Along with great courses, look for out-of-class experiences that offer practice in making HSJs. Internships provide that kind of learning opportunity, as do the right kinds of extracurricular activities, particularly those that allow you to serve and lead in areas related to your career interests.

In addition, your major may offer opportunities for fieldwork. Some majors, such as elementary and secondary education and nursing, require it. So does geology. Fieldwork, in which professors take students out into the world where they will work, provides tremendous learning opportunities. That certainly was true for me. For all I gained from great teachers in the classroom, my best geology learning experiences came during my summer of required field camp.

In fact, I learned a lesson on my very first day of field camp that may have been worth as much as all of my time in class put together. About twenty of us soon-to-graduate geology students were loaded into vans and driven from the tiny southern Utah town of Gunlock out toward the desert. Every half mile or so, one of us would be dropped off and told to make a simple map of the rock formations in the area.

When my turn came, I got out of the van and found myself standing in a cow pasture. (There weren't cows there at the time, but I could see plenty of organic evidence that it was a pasture.) I looked around and felt sure I was the victim of a mistake—or even a prank. There wasn't a rock in sight. I dutifully walked the area, hoping to find something to

work on. The ground was entirely covered with grass; there was absolutely nothing for a geologist to map. So I sat down and waited for the van, which was due to pick me up at noon.

While I waited, my frustration grew. Why, I thought, would they waste my time this way? Southern Utah is famous for fantastic rock formations; I could see great mapping opportunities down the road in either direction. What was I doing in a pasture?

When the van came and delivered me back to our base camp, I made a beeline for our faculty leader, Professor Lehi Hintze. Professor Hintze was a handsome, silver-haired gentleman a few years from retirement. He had been leading geology field camps for decades.

Fortunately for me, Professor Hintze had learned great patience in all those years of working with inexperienced students. When I launched into him, complaining about having spent the morning in a cow pasture, he said nothing. In fact, he just smiled a bit. That made me angrier still. "Are you telling me that I'm supposed to map that pasture?" I almost shouted.

"Yes," he replied calmly.

"How in the world can I do that?" I shot back.

"Dig," he said. I was dumbfounded. I stared for a moment, wondering if he was putting me through some kind of new-student hazing. But he seemed to really mean it.

"How am I supposed to dig?" I finally sputtered. "All I have is my rock hammer."

"Borrow a shovel," he answered.

That day, after four years of classroom study,

I started to become a real geologist. I swallowed my pride and borrowed a shovel. The van took me back to the pasture, and I spent the afternoon digging. Sure enough, there were rocks under all that grass. When I dug down far enough, I even found the bedrock formations that allowed me to create my first geologic map. I returned to camp that night victorious (though ashamed for the way I had acted in the morning).

LESSONS ABOUT ANALYSIS SKILLS, PEOPLE SKILLS, AND MORAL SENSE

That first day in the field was critical to my training as a geologist because it began to put my classroom learning into perspective. But it did more than that. It also began to build my HSJ capability. In the pasture I learned important lessons about analysis skills, people skills, and even moral sense.

I learned, for example, one of the most important of all analysis skills—that you have to dig through the "dirt" to get to the "bedrock" of most analytical problems. A challenging organizational problem, for instance, will never come with the essential information laid out, like an exercise in a textbook. You have to dig for the data you need.

The pasture experience also taught me something about people skills. I learned the

Even seemingly precise jobs like accounting involve some guesswork. Accounting statements may look cut-and-dried, with everything detailed down to the last dollar. But when accountants state the value of something complex, such as a bundle of home mortgages, they can do little more than make a best guess. The world learned that the hard way in 2008, when many of the largest banks failed because of their reliance on overvalued mortgages.

danger of attacking someone on suspicions of bad faith. I had assumed that Professor Hintze, whom I had never met before field camp, was out to get me. Because of this rash and unfounded assumption, I nearly ruined what turned out to be a great, lasting friendship. I also learned, from Professor Hintze's undeservedly gentle reply, how people of great character can, when they choose, suffer fools kindly.

Finally, that day of mapping in the pasture also taught me a bit of moral sense. It turns out that, even with a lot of digging, I couldn't be exactly sure of what the rock formations looked like at every point of my map. Like so many things in life, geologic mapping requires some educated guessing.

The key, in those difficult situations, is not only to make an honest guess but also to be honest in *saying* that you're guessing. A geologist does that, for example, by using dotted lines instead of solid ones when it's not clear which way the rock formations are going at a particular place.

On my first attempt at drawing the geologic map of the pasture, I drew all solid lines. I wanted to impress Professor Hintze with my certainty. But then I remembered complaining to him that it was impossible to find *any* rocks in my pasture. I imagined how Professor Hintze might respond to a student who knew absolutely nothing at lunchtime but by dinnertime knew everything. With that thought in mind, I drew a new map, one with lots of dotted lines. My new map wasn't as impressive as the ones made by classmates in areas with all exposed rock formations, where it was easy to draw solid lines. But my map was true to my area and the guesses I had to make about it.

YOUR GRADUATION PRESENT

In the end, the rules for being the general contractor of your college education are straightforward:

1. Always have a career dream.
2. Always have a major.
3. Customize your degree.
4. Find the best teachers.
5. Do your best work.
6. Connect your degree to what comes next.
7. Get all the HSJ skills you can.

Putting all of these rules into practice isn't always easy. In fact, the different and sometimes competing purposes of universities can sometimes make it quite hard to apply them. You can't expect your professors or even your academic advisers to provide everything you need. But if you choose the right school and keep the rules in mind from the beginning, you stand a great chance of success.

And if a person gains more knowledge and intelligence
in this life through his diligence and obedience than another,
he will have so much the advantage in the world to come.

DOCTRINE AND COVENANTS 130:19

ongratulations! You're going forth armed with a great plan for your college experience. But it doesn't end here. At some point, you'll be deciding whether to aim for more schooling or head straight to the workforce. (More discussion of those decisions is available online at majordecisionsforcollege.com.) Whatever you choose, learning should be a prominent goal throughout your life, not just in school or your job.

"The object of this existence is to learn. . . . How gladly would we understand every principle pertaining to science and art, and become thoroughly acquainted with every intricate operation of nature, and with all the chemical changes that are constantly going on around us! How delightful this would be, and what a boundless field of truth and power is open for us to explore! We are only just approaching the shores of the vast ocean of information that pertains to this physical world, to say nothing of that which pertains to the heavens, to angels and celestial beings, to the place of their habitation, to the manner of their life, and their progress to still higher degrees of perfection."[1]

PRESIDENT BRIGHAM YOUNG

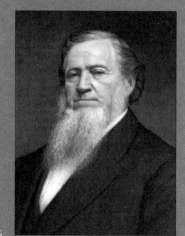

My father has said it this way: **"No service that matters can be given over a lifetime by those who stop learning.** A great teacher is always studying. A nurse never stops facing the challenge of dealing with something new, be it equipment or procedure. And the workplace in every industry is changing so rapidly that what we know today will not be enough for tomorrow. Our education must never stop. If it ends at the door of the classroom on graduation day, we will fail. And since what we will need to know is hard to discern, we need the help of heaven to know which of the myriad things we could study we would most wisely learn. It also means that we cannot waste time entertaining ourselves when we have the chance to read or to listen to whatever will help us learn what is true and useful. Insatiable curiosity will be our hallmark."[2]

Anticipating the argument that there is too little time to keep learning after careers have started and families have come, he added this time-management counsel: "Too often we use many hours for fun and pleasure, clothed in the euphemism 'I'm recharging my batteries.' Those hours could be spent reading and studying to gain knowledge, skills, and culture.

"For instance, we too often fail to take advantage of the moments we spend waiting. Think of the last time you sat in a barber shop or a beauty salon or the waiting room of a doctor's office. It is so

easy to spend time thumbing through any magazine that is stacked on a table there. In fact, if you think about it, you will remember how you wondered where they get those out-of-date magazines. There is much valuable reading you could do if you took a book with you to fill those islands of time. . . .

"It takes neither modern technology nor much money to seize the opportunity to learn in the moments we now waste. You could just have a book and paper and pencil with you. That will be enough. But you need determination to capture the leisure moments you now waste."[3]

Your HSJ skills will open a world of fulfilling possibilities. You'll find that you can not only provide the necessities of life for those you love but also find deep meaning in your work as you serve others and continue to learn. Education makes this possible. Whatever your career objectives and your personal capabilities and interests, you need to be a "lifetime student." That means both formal schooling and also lifelong learning.

Remember, you're a child of God, destined to become as He is and to do the things He does. As Brigham Young put it: "When we have lived millions of years in the presence of God and angels, and have associated with heavenly beings, shall we then cease learning? No, or eternity ceases. There is no end. We go from grace to grace, from light to light, from truth to truth."[4] Our Father's work involves the greatest of all high-stakes judgments. You have the potential to become like Him and to help in that work, and your education will help you realize it!

---

[1] In *Journal of Discourses*, 26 vols. (Latter-day Saints' Book Depot, 1854–1886), 9:167.
[2] Henry B. Eyring, "Education for Real Life," *Ensign*, October 2002, 19.
[3] Ibid, 19–20.
[4] In *Journal of Discourses*, 6:344.

INDEX

Accounting, 100–101, 233
ACT test, 82–83, 132
Adjunct professors, 196
Admission percentages, 131–32
Airline employees, 43–46
Analysis skills, 64–65, 103–7, 228–35
AP (Advanced Placement) classes, 94–98
Applied technology training, 72–76, 99–103
Apprenticeships, 73–74
Aristotle, 228
Assets and liabilities, 100–101
Associate's degree, 119–20, 186–87
Athletic teams, 116, 126–27
Autopia (Disneyland attraction), 12

Babe Ruth, 145–46
Bachelor's degree, 119–20, 176–87
Bangerter, William Grant, 8
Baseball games, 144–48
Beck, Julie Bangerter, 8
Biases, 107–8
Biology major, 184–86
Boise State University, 116
Boston Red Sox, 144–48
Bray, Martha, 55–57
Buffett, Warren, 48–49, 102, 105, 172
Business major, 158–59
Business skills, 179–80

Calculus, 98, 104
Campuses, visiting, 138–43
Career dreams, 156–63
Children, encouraging education for, 7–9
China, 32–33
Choosing colleges: sports teams and, 116–18,
    126–27; transferring and, 118–20; friends
    and, 121–23; location and, 123–24; tuition
    and, 124–25; rankings and, 127–36; student
    placement and, 136–37; visiting campuses and,
    138–43

Church institutes, 142
Clark, Kim, 190
Classes: attending, 138–40; preparation and
    participation in, 210–11; seeking guidance in,
    212–15; high-stakes judgments and, 228–30
College(s): high-stakes judgments and, 67–69;
    value of, 73–77; cost of, 77–80; acceptance
    to, 81–84; finishing, 84–85; Sandra's success
    in, 86–87; Craig Moor's success in, 88–91;
    Advanced Placement classes and, 94–98;
    vocational education and, 99–103; transferring,
    118–20; local, 123–24. See also Choosing
    colleges
Communications major, 158–59
Competition: for jobs, 24–26; machines and,
    26–30; globalization and, 30–33; threats and
    opportunities of, 33–35; high-stakes judgments
    and, 63
Computers, 26–30, 31, 35
Concurrent enrollment classes, 99
Co-ops. See Internships
Cowdery, Oliver, 157
Cow pasture, rock formations in, 231–35
Credits/credit hours: transferring, 118–20; for
    majors, 182–86
"The Curse of the Bambino," 145–46
Customization, of college degree, 176–87, 235

Decision making: investment banking and,
    38–39; Nintendo Wii and, 40–41; high-stakes
    judgments and, 43–53; career dreams and, 157
Degree, customizing, 176–87, 235
Dell, Michael, 73
Doyle (draftsman), 28–29
Draftsmen, 28–29

Earning power, 22–23
Education: importance of, iv–v, 18–24, 67–69;
    Joseph Smith and, 7; opportunities for, 10–11;
    divine guidance in, 12–15

Einstein, Albert, 21

Elective courses, 167, 176

Embree, Glenn, 170

Employment: competition for, 24–26; placement in, 136–37; customizing your degree for, 179–80

English, 103–6

Executives, 46–49

Externships. See Internships

Extracurricular activities, 209, 219, 230

Eyring, Caroline Romney, 7–8

Eyring, Emily, 219–21

Eyring, Henry: on children and parents' education, 9; education of, 19–21; on importance of education, 22–23; on working with machines, 35; on spiritual rewards, 59; people skills and, 109–10; on choosing career path, 160–62

Eyring, Henry B.: on Joseph Smith, 6; on educational opportunities, 10–11; on divine guidance, 14–15; as physics major, 160–62; on lifelong learning, 239–40

Eyring, Henry Christian (H.C.), 222–23

Eyring, Mildred Bennion, 62

Eyring, Sarah, 110

Farming, 88–90

Fieldwork, 230–35

Fiesta Bowl, 116

Free trade, 32

Friends, 107–9, 110, 121–23

Fuller, Mark, 65, 108

Gas, pumping, 109–10

Gates, Bill, 73

GED (General Equivalency Diploma), 83–84

General education: credits, 119–20, 167; courses, 197

Geology, 170–71, 231–35

Globalization, 30–33, 51

God, guidance from, 12–15

Gordon, Jim, 192–93

Grades: college acceptance and, 82–83; importance of, 207; grading, 209, 215; retaking classes to improve, 210; learning and, 213; wrangling over, 214–15

Graduate school, 228

High school: high-stakes judgments and, 68; college acceptance and, 81–84; vocational education and, 99–103; fundamental skills and, 103–12

High-stakes judgments: investment banking and, 38–39; Nintendo Wii and, 40–41; salary and, 43–53, 58–63; matrix exercise, 52–53, 69; increasing capabilities and, 54–57; fundamental skills for, 64–67, 103–12; college degrees and, 67–69; choosing classes based on, 228–30; fieldwork and, 230–35

Hintze, Lehi, 232, 234

I Love Lucy, 210

Immigration, 30–31

India, 32–33

In-state colleges, 123–24

Institutes, 142–43

Intelligence, 5

Internet, 31

Internships, 219–25, 230

Investment banking, 13, 38–39

Jerome (investment banker), 38–39

Job market, 24–26

Johnson, Sid, 74–75

Kant, Immanuel, 228

Lawn mowing, 25–26

Leadership, 108–9

Learning: Joseph Smith and, 6, 7; lifelong, 238–40

Lee, Rex, 139

Liabilities, assets and, 100–101

Living standards, 19

Local colleges, 123–24

Machines, 26–30, 35, 51

Majors: choosing, 158, 166–73; master's degree and, 177–78; employment and, 179–80; credit hours required by, 182–86

Market competition, 24–26

Master's degree, 177–78

Math, 103–5

McKay, David O., 202–3

Minimum wage, 24

Minors, 167, 181

Miyamoto, Shigeru, 64

Money: time value of, 79–80; for college, 80. See also Salary

Moor, Craig, 88–91

Moral sense, 66, 110–11, 228–35

Mothers, high-stakes judgments and, 60–63

Networking computers, 30

Newspaper, 219

New York Mets, 144–48

Nintendo Wii, 40–41, 64–67

Note taking, 211

Odoardi, Andy, 94–95

Opportunity cost, 79

Parker, Donna, 95–96

PC networking, 30

People skills, 65, 107–10, 228–35

Perceptions, 144–48

Physics major, 160–62

Pilots, 43–48

Pioneers, education and, 7–8

Placement, of graduating students, 136–37

PlayStation, 40

Plotters, 28–29

Political science, 168–69

Postgraduate education, 177–78

Professors: characteristics of great, 138–39, 202–3; influence of, 190–93; non-tenure-track, 194–95; responsibilities of, 194–95; RateMyProfessors.com and, 197–200; as mentors, 200–202; seeking help from, 213–15; high-stakes judgments and, 229–30

Rankings, for colleges, 127–36

RateMyProfessors.com, 197–200

Research, professors' requirements for, 194–95

Research assistant, 202

Resurrection, 5

Rewards, for service, 58–59

Ritchie, Bonner, 144–48

Rock formations, 231–35

Roommates, 122–23

Ruth, Babe, 145–46

Salary: understanding, 42; high-stakes judgments and, 43–53, 58–63; of college alumni, 136–37

Sandra (college student), 86–87

SAT test, 82–83, 132

School building, 7

Service, rewards for, 58–59

Shower, thinking in, 160–61

Smith, Joseph: Henry B. Eyring on, 6; learning and, 7

Socrates, 228

Sony PlayStation, 40

Sports teams, 116, 126–27

Stock market, investment banking and, 38–39

Student-led organizations, 219

Student loans, 208–9

Study time, 207

Syllabus, 213

Technical schools, 72–76, 99–103

Technical skills, 179–80

Television, 60–62

Tenure, for professors, 194–95

Test scores, college acceptance and, 82–83

Text books, 78

Time, wasting, 239–40

Time value of money, 79–80

Transferring colleges, 118–20

Transportation, 31

Truman, Harry, 106–7

Tuition, 124–25

Unpaid internships, 219–25, 230

Video games, 40–41, 64–67

Vocational education, 72–76, 99–103

Washington, George, 112, 172–73

Wealth, creation of, 19

Wii, 40–41, 64–67

Williams, Ed, 170

Working, 208–9

World Series, 145–48

Writing, 105–6

Young, Brigham, 238, 240

PHOTO AND IMAGE CREDITS